This
Body
I Wore

FARRAR, STRAUS AND GIROUX

New York

This
Body
I Wore

A Memoir

DIANA GOETSCH

Farrar, Straus and Giroux
120 Broadway, New York 10271

Grateful acknowledgment is made for permission to reprint the
following material:
"Jake," copyright © Emily Carmichael, used by permission of the author.
"Upstairs" and "Back Flip," from *Nameless Boy*, copyright © 2015 Diana
Goetsch, used by permission of Orchises Press.
Excerpt from *Girlhood*, copyright © Carolyn Hays, used by permission of
the author.

An early version of "Writer in Residence, Central State" appeared in *Rattle*.

Library of Congress Cataloging-in-Publication Data
Names: Goetsch, Diana, author.
Title: This body I wore : a memoir / Diana Goetsch.
Description: First edition. | New York : Farrar, Straus and Giroux, 2022. |
    Summary: "A memoir of one woman's long journey to late transition, in
    an era before real community or appropriate language was available to
    help her understand herself" —Provided by publisher.
Identifiers: LCCN 2021059968 | ISBN 9780374115098 (hardcover)
Subjects: LCSH: Goetsch, Diana. | Transgender women—United
    States—Biography. | Poets—United States—Biography. | Gender
    transition—United States.
Classification: LCC HQ77.8.G34 G64 2022 | DDC 306.76/8092 [B]—
    dc23/eng/20220202
LC record available at https://lccn.loc.gov/2021059968

Our books may be purchased in bulk for promotional, educational, or
business use. Please contact your local bookseller or the Macmillan
Corporate and Premium Sales Department at 1-800-221-7945, extension
5442, or by email at MacmillanSpecialMarkets@macmillan.com.

www.fsgbooks.com
www.twitter.com/fsgbooks • www.facebook.com/fsgbooks

10 9 8 7 6 5 4 3 2 1

This is a nonfiction account, though in some instances names and other
identifying information have been changed.

for my grandmother

You're not free if you don't know me.

—SINÉAD O'CONNOR, "THE HEALING ROOM"

Contents

A Note About Language

This memoir spans several decades, during which trans people in the United States referred to themselves in various and changing ways. To take one example, in the 1980s the terms "crossdresser" and "transvestite" were practically interchangeable. Today the latter term is generally frowned on, while the former is still accepted. Likewise, some of today's conventions are bound to become problematic for future readers.

In this book I sought to use terminology authentic to the era of each experience. As I, and others around me, tried to make sense of our identities, language was part of what shaped our reality. We misgendered and deadnamed ourselves left and right, in part because words like "misgender" and "deadname" had yet to come into use. By the same token, words matter, pronouns matter, misgendering matters, and for those who are aided by trigger notices, this is to respectfully advise you.

This
Body
I Wore

Prologue: Stepping Out
1987

One hot summer day crossing a street in Brooklyn I thought, *Maybe it would be better if I were dead.* The thought had never visited me before, and yet I knew why it was here: I'd run out of road.

On the surface, my life may have appeared promising. I was twenty-four, healthy, and had just begun a career as an English teacher at Stuyvesant High School. But inside I felt desolate. After two years in New York City I didn't have one close friend. My attempts at romantic relationships had all ended before we'd even had sex. My isolation made no sense to me. It felt like a punishment in a bad dream that didn't include the crime I was being punished for. I envied people I saw together, laughing on park benches, at sidewalk restaurant tables, playing tennis in Central Park, lined up outside the Beacon Theatre. I overheard two people on the subway making plans to go to the beach, and it lacerated me. A childhood friend wrote to tell me her husband had suffered a collapsed lung, and I even envied *her*—fretting in a hospital waiting room with more purpose to her life than I could fathom.

But here was something new, albeit morbid: *Maybe it would be better if I were dead.* And on the heels of that thought came another: *If you're going to die, you might as well step out once as a woman.* The two thoughts had hit me in the time it took to cross Adams Street, a four-lane road that led to the Brooklyn

Bridge. I did an about-face, recrossed those lanes, and headed to a women's shoe store off the Fulton Street Mall. I'd passed that store many times, noting a sign advertising wide sizes.

"We get men in here all the time," said a young salesgirl, mercifully. I selected a pair of cream-colored pumps. The salesgirl brought me to a chair near the stockroom, away from the windows, and handed me two nylon footies. My heart, which had been racing in fear, shifted into excitement. The pumps fit snugly. I looked down amazed, the arch of my instep looked just like a woman's. I took a few steps and walked quite easily, even though I'd never walked in heels.

I brought the shoes home to my apartment and began the process of readying myself to go out as a woman. I had accumulated some clothes I liked to put on in private, a few outfits, underthings, makeup, and a wig. I kept much of it stuffed high in a corner of my one closet, an elbow-deep recess in the wall covered by a sheet of plywood that latched like a screen door. I lived in a brownstone that had been converted into a men's rooming house. My apartment was the only unit with a kitchen and bathroom. Mrs. Caruso, the elderly landlady who lived downstairs with her nephew, Pat, and a poodle named Kevin, thought it her right to go snooping in my room when I was out. She called it straightening, and so I asked her not to straighten. *Had she gone into that closet and seen my women's things?*

Shaving my legs in the bathtub felt ecstatic and illicit. With each stroke of the blade, I feared the authorities would storm in and arrest me for a crime against nature. My calves and knees looked surreal in their hairlessness, while the startling amount of body hair, swirling on top of the soapy bathwater, threatened to clog the drain.

After getting dressed, I took down a heavy round mirror

from the wall and propped it against a doorframe to behold my whole body, from a strange angle, turning this way and that. I had on a long-sleeved gold lamé blouse and matching skirt, to go with the cream pumps—I actually thought I looked great.

I planned to go to the Eulenspiegel Society, an S&M association whose gatherings on East Fourth Street I'd seen advertised regularly in the back pages of *The Village Voice*. Cruelty didn't turn me on, but "sissies" were explicitly welcome there, and no doubt fit into any number of role-play scenarios. Those didn't interest me either, but if someone offered to lick my shoes I'd figure out how to deal with it.

I stood on the stoop of that brownstone, several steps above the street, waiting for the car I'd called. I prayed it would arrive before anyone came out the door behind me. The car would be coming down Court Street and making a right onto my block. People in Brooklyn Heights didn't hang out on their stoops, though for all I knew a hundred pairs of eyes could have been watching me from windows.

The evening had turned cool, and the breeze on my legs and up my skirt was another unprecedented thrill, like wind on another planet. Every nerve ending in my skin was lit. The curtains of the front apartment, just a few feet away, were pulled aside, enough for the man behind them, an old navy vet, to peek out. Those curtains closed and opened again a few more times. *Where is that car?* In winter, whenever the old man came in from the cold, I heard him wheezing for several minutes through the thin wall separating our rooms. Each wheeze turned to a rattle at the bottom—or perhaps he was weeping. I could never tell, and the mystery of his suffering made the sound unbearable, like an animal being tortured.

When the car arrived there was already a passenger in it, a woman also going to Manhattan. "Where is *he* going?" she said to the driver, not one bit happy when I'd joined her in the back seat. I didn't say anything or look at her. If she called me a pervert I wasn't sure I could honestly disagree; being out in women's clothes was, moment by moment, the biggest turn-on I'd ever experienced. The car pulled up to a curb in lower Manhattan to drop off my disgusted fellow passenger. I glanced at her as she climbed out—a frail lady in black.

I WAS ALONE now, being driven through Manhattan at night. I thought of all the times I'd gazed at women hailing cabs on the avenues of New York. Ladies in dresses and coiffed hair, young women in aerobics tights with thick ponytails, businesswomen in sheer stockings and pumps, red nails on a door handle, a symphony of bend and swivel, shift and pivot, keeping legs together, settling like a bird in a nest, then safely shutting the door as they tell the driver their address. Witnessing this, or *any* moment from a woman's day—smoothing a skirt, checking lipstick in a mirror—could put me in a stupor. Whoever the particular woman was, she was likely having a day full of ordinary worries and distractions, though I couldn't shake the belief that all women were citizens of a better world, living superior lives moment by moment, simply because they were women.

And now I was one of them—sort of, approximately— enough, anyway, for people on the street to assume there was a female passenger in the back seat of a car rolling by in the night. I looked down at my hairless legs, glowing and dimming with each passing streetlight. I rested a hand on my thigh, which sent shudders of pleasure through me. I recrossed my legs, felt flesh rubbing flesh through nylon, and shut my eyes in ecstasy.

We pulled up to the curb on East Fourth Street. I paid the driver, thanked him in a falsetto British accent, and stepped out into the night. Walking to the door of the Eulenspiegel Society, I was too consumed with every sensation and foot-fall, and with all that awaited me, to register something every bit as momentous: I might have just saved my own life.

Part
ONE

Woman Good Man Bad
1984

I am lying facedown on a futon on the floor of my attic room in the off-campus house I share with three English majors. *Glenn Miller's Greatest Hits* is playing on my turntable— swing music jubilant enough to make a country forget a war.

"I can't believe you have Glenn Miller!" Ravi had said in a swoon when I put it on. Ravi is perched on my buttocks giving me a back massage. Sometimes he just caresses me, or leans down to kiss my neck or shoulder.

"That feels good," I say.

He nudges me to turn over, then plants a soft kiss on my lips.

"So I've got news for you," he says.

"What?"

"You're not gay."

"No?"

"Definitely not," he says, looking down at my crotch.

RAVI AND I met in a critical theory seminar taught by Gayatri Spivak, a star professor on loan from Emory University. For two and a half hours every Monday evening, otherwise accomplished scholars sat dumbfounded while this postcolonial deconstructionist (who was also quite sexy) goaded us to "defetishize the concrete." "You Americans," she observed, after lighting up a Marlboro, "bristling at a little cigarette smoke, while your government shoots microwaves through you." She had once dismissed us early so she could take an overseas call from Jacques Derrida. Ravi was among the few with the courage to speak in that class, and his elegant accent—he was Indian South African—seemed to lend gravitas to the simplest assertion. He was loose-limbed, with a thick beard and pretty eyes. He liked to tease me with clever digs and smiles, giving my shoulder a flirtatious poke each time we ran into each other.

The first time I seriously wondered if I might be gay, I was standing at the entrance to the Center for the Arts on a crisp fall afternoon. And who do you think came walking along with his macramé bookbag slung across his hip?

"Hi Ravi."

I HAD A history of people assuming I was gay. I'd befriended a gay kid in a high school where you were either homosexual or homophobic. I was madly attracted to girls, but never had a steady girlfriend. When I entered Wesleyan University I didn't quite get the memo that the main point of college was hooking up, despite all the sex going on in my coed dorm. Walking down the hall on any Saturday night, I heard U2 and sex, Bob Marley and sex, sex between bong hits, bedsprings creaking to Michael Jackson and Fleetwood Mac, headboards knocking into walls and reverberating through the cinder blocks. Even Tilly, who called her pastor each week from the hall pay phone, was moaning in alternate waves of what sounded like panic and relief.

Late in the spring I met Odette. I'd seen her often in the dining hall, long-legged and accident prone, crashing into furniture, spilling things from her tray, which caused her to laugh and drop more things. She gravitated to a table of her dorm friends who liked intellectual debate. When a loud obnoxious guy claimed Descartes "proved" the existence of God, Odette scoffed at him, her chin jutting out sharply as she delivered a dismissive quip with a backhanded sweep of her arm. She was a consummate contrarian.

She was one character among many, until the day—*how does this happen?*—I couldn't take my eyes off her. I introduced myself. We talked for a while as the dining hall emptied out, and she showed a side of herself that was tender, polite, even a little shy. A few days later I looked out my dorm room window and saw her sitting cross-legged in the little graveyard on top of Foss Hill, typing on a manual typewriter. She had the long back of a swimmer. She kept stopping to mark the page with a pencil. The marks were accents—she was typing in French, I discovered, when I walked out to say hello.

On our first date we sat in a booth in a dive bar down the hill in Middletown. We talked for a while, until a long silence wiped the smiles off our faces, and we plunged nakedly into one another's eyes. The two of us lasted six months, through the summer and into the fall. We wrote love letters, traveled together. People knew us as a couple, though she hadn't broken up with Ben, her high school boyfriend, who was down the road at Yale. I rarely brought it up, fearing she'd choose him over me. Each time she hopped in her car and drove off to visit him was a fresh humiliation.

Worst of all, we hadn't consummated our love. We never advanced past foreplay, and neither of us broached the subject in conversation. For my part, I was a virgin and terrified of sex. I assumed it was just a case of extreme shyness. I was immensely turned on by Odette, who I hoped would enable me to cross the threshold into sexual experience.

The problem was she wouldn't touch me. We'd kiss, and press against each other, I'd feel up her breasts and buttocks, and hear her heavy breathing, but she would hardly reciprocate my touch, and my penis seemed to be off-limits. Was she putting a lid on sex with me until she made a decision about Ben? Or was she waiting for me to take control? Did the contrarian in the dining hall, and the scholar in the graveyard, have a Victorian policy of never initiating anything in bed?

There were so many times I could have asked or said something, but I froze. She never spoke of sex either. Despite a deep and obvious love, we withheld ourselves from each other. In my pain and confusion I started to resent her. I didn't speak of that either, though I wrote hateful things in my journal. On a fall day in my sophomore year, feeling particularly tortured, I walked to the coed frat house where she lived. I arrived in tears. She hugged me hard and said, "I think you need to break up with me." Breaking up should have been a relief, but it was devastating.

I PURSUED OTHER girls, though never for long. Asha, from Trinidad, was smart and enchanting. We danced close at parties, alternating back to front. I vaguely remember getting up from her mattress on her dorm room floor after just a few kisses, and making an excuse to leave. Dina had dark curly hair and large almond-shaped eyes. She was two years younger than me, and kept her tights on in bed (her mother's orders). I was relieved just to spoon all night. Tonya was tall and quirky, had acne, was beautiful, and always wore jeans.

We met as sophomores in a European Intellectual History class, had a long flirtation, and didn't make out until I visited her in Boston after college, after which we quickly lost touch. I lost Patrice in a cornfield. We pulled over to the side of the road and waded into separate rows of corn. We must have found each other before driving back to campus, but all I remember is losing her. Nina liked studying with her door open and her stereo on. On a whim I drifted in from the hall and offered her a shoulder massage. From the way she surrendered to my hands I knew it could have gone further, yet I drifted back out the door.

I kept to myself. I went for long runs. I emptied the trash early in the morning at the high-rise dorms (a work-study job no work-study students would take). I studied way too much. When my eyes were bleary from reading, I'd wander aimlessly in Middletown. I was grateful when it rained because I wouldn't have to see my peers necking on campus lawns. I couldn't figure out what was keeping me isolated. I'd scribble notes in the margins of philosophy tomes I was reading, as though I'd found clues.

One morning walking across campus I passed a girl I'd once made out with, another at the mailboxes in the student center, a third on my way to class. Each time, we briefly made eye contact, but didn't speak. I barely remembered I'd kissed them. *This place is filled with ghosts*, I thought, not realizing *I* was the ghost, shuffling through Wesleyan in a fugue state.

KATE WAS A pale, stoic freshman in the Zen Buddhism class I TA'ed as a junior. She said she had a dashiki that might look good on me, and invited me to her room. We started kissing on her bed, but then she pulled away to give full disclosure: "I'm fucking my high school English teacher," she said. "That's why I go to New York every weekend." She was also friends with his wife, and babysat their kids, so she figured she should probably cut things off with the teacher. She said this all without a hint of affect or emotion. (Maybe that's what drew her to Zen.)

Sitting on the bed beside this slim-hipped girl, who looked no older than sixteen, and whom I'd assumed was a virgin, I was overcome with fear. Partly I feared for her in her situation, but mostly I feared for myself. Everyone but me was fucking. Something was very wrong. I didn't tell Kate or anyone else I was a virgin. If that news ever got around it would only deepen my shame, and leave me feeling more cursed than I already was.

I woke up late the next day in my own room and startled myself in the mirror: I still had on Kate's brightly striped dashiki, which made me look ridiculous and pale. I drew closer to the mirror, examining the blond and reddish whiskers in the beard I was growing. And something else: my hairline had become shockingly high at the temples. *When did that happen?* I ran my hand through my hair, pulling it back repeatedly, examining the impending catastrophe.

I BEGAN TO wonder if I was gay. I didn't particularly want to be gay, but I wanted an answer to why I froze up with girls. I was also depressed, insomniac, and vexed by headaches. Actually it was one continuous headache, the tension and volume rising late in the afternoon each day. A chiropractor diagnosed me with TMJ—Temporomandibular Joint Disorder (or Totally Messed-up Jaw). He couldn't tell me what was causing it, just that it had a lot of "stressors," one of which was stress.

A campus therapist, a thin guy in a sweater who jotted notes on a clipboard as we spoke, rendered his evaluation: "Your problem is you're an angry man, you complain incessantly, you look down on others, and so you have no friends." He then informed me that the university alloted three mental health counseling sessions per student, and this concluded our third session. Then the asshole, who'd diagnosed me as an asshole, wished me luck.

Was I angry because I didn't want to face being gay? Yet it was women, never men, who caused me to lose my page in the library as I saw them glide across the room in colored tights and miniskirts, stepping through columns of sunlight from high windows. A random glimpse of femininity could wipe out all sense of who I was. At times it felt violent. One moment I'd be sitting calmly in class, then the sight of my philosophy professor brushing the locks from her face with slender fingers set off a depth charge planted in my chest.

Susan Lourie, a massage therapist I went to for the headaches, told me I needed to stop weight training and running long-distance. She was also a dance professor, so I started taking her modern dance class. "I didn't know you were a dancer," people told me. I told them I wasn't. But my body took to dance, which felt liberating and sensual. And I liked wearing men's dance tights, though I wished they weren't so thick. I wished they were women's.

I still had the pair of purple tights Odette had loaned me one Halloween. I'd worn them, with running shorts and a carnival mask and lipstick, to a couple of parties, where people couldn't recognize me *or* my gender—not at first. I kept those tights in a drawer, along with some panties, and a few other girly things I'd found left behind in the laundry room. Putting them on brought me comfort, and I fantasized about being a girl. I'd fantasized all my life about being a girl. Mrs. Rowe, my high school art teacher, had introduced me to the word "androgyny." "Everyone needs to be androgynous," she proclaimed. I told myself that wanting to be a girl meant I was androgynous, and all the more secure in my masculinity, though by my junior year at Wesleyan nothing really made sense.

I knew it was pretty messed up, and not exactly romantic, to ask a gay man to help me determine if I was gay. I half expected Ravi to administer a postcolonial tongue-lashing when I propositioned him. But all he did was smile, and ask what I was doing Friday night. We went to my attic room, where I put on Glenn Miller. "OK if we take this off?" he said, lifting my shirt. I took off his too. He didn't try to kiss me—I think he saw how nervous I was. He suggested we start with a massage. He was wonderfully tender, but I wasn't excited or turned on.

"Too bad," he said, lying beside me on the futon.

"Too bad," I said. On the stereo, a band singer was crooning "My Prayer," a vapid song of endless love.

"If it was any man," I said, "I'd want it to be you."

"I can't believe you have Glenn Miller."

I DETERMINED TO plumb the mysteries of gender, equipped with the Wesleyan course catalogue, which cross-listed courses from various departments under the category of gender studies.

One was Psychology and Literature, taught by Mike Rodney, a popular professor among radical feminists on campus. Professor Rodney was a stocky, balding, bearded man who lived communally in a house of women. I heard him once fleetingly claim he *was* a woman. (I would have loved to hear him elaborate on this, though he never did.) He was missing two fingers on his right hand—trigger fingers, it was rumored, which he'd chopped off in the 1960s to avoid the draft. The absence of the fingers wasn't easy to spot; he kept his right hand perched at his hip, just above the pocket of his blue jeans, where fingers could be tucked inside that pocket.

It was also not easy to see Mike Rodney as a woman, no matter how glamorously he stroked the flyaway hair growing out the sides of his bald head. Though I did once glimpse . . . something. We were alone in the men's room of Fisk Hall, the old psych building, standing a few urinals apart. "Hi," he said, looking over at me. His eyes, when I met them, were sort of misty and alluring, like bygone female movie star eyes. I stood there awkwardly, unable to pee, until he'd finished and left the bathroom.

Professor Rodney had assigned us some Freud, in order to prepare us for when other professors tried to ram the father of modern psychology down our throats. On the subject of penis envy, he said, "Now if I were to turn around to reveal a third arm growing out of my sweater"—he pivoted comically to the side—"would anybody here *envy* that?" The female students laughed and applauded. The few guys in the room smirked and stayed quiet. I didn't object to this professor's interpretations, though I wished the class was just that—a class— and not a pitched battle. Male authors on the syllabus were there to be criticized, while the women were feminist heroes.

It reminded me of the talk show spoof I'd seen on *Saturday Night Live*, where Jane Curtin played a host who said, "Welcome to *Woman Good Man Bad*."

"Woman good man bad" was *already* my worldview. As a child, it never escaped my notice that it was always boys doing the fighting, getting dirty, getting in trouble, sitting glumly on the bench outside the principal's office. Whereas girls were graceful, clean, kind, with exquisite handwriting. You could maybe map these impressions onto feminism, though the fact that I considered girls incredibly fortunate, and wondered if boys were so angry and violent because they didn't get to be girls, was not a particularly feminist viewpoint. And despite examples to the contrary—boys who were sweet, girls who were brutal—nothing put a dent in my prejudice that male equaled bad, and female equated to good.

Nothing until Wesleyan, where I watched radical feminists attack women who chose to shave their legs or wear makeup, calling them sellouts, which was nothing compared to how they treated men. I was called a "potential rapist"—to my face, more than once—by women who didn't even know me. I knew it couldn't have been personal, and that some of them had likely been raped, and all had been given a raw deal by a patriarchal culture. Yet their hostility felt *very* personal to me, and physically nauseating.

Needless to say, I didn't learn a thing about gender in those classes. Except perhaps this: "gender is primary." I encountered that phrase in a journal article about an experiment where a person seated with their back to a door was asked to guess about the identity of another person stepping into the room. The results led the researchers to conclude that, in the split second we come upon a stranger, the first thing we seek to determine—prior to race or age or class or anything else—is gender. I can't say if it was good science, but it was compelling reading. And that slogan—"gender is primary"—led to a haunting thought: *If gender is unmoored, what happens then?*

SENIOR YEAR CAME and I grew nervous about my future—nervous I didn't have one. I was surrounded by high-achieving peers headed for law school, med school, business school, internships, and nonprofits fighting to defeat hunger and save rivers. I felt like someone who couldn't get past the decision of what to make for dinner, only instead of dinner it was the rest of my life, and I wasn't sure I was hungry.

I didn't even have a major until I was a second-semester junior, when the dean of students—Dean Denise, we called her—phoned to tell me I needed to pick one. That was news to me. I didn't think you needed a major at a liberal arts college. "Yes," said Dean Denise, "you have to have a major." I asked for a week to think about it. I looked over my transcript, which included courses in Zen Buddhism, German philosophy, existentialism, music theory, physics, astronomy, linguistics, Virginia Woolf, African American literature, acting, dance, drawing, Italian. It looked like someone preparing to go on *Jeopardy!* Several of the classes had been taught by religion professors, so if the department chair signed off, maybe I could cobble together a religion major.

"Come on in," said Professor Crites. He was sitting at his typewriter smoking a pipe. "The past comes at you from right out of the future," he said, reading from what he'd just typed. "Totally," I replied. Steven Crites, a minister and Hegel scholar, was a short plump man with a white beard who sometimes wore lederhosen. Other religion professors included

Ron Cameron, who read the gospels brilliantly and dynami-cally, as though they were ESPN highlight reels, and the mysterious and charismatic Jim Stone, whose course on phenomenology blew students' minds and caused several to drop out. What a great department! "You're going to need a class in early Christianity," Professor Crites said through pipe smoke, while signing my form. So I became a religion major, which sounded cool when I said it at parties to English majors, who were a dime a dozen at Wesleyan.

Around this time I came to know Sara Cohen, another religion major, who'd just returned from a semester in India. Sara was a short, butch, badass bisexual with a great wit. When sloppy thinkers aired their arguments, she would pa-tiently wait for them to finish before posing a simple question they couldn't answer. She'd been a youth tennis champion, and maybe this had something to do with her confidence. Or maybe it was because she drove a Mustang. "Find your people," Ms. Collins, my high school writing teacher, had once advised me. It was my senior year in college, and I still hadn't found my people. But something I couldn't place felt familiar about Sara, some type of tribal recognition, though I couldn't name the tribe.

We took her Mustang down to New York City on a whim one Saturday night. It was already late when we arrived at the Hellfire, a basement S&M club where Sara's older sister was a bartender. Rivka resembled Sara, but presented more fem-inine. When she wasn't bartending she worked at Womero, a women's erotic video company that had a small office on lower Broadway.

"Want to see my new piercing?" she asked.

"Sure," said Sara. Rivka hiked her leg onto the bar and lifted her skirt to display a small silver ring through her labia.

Sara and I strolled through the grotto-like club, observing various scenes going on, but we didn't stay for long. She asked if I wanted to go to the 2020 Club, a three-story after-hours place she'd been to once. She said there were drag shows there. "Sure," I told her, trying to act nonchalant. *Drag shows!*

When we got there it was fairly dead. Only the ground floor was open. There were some plastic chairs around tables, and large tropical potted plants. It felt like somebody's patio, even though we were indoors. Ordinary-seeming people conversed in sparse groups of two or three. There wasn't much drinking, which could have meant they were instead doing drugs. Maybe we'd arrived too early, or on the wrong night— though how could Saturday be the wrong night?

A tall thin waitress wandered into the room, eventually coming over to take our order. She spoke in a deep, yet effeminate voice. When she returned with our drinks in plastic cups, we asked her if there were going to be drag shows that night. "Probably not," she said. I noticed a few other waitresses gathered in a corner—or perhaps they were performers. They wore slinky dresses with high slits, or bandage skirts and low-cut blouses, platform shoes, bright lipstick, big earrings. I didn't know if they were drag queens or transsexuals. I preferred to imagine they were transsexuals, and living as females, though the idea of transvestites, transforming in order to work, thrilled me as well. It was the first time in my life I'd been in the presence of such people, and I was spellbound. They, on the other hand, seemed bored, standing around smoking, or sitting with a leg crossed on a slow night. One or two were always wandering off or wandering back. I pictured them retiring to an inner sanctum, where they lived in a parallel universe doing whatever transsexuals do.

I wasn't sure what interested Sara about the 2020 Club.

We kept our desires private that night. I suppose the desire to flee the campus of "Diversity University" (Wesleyan's nickname for itself) and mix with actual freaks and transgressors who lived on the edge was enough to have in common. We tried striking up conversations with others, but mostly we just observed: two wide-eyed kids, alone together, nursing drinks after-hours in New York City, where anything could happen— though not much did, not that night.

(I would try several times to return to the 2020 Club, but the place eluded me. Even that night, we had cruised back and forth along the block on Houston Street where the address should have fallen. Eventually someone told us we were on *East* Houston Street, and directed us west, to the right block, where we found an unmarked door. Years later, I discovered I had the name wrong the whole time: it was the 220 Club, at 220 West Houston. By then it had disappeared like a mirage.)

When Sara and I emerged it was bright morning on the planet of Manhattan. We drove through the Lincoln Tunnel, past Giants Stadium, to her parents' house in Wayne, New Jersey, to get some breakfast and sleep. Her parents were wealthy orthodox Jews, who kept separate sets of plates for meat and dairy.

"Rivka pierced her labia," Sara reported over coffee and bagels.

"Oy," said Mrs. Cohen somewhat nonchalantly. Neither she nor her husband seemed easily rocked by anything. They were very warm toward me, and asked a lot of questions about my family, my future.

"Sorry you got the third degree from my parents," Sara said in the car on the way back.

"It's OK. Were they looking at me as marriage material?"

"Probably," she said, rolling her eyes.

I WISH I'D met her when we were freshman, and we'd gone through college as friends. It was already the spring of senior year. Soon Sara would be heading to Colorado, to Naropa (the only Buddhist university in the country) for grad school, and she was psyched. The weekly round of campus parties had taken on the feeling of a last fling, and, never having had a first fling, I avoided them. I spent Easter Sunday alone in Olin Library, rereading the entirety of *Thus Spake Zarathustra*.

Unable to envision a future for myself, I went to see Henry Abelove, my favorite professor, to ask him what I should do. Professor Abelove, a small bespectacled man with thinning red hair, was openly gay, and taught amazing courses in European intellectual history, the history of sex, and Thoreau. He was a hero to a lot of students. Not long before I came to Wesleyan, the university tried to deny him tenure, and students spray-painted their protests in giant letters on the walls of the brand-new Center for the Arts.

"Come in, Mr. Goetsch," Professor Abelove said, offering a gap-tooth smile, and his warm hand to shake. After I told him how lost I felt, he said, "Why don't you buy some time?" and suggested I apply to grad school and see if anyone would give me money. He told me that he also felt lost when he graduated—"depressed, actually"—and that's what he did.

I sent out a dozen applications to graduate departments of American Studies (a broad and fairly new field I chose for maximum freedom). Several colleges accepted me, but

NYU was the only one that offered money. So my decision was made: New York was beckoning, and suddenly the future seemed open.

"Well, it's the biggest city," Professor Abelove said when I told him, "and it's the best city." I assumed he meant the best city in which to be gay. I knew I wasn't gay, though it was still the best city.

The Admirer
1985

I am waiting near the reference counter of the Main Reading Room of the New York Public Library. A few minutes ago I handed one of the librarians several slips of paper, almost all of which contained the word "transsexual," along with call numbers I'd looked up in the catalog room. I do not think my hand was shaking when the librarian took the slips from me, nor do I think she stared long at what I wrote, before sending the slips through pneumatic tubes to an underground city of research stacks.

It is July, I just turned twenty-two, and at the end of the summer I will begin graduate school in American Civilization at New York University. In the meantime I am filling gaps in my American literature reading, which include Melville's *Moby-Dick*, Thomas Wolfe's *You Can't Go Home Again*, and Gertrude Stein's *Three Lives*. I am also reading Aldous Huxley's *The Art of Seeing*, a book about how the novelist staved off blindness through a series of self-taught eye exercises. I am going nearsighted, perhaps due to all the reading I'm doing while working as a doorman at Park Avenue and Ninety-Second Street. I operate the service elevator in the back of the building. When there are no contractors or deliveries, I park the elevator manually between floors, where I can't be found, and sit on an upturned milk crate under a bare bulb reading about Ishmael in the crow's nest of the *Pequod* gazing out at the horizon. New York has no sky, said Gertrude Stein. My horizon is limited to the next city block, or the wall of an elevator, which may also be why I'm going nearsighted.

In the evenings I take jazz dance classes with Arthur Goldweit at the Douglas Wassell School of Ballet and Theater Dance, where you can buy a ten-class card for $70. The studio is at Broadway and Fifty-Third Street, and has a set of windows directly over the billboard of the Ed Sullivan Theater. It is among the last of the old dance schools in the theater district. In 1993, CBS will buy the studio out, move *The Late Show with David Letterman* into the theater below, and convert the dance school to a greenroom.

I like Arthur's movement. He is a protégé of Ronn Forella, who is somewhat of a backstage legend. Supposedly, Ronn was the teacher Bob Fosse sent young dancers to, when Fosse spotted raw talent that needed training. You can see some of those Fosse-esque lines in Arthur's choreography, which is catlike and sensual. One day a thin man with gray hair stood at the door watching us. At the end of class Arthur invited the man in and said, "I'd like to introduce you to Ronn Forella." I will take Ronn's class just a few times ("No one moves like the master," Arthur says) before he dies of AIDS in 1989. He will compliment my talent, and bequeath to me, unceremoniously in the men's changing room, his white canvas jazz shoes. ("Hey, what size are ya?")

I am in New York, the city where I was born. My family moved out to the suburbs when I was five, but I'm finally back. I hear my name called, and step to the reference desk to pick up the books and journals that have arrived from below. I find a spot at the end of one of the long tables, where I begin to pore over articles on transsexuality, hunching my arms and shoulders around the pages to shield them from the sight of the scholars who populate this magisterial room.

I WENT TO the New York Public Library to research my fucked-up self. Writing this now, I could say I was there to research my gender identity, but at the time there was no language for this—other than pathology and deviance. I read clinical studies that sought to link sex hormones to brain formation, articles full of Latinate terms in long dense paragraphs trying to suss out which cultural factors (poverty? geography? religious fundamentalism?) or family patterns (birth order? absent fathers?) correlate with transsexuality. I read about the "Benjamin Scale," Dr. Harry Benjamin's method for distinguishing "transvestites" from "non-surgical transsexuals" from "true transsexuals," and "homosexual transsexuals" from "heterosexual transsexuals," all of which made my head spin. I pictured Dr. Benjamin's forlorn specimens crouched behind curtains in a secluded wing of a laboratory, waiting timidly to be examined. Back I went to the catalog room, up came more scientific literature, not a word of which was helpful to me.

I would be left to my own wits, though I had the city itself—"the best city"—at my disposal. Looking through the back pages of *The Village Voice* I occasionally spotted notices for a crossdressing "event" or "TV nite," and ventured out to an inconspicuous bar in the outer boroughs, a dive on a Wall Street block deserted after five, a furtive lounge behind an unmarked door on the Bowery. Someone periodically booked a midtown hotel suite for "TVs, TSs and admirers" to gather. You had to "call for location" and it cost $30 to walk in if you were an "admirer," which I suppose I was.

I saw only transvestites, no transsexuals, at these advertised events. The transvestites who were the most done up—completely shaved and cinched and painted—seemed paradoxically to be the most naked, perhaps because their preferences were so plain to see. Or perhaps they made *me* feel naked, just for being there. The rare ones who could, if they wanted, blend seamlessly as women in public, had me awestruck. They possessed the superpower of invisibility—though no one used that word. People instead said, "passable," "extremely passable," or "unclockable," in which case they could live in "stealth," or "deep stealth." No one in stealth was likely to show up at such events, lest they be clocked.

I began going to more brazen places, drag shows in gay bars, and hard-core tranny clubs featuring stripping, drugs, and prostitution. Club Edelweiss on Eleventh Avenue, which was constantly being raided by the police, was frequented by pre-op Black and Latina transsexuals, many of whom towered above me in platforms and heels and had curves made of silicone. They were not shy. One told me straight out she was saving for her operation, though she still wasn't sure she'd go through with it because she'd be out of business without a cock. I wanted to talk more but she said, "I'm here to make money," and stepped off when she saw I wasn't buying. At Edelweiss they were doing business—sucking and fucking—in the basement, the bathrooms. They were soliciting at the diner next door, and out by the highway.

I recall a second Edelweiss in the middle of a block in Chelsea, which didn't stay in business long, and featured a lot of Asian pre-op girls. They were drama queens, though demure and petite compared to girls at the other Edelweiss. Their voices were thin and sandpapery. Many were stunningly passable, and some of them lived full-time as women, selling themselves while waiting for the prince who would pay for their surgeries and love them forever.

Despite the seediness, these places were made of dreams. The chasers dreamed of girls who were the answer to all their libidinal prayers, who would do things they could not ask of the women in their lives. I just stood around beholding girls who had *pronounced themselves* girls, rechristened themselves with female names, and bestowed on themselves the wardrobes and lives of girls. Every feminine movement and step, every glance they took in the mirror (there were a lot of mirrors) seemed like a sacrament of self-nourishment.

I was particularly captivated by a Filipina girl named Favia. She was short and slender with a doll face and wavy hair in a cute bob. Talking to Favia was both intoxicating and frustrating. She was in perpetual motion, vigorously chewing gum, pumping one crossed leg over the other, checking her face in a wall mirror, gazing everywhere but straight ahead. When I told her I also liked to dress in women's clothes, she literally turned her back on me. But before long she resumed giving me sidelong glances, perhaps not giving up on a possible trick. At closing time, when the remaining crowd was ushered into the street, Favia hoisted up her blouse to display foam breast forms duct-taped to her flat little chest. I think she did it to signal she was a pre-op, which is what most chasers wanted. But to me it was a shocking act of self-cancellation. My shock must have registered on my face because she pointed at me and laughed. Her laugh was an extended theatrical cackle, during which I thought I glimpsed an angry little boy who kept switching into a glamorous woman, tragically cursed.

There was another Filipina girl named Leilani, who didn't mind when I told her I wished I was dressed like her. She even called me *gurl*, teasingly, sensing I would like it, and I did. She was my height with large eyes, straight bangs, and feathery hair to her shoulders. I wasn't sure if Leilani was a transvestite or a pre-op transsexual—if she lived as a man or a woman—and I didn't know if she was a prostitute. But she wasn't looking for money the night she came back with me to Brooklyn. She made that clear, and I told her I wasn't interested in sex, though I wasn't against getting in bed and snuggling. Her body was disappointingly hard and bony, and I soon dozed off.

"So how come you don't just dress and go out, *gurl*?" Leilani said, getting dressed the next morning.

"I wish," I said from the bed, "but what about all this chest hair?"

"Oh sweetie, just shave it."

"And leg hair. How would I ever explain shaved legs to—"

"To *who*?" she said, pulling a sleeveless top over her head.

"To a girlfriend."

"You don't have no girlfriend, *gurl*."

With each item she put on, Leilani was transforming magically into an ordinary pretty woman. She inserted dangle earrings, then fished her sunglasses out of her bag, placed them on top of her head, came over, and said, "Give me a hug." When I got close she planted a kiss on my lips and laughed. "See you around, *gurl*," she said, and was gone.

MY ENCOUNTERS WITH transsexual women were as fleeting as those I'd had with women in college. There was a Black singer named Donna who performed in drag shows, though it wasn't exactly drag for her, and she didn't need to lip-synch because her own voice spanned four octaves. Donna lived in a tiny second-floor studio overlooking Tompkins Square Park in the East Village. She seemed to become a different person when she removed her wig to reveal a close-cropped receding Afro.

I met a six-foot-tall white transsexual with long straight hair who'd run an ad in the personals saying she was post-op. She told me on the phone she was a call girl, but assured me the ad wasn't for business, but for her, and I believed her. We met at the Roosevelt Hotel, but only briefly because her schedule had changed. She needed to take a car service to Queens for a "date," but she told me it shouldn't take long, and invited me to take the ride with her.

We pulled up to an apartment building in Bayside. It was raining lightly, and just getting dark. I'd lived in Bayside, briefly, when I was three or four years old. As I waited for her in the back seat, I gazed up through the drizzle at apartment windows as their lights came on, and suddenly I felt very old. Afterward we went to her apartment. I can't recall where it was, only that it was tiny, with a bathtub in the kitchen. I remember sitting on a bed and watching her move through the narrow space with a slow, almost studied grace, as if her feet were breakable. She felt rail-thin when I hugged her. I thought of anorexia, and heroin, and feared for her. I wonder what she thought of me, and what it was I wanted.

It was never sexual, and they weren't glamorous. But they were otherworldly, and I got a contact high from being around them and seeing them in their lives, even if their lives were doomed. Few of them could have conventional jobs or careers; many wouldn't live past forty. (Donna would die of AIDS in 1993.) Still, they were Magellans, going for broke, determined to live female lives, despite having been bullied and tortured to conform, and thrown out of schools and families. They are the boldest, most unheralded people I will ever know.

IN THE MEANTIME, I was on a quest to be ordinary. I would have liked very much to attract and date women, to someday marry and go through life in a family more loving than the one I'd grown up in. But I wasn't meeting women—an unusual state of affairs for someone young and single in New York in the 1980s. I didn't find myself at many parties. I didn't hang out in bars or go to clubs, and when I did the thought of a pickup line slithering out of my mouth made me cringe. The last thing I wanted was for a woman to see me as a creep.

I could never see what women saw in men. Theoretically, I knew that most women were heterosexual, and therefore desired men, but I had a hard time believing it. I might have disconfirmed this at Union Square when, after sprinting to catch a downtown train, and knifing through the doors just as they were closing, I found myself face-to-face with a beautiful woman about my age openly gazing at me. It was a full train on a hot day. I had on a thin black T-shirt. My chest heaved slightly from the sprint, my arm grasping the rail overhead was well-muscled and perspiring slightly. She took me in with her eyes, and gave me a look that seemed to say, *You don't need a pickup line for this.* Yet still, a shyness, or maybe fear, came over me, and I looked away. She got off at the next stop, and I regretted my failure for years.

My dates were few and far between, and so each one felt like it had a lot riding on it. I was attracted to all kinds of women, though the more feminine women were trickier to relate to because in addition to wanting them, I wanted to be them. A woman might sense something *off* about me she couldn't quite place. Perhaps I complimented her makeup, or she noticed me noticing her nails. Soon her eyes, which initially widened to take me in, narrowed in suspicion. One date spun out of control when I asked a woman how she dressed for work.

If a woman gave a signal that she wanted to have sex, I often missed it. It was only later, when I was alone again, that her interest seemed obvious in retrospect. One exception was Paola, a curvy Puerto Rican grad student I met on the R train. We exchanged numbers, and on our first date she brought me back to her place in Astoria. I was turned on and quite hard when we got in bed. We started kissing, touching, but as her breath quickened, and her hips started to heave, a bodily fear arose. The fear gave way to numbness, and soon I was just going through the motions. There was nothing about Paola that didn't turn me on—in fact, I was still hard—but I wasn't really there and she knew it. I thought of telling her that I was a virgin, though I felt too powerless to speak. The two of us lay still for a while, in the dead silence of whatever had sabotaged me, then she turned over and went to sleep. "Maybe you are 'omosexual?" she suggested gently the next morning. I told her no, but dressed and left without trying to prove her wrong. It had been a terrifying night.

"It's so good to be with a body," I blurted out, my first time with Janet, a thirty-year-old massage therapist I'd met while looking for an apartment. She waited until the next morning to say, "I am not 'a body.'" I was shocked I'd said that, and ashamed. I was becoming estranged to women's bodies, their soft skin and flesh, aureoles many times larger than mine. How pitiful: to be so consumed by women, yet so removed from their company.

Arthur, my jazz teacher, fixed me up on a blind date with

one of his roommates, an actress who was, he assured me, drop-dead gorgeous. He was correct, she was also intelligent and kind. We met at a Greek restaurant in Tribeca. The date seemed to be going fine until she asked how long it had been since my last relationship. The question took me by surprise. A dread came over me. My heart raced, I began to perspire, and couldn't speak.

"Are you OK?" she asked. I couldn't answer that question either.

"I think I'd better go," I finally said. The words coming out of my mouth shocked me. What man in his right mind would end a date with a woman this desirable?

"Maybe you'd better," she agreed.

COMING TO NEW YORK, I felt the same excitement a lot of young men feel arriving in this city, hungry for love and for adventures that will set the course of their lives. In a sense, I'd come to the same New York as F. Scott Fitzgerald, Thomas Wolfe, Langston Hughes, Truman Capote, Bob Dylan. Also Harry Gordon, my maternal grandfather, who grew up in the Catskills, and made a beeline for Brooklyn as soon as he was old enough to work. He started out as a stock boy in a grocery store on Flatbush Avenue. On weekends he got together with buddies and cruised the boardwalks of Coney Island, where one night he met a girl from Bensonhurst named Gladys Lichtman—my grandmother.

I say *young men* because, despite my confusion, maleness was all I knew. I was assertive, competitive, athletic, walked and spoke like a guy. Like so many boys around me, I'd grown up fixated on sports, girls, and the freedom of a car. I identified with Bruce Springsteen "riding out tonight to case the promised land," and Billy Joel proclaiming that "a young man is the king of ev'ry kingdom that he sees." That's what it felt like coming to New York, where I wanted to know every block, explore every bookstore and concert hall, throw myself into the night, meet smart, beautiful women, and find heaven.

But there was another set of dreams churning in me, and they had their own power. Unlike the masculine drumbeat, the call of the feminine had no discernible source, no promise of a future, no scaffolding of culture to support or explain it. Not yet, not unless you count an infectious little tune by Lou Reed about a transsexual who hitchhiked across the country and took a walk on the wild side.

After a year in New York I sensed my life depended on reconciling these two sets of dreams, though I didn't know how. But New York affords opportunities for working out such things. The city feels like a stage set, where nearly everyone is anonymous, so you can be anyone going anywhere. Most of the seven and a half million New Yorkers remember where they were late on a Saturday night in October, when Mookie Wilson hit a slow-rolling grounder that miraculously dribbled through the legs of Red Sox first baseman Bill Buckner, and the Mets came from behind in the bottom of the tenth to win Game 6 of the 1986 World Series. I watched it in a bar off Park Avenue South, a bar full of screaming men. Half of us were dressed as women.

The Fabric Factory
1987

The Fabric Factory bar on West Forty-First Street has a dressing room in the basement for men who arrive in trousers and polo shirts carrying duffel bags, and appear an hour later at the top of the stairs in gowns or skirt suits, teetering in high heels like newborn colts. Though most arrive already dressed as women. They come from as far as Pennsylvania and Massachusetts. They have shaved and prepped themselves all afternoon, appropriated clothes from their wives' closets, snuck out to their cars at dusk, braved the stares of highway toll takers, risked getting pulled over by troopers. By midnight they have five-o'clock shadows.

I take the subway from Brooklyn. I'm safe on mass transit, I tell myself, as long as I go all out, like an actor who fully commits. Even if the material is flawed, people respect the effort. Some riders look at me, then look away, and those who don't notice me at all—well, that's even better. I dress like an ordinary woman coming from work. Most crossdressers overdo it in some way—a crazy wig or garish makeup, a too tight outfit or stiletto slingbacks they can't manage. Not that I don't respect whatever turns them on; I just happen to get turned on by blending. I'd like, with my first step inside the Fabric Factory, to be seen as a woman who entered the wrong bar.

There's a contingent of Filipino pre-ops who hang out near

the front window. They wear little slinky dresses and speak to each other in rapid-fire Tagalog while tossing their hair and checking themselves in compact mirrors. There's a small lineup of chasers who lean against the opposite wall deciding— sometimes for hours—which girl they will approach. (If one of them asks to buy me a drink I might accept, but I'll tell him it's only a drink.)

There are TVs from a suburban New Jersey support group, who drink together in a small pack, and seem like they could be tailgating at Giants Stadium. There's Vicky from Long Beach, who supports an aging mother and a kid in college by working a security job. She wears see-through tops and miniskirts over bare legs and speaks in a saccharine falsetto.

There's Adele, a married TV who is smart and stable and ten years my senior. She's neither ugly nor stunning, wears designer labels, is quite ladylike, and fairly passable. I like talking to Adele. Sometimes she brings her wife, Mara, who is plump with a pretty face and is often the only GG ("genetic girl") in the bar. She and Mara have no children, and use an entire bedroom of their house as a closet. I picture aisles of stylish clothes, like a small store the two of them share.

Stephanie, from Long Island, wears fake daggerlike nails, a long black wig, heavy makeup, and supershort skirts, but cancels these efforts by walking and talking like a building contractor in stilettos, which she is. She shows up maybe once a month, drinks a lot, and discusses her truck. We envy her size 7½ feet.

Kayla, young, tall and pretty, visits from Tennessee a few times a year. She is on a mission to compete in drag beauty pageants, and is on hormones to grow breasts to help the cause. After she wins one, she promises us, she'll stop the hormones. She's unbuttoned her blouse just low enough to display smooth chest flesh and the budding of some cleavage, a sight that fills me with shock and envy. In Tennessee Kayla lives as a man named Ken, who binds his breasts in Ace bandages to patrol center field for his company softball team.

Stan, a Vietnam vet, wears Mary Jane flats, a black page-boy wig, a shapeless cotton frock, and has no girl name. The first time I saw him he was handcuffed to a young Black woman who hardly spoke. I couldn't quite figure out their dynamic.

There are drag queens who drop by after their midnight shows at Hell's Kitchen bars—gay boys as tall as NBA forwards who wear hip pads and butt pads and have racks you could fold laundry on. They talk exclusively to one another, as if they are royalty.

If we're lucky we may get a visit from International Chrysis, who *is* royalty. Salvador Dalí's one-time transsexual muse, often seen on Page Six of the *New York Post*, and rumored to be dating some Hollywood actor, Chrysis trails her entourage of taciturn queers, her red cheeks puffed around a small chiseled nose, her cleavage carved deep from mail-order progesterone that will overtake her liver in two years' time.

WE COME TO the Fabric Factory like animals to water. Whether we drink or not, whether we mingle or dance or sit alone in a corner just enjoying the feeling of being in our clothes, we are nourished. Every time we hear the pronoun "she," and realize it's us, there's a shock and shiver of life.

We tell one another how we got through our week. The hiding, the purging, the fear, the thrill. Someone's wife was in tears again, threatening to leave. Someone was spotted by a cop while getting dressed behind bushes in a vacant lot—though the cop mercifully left her alone. We share our confusion: how can we love sports and car engines and also love this? How can we love women, and also this? "I consider myself a lesbian," says a huge crossdresser in a yellow prom dress.

We talk about how we handle our families (those who have families) and church (those who attend). We trade advice on how to create cleavage, cover beard shadow, fill bras, tuck our genitals, what to tell our coworkers who ask about our long nails ("I play guitar"), our long hair ("I'm in a band"), our shaved legs ("I'm a cyclist" or "a swimmer"), our tweezed eyebrows ("I don't know what you're talking about").

We tell each other where we shop—thrift stores with dressing rooms, the clearance racks at the Brooklyn A&S, a Naturalizer shoe store on Fifth Avenue specializing in wide sizes, the wig salon in a hidden alcove on the seventh floor of Macy's. Most of us have visited Lee's Mardi Gras Boutique, the "transvestite supply store" on West Fourteenth Street, reachable only by a private elevator sent down when you ring the bell. The merchandise is overpriced, maybe because most of the customers are too scared to go anywhere else. When I tried on some things and decided not to buy them, Lee said, "Sweetie, you can't just come here and play dress-up," and I haven't shopped there since. There's talk of a ladies' boutique out by the Pennsylvania state line, where angelic saleswomen bring you things to try on in the back. A few crossdressers get everything by mail, having found catalogs that ship to customers in—praise God—unmarked packages. "I shop anywhere," Adele says with a shrug. "They just want our money."

We report on places we can go. Someone found a midtown hotel bar that doesn't mind our presence. Someone found a diner in Queens. There's the Pyramid Club in the East Village, a big loud punk goth queer grungy den of who-the-fuck-cares. Sally's Hideaway, a couple blocks north and across from the New York Times Building, has drag shows, drugs, and prostitutes, or you could stick by the bar and just smoke and drink. Club Edelweiss is too hard-core for most of us, though there are always some stunning transsexuals there. Tranny Chasers (that's actually the name of the place), belowground on Seventh Avenue South, is more tame.

In the months since stepping out for the first time I have been to nearly all these places, though there is nothing quite like the Fabric Factory, eclectic, warm, and welcoming. Like your first Little League field, it is both a home and a destination. A man can wander aimlessly in a city at night, but a lady needs a destination. During the week, Garment District executives come here to drink their lunches, but every Saturday the Fabric Factory is ours, and the disco ball in the middle of the ceiling shines its ever-receding facets on the faces of people we are twenty years away from having any respectable words for.

Roy, the mustachioed Australian bartender who runs the place, is jovial, happy to profit from all the perfumed bacchanalia. He's also happy to let Vicky from Long Beach be our DJ, and Vicky is a horrible DJ, whose playlist never makes it past the disco era.

"LAST CALL FOR alcohol!" Roy shouts at a quarter to four, and Saturday night at the Fabric Factory is about to come to a halt. Soon the lights go up and Roy starts chanting, "GTFO!" But we don't want to leave. Pre-op girls approach bashful chasers and they haggle over the price of a blow job.

"Thirty bucks, in the bathroom."

"GTFO!" Roy shouts. "You don't have to go home but you can't stay here."

"Twenty-five, in my car."

"Where's your car?"

"GTFO!" Roy shouts, then breaks it down: "Get the fuck out!"

We stagger onto West Forty-First Street into a false dawn radiating from Times Square, and scatter like roaches down midtown blocks. Some head for the subway. Some get behind the wheel to drive back to the suburbs. Others climb in cabs headed downtown to after-hours clubs, where "ladies" get in free, then get in trouble. This is who we are every Saturday, when we put on other names, and bargain with urges that run our lives like bullies in the shadows.

The Limelight
1988

In the ladies' room of the Limelight there is a lounge, away from the booming and strobe-lit dance floor, separate also from the stalls and sinks, a soft-lit room with plush couches where women can set down their drinks, put up their feet, compare notes about their nights, their dates, and warn each other about the creep on the dance floor. It is a place of female refuge, and it's my favorite place in the world.

"You're beautiful!" someone says.

"Thanks!"

"So do you go out like this all the time?"

"I wish."

"Can I see a picture of you as a man?"

I pull my wallet from my bag and show them my driver's license, where they see a smiling guy with a receding hairline and the shadow of a goatee.

"Oh my god, look at him!"

"Let me see!"

"Cute!"

They look at me again. "So why do you do this?"

"I just like to."

"Look at his legs. I wish I had legs like that."

Some will share with me what they share with their girl-friends, confessing their insecurities about their looks, their misgivings about their boyfriends and fiancés. They want to know why men do the things they do.

"Because you put up with it."

"Oh my gawd, he's right!"

I can tell by their accents who is from the suburbs.

"So you're gay, right?"

"Think about it," I say, displaying a shaved leg and pointed foot, "what gay man would chase this?"

"So then . . . what?"

In the ladies' room of the Limelight they are confused about me, and yet I am welcome. I am a "New York experience," part of the tale they'll tell when they return to work on Monday and someone asks, "How was your weekend?"

"So where do you perform?"

"I'm not a drag queen."

"He looks like Barbra Streisand."

"Who does your makeup?"

"I do my makeup."

"You're good."

"So are you," I say. "You've got great eyes."

I get phone numbers when I'm out this way—more than I ever get as a man. There's always someone who wants to meet the guy in the driver's license photo. But a day or two later, when I dial the number jotted on the bar napkin, the voice on the other end is startled to get a call back from her wild Saturday night.

"Remind me again who you were?"

"We met at the Limelight, in the ladies' room."

"Oh yeah. So what were you doing in the ladies' room?"

Oddly, it made sense to meet women while wearing women's clothes. I only spoke to the ones who came up to me, and when they beheld my most shameful secret and still wanted to give me their number, I felt I'd already cleared a big hurdle. But in the sober light of Sunday, the man in the ladies' room was never boyfriend material. It was the late 1980s, people were terrified of AIDS, and straight women especially wanted nothing to do with a man who could be gay—*no matter what he tells you.*

AFTER A YEAR or so of going out dressed, I'd begun to matriculate to more mainstream places. I would still start the evening at the Fabric Factory or some other TV enclave. I'd arrive around ten, have a drink, and see if any of my compadres were up for venturing out. Kayla from Tennessee once came with me to the Limelight. Adele was game, and sometimes Stan. We might go down to Kelly's Village West, a laid-back lesbian-owned bar on Leroy Street. "What'll it be, ladies?" the bartender there said, so effortlessly it took my breath away. We might go to the Flamingo East, on Second Avenue, just below Fourteenth Street, which attracted an artsy, eclectic crowd. Stan and I once saw a drag king show there, and met an excitable Japanese woman named Kazumi who dressed in couture and said she was an artist, but wouldn't say what kind—just an artist. "Are you ooman? Are you man?" Kazumi kept asking, with a bemused smile. Later she invited Stan and me for drinks at a large nearby apartment she sublet with another Japanese woman.

Walking there, I had visions of making out with Kazumi. (I also had visions of a closet full of couture clothes, some of which might fit me.) When we arrived, the apartment was populated with others from the Flamingo she and her roommate had invited over. There was a lot of vodka, cocaine, and

loud techno music. There would be no making out with Kazumi. "Ooman? Man? Who can say!" she screamed over the
noise, more wasted than confused.

I loved being in mainstream places and meeting people of
every stripe. I loved being asked to join them, to accompany
them to another club, or a late-night diner or pizzeria, where
we'd hang around discussing art or politics. Sometimes the
night carried me on its back like a great wave, and I wouldn't
get home until dawn.

I wish there had been more of those nights, and that I'd
become friends with some of the people I'd met. But nothing ever took hold. Even if we'd kept in touch, they might
only have been party friends, and I wasn't much of a partyer.
New York nightlife centered on cocaine and casual sex—
things I stayed away from. I didn't generally enjoy going to
bars or clubs; they were just the only places where I could go
crossdressed.

Had I been gay, and part of a different social scene, there
would have been more space for my femininity. In gay bars
I occasionally saw drag queens on their nights off who still
wore some makeup, a pair of dangle earrings, or high heels,
blending femininity into their everyday lives. Watching drag
shows, I wondered how much of the day each queen spent
en femme. The less cartoonish ones, who grew out their hair,
may not have been the most skilled performers, but they sent
my mind racing. Performing was never as exciting to me as
being.

I WAS OF two minds. Part of me wanted to normalize
crossdressing—why did my feminine expression have to be
deviant?—while another part of me suspected its essence lay

in trespassing, and the charge that comes from doing "the wrong thing." If a night out grew lonely or boring, I'd periodically remind myself of the audacity of being in a dress. I'd recross my legs, check for a run, or gaze at my polished nails, just to feel my heart quicken. Walking home from the subway, I'd slow down to feel every step, the sublime rocking of my hips and ass with each click of my heels—a woman's sound that stirred my blood—and the whisper touch of stockings as my thighs scissored importantly past one another.

My crossdressing seemed to have the hallmarks of an addiction. Like an alcoholic who develops tolerance, I no longer found it satisfying to stay inside the safe confines of the Fabric Factory. I seemed to need more risk, a higher level of sensation, to achieve euphoria. The more widely I ventured, the more I risked running into someone from work. It would not have surprised me to see a male teacher among the chasers at Club Edelweiss or the Fabric Factory. A high school student with fake ID could easily wander into Webster Hall or the Pyramid Club and spot me in a wig and a dress. A female colleague might discover me riffling through dresses in the clearance section of Macy's, or shopping the ladies' floors of Century 21 or Syms. Isn't it a sign of addiction when a behavior jeopardizes your employment or compromises your values?

I had goals of marriage and family. I had no idea how to pursue a life that included female love and companionship, but I assumed it started with putting an end to dressing and growing out my body hair—otherwise how could I explain shaved or stubbly legs to a date? Dressing made it hard to date and have a sex life. At times I suspected that was its unconscious function—to keep me far from sex and intimacy. When I heard other crossdressers refer to themselves in the third person as "my girlfriend," it sounded silly, and a little creepy. Yet dressing was as time-consuming and as costly as dating—the shopping, the shaving, the beard cover, the makeup, the outfit, no the other outfit, the going out.

Sometimes in my optimism I told myself that dressing was just a temporary thing, an hors d'oeuvre to tide me over while I waited for the feast of life to begin. Though I had no idea what exactly that feast would consist of, nor when it would be served.

These two views of dressing—healthy vs. destructive— were at war inside most of the crossdressers I knew. We commiserated, and we were kind to one another. I'd never call what we had "community," maybe because we didn't trust what drew us together. None of us understood where cross-dressing came from. All too often it felt like a perversion and a curse, and the person you commiserated with might disappear for months—or *you* might.

The gay community, which was being decimated by AIDS, was still a community. The pink and black SILENCE=DEATH posters wheat-pasted all over New York City told them it was vital to come out. There were nightclubs and businesses, newspapers, districts of cities, and entire towns on Fire Island and Cape Cod devoted to their lifestyle. Whereas crossdress-ers had just a few bars catering to us one night a week, bars that blinked in and out of existence. (The Fabric Factory wouldn't make it into the 1990s.) There was no daytime life for us, and many of us hibernated during summer months, when makeup and beard cover would melt off our faces, and wigs and shapewear would cook us. Most of us preferred to keep this pocket of our selves sealed off from other pock-ets. We'd talk to each other about our lives, but there was no thought of ever meeting someone's friends or family, and little chance of us getting together outside of our nocturnal haunts. People were reluctant to give out phone numbers, for fear of who might pick up or hear a message on an answering machine. (This was before cell phones and texting, which no doubt would have helped us connect.) In place of community, we settled for an evening's camaraderie.

I once was out with Stephanie, the building contractor from Long Island, when she'd had way too much to drink. I sensed that dressing traumatized her, and that she drank to get through it. She was especially wobbly on her shoes when we walked out of a Hell's Kitchen bar around closing time. She bent over and vomited on the sidewalk, holding her hair from her face with one hand, while clutching her pocketbook under her other arm. We started walking again. I asked if she was OK. She quietly told me "Yeah," then threw up twice more before we reached the corner. I wasn't going to let her drive back to Long Island. After some protests, she agreed to crash at my place, and we took a cab to Brooklyn.

I saw a thick crop of flattened-down hair when she emerged from my bathroom, having removed her wig and washed her face. She still had her skirt and pantyhose on, and was bare from the waist up. Her torso was long and well-muscled. "Call me Steve," he said, and I told him he could call me Doug. I gave him a pair of pajama bottoms, took down a spare mattress I kept standing against a wall. (I'd tried to get Mrs. Caruso to take that mattress away when I discovered the sofa opened into a bed, but she refused, saying, "This is a furnished apartment.")

The next day I made us coffee. We talked a little about Long Island (I grew up on the north shore, he lived on the south shore), a little about where we shopped for clothes. He was polite and reticent—the silent type. He was also badly hung over. I loaned him a T-shirt, some old jeans, a pair of cloth Chinese slippers. I gave him a bag for his women's clothes and pocketbook. He thanked me, gave me a stiff hug, and left for Manhattan, where his truck was still parked. I never saw him—or Stephanie—again.

I got to know Stan a little bit. He was a factory supervisor at a canning company in Queens, and lived in Cobble Hill, one neighborhood away. He was fifteen years older than me and well educated, with a British air, a thin-lipped smile and a habit of saying "Indeed!" in place of something more like "Wow!" He invited me to play squash with him at the St. George Health and Racquet Club, where he was a member. Two men with shaved legs, competing.

He had gotten involved in a long-distance relationship with an attorney from Vermont named Linda. Linda was in her forties and pregnant with their baby. She may not have known about Stan's crossdressing; on the eve of one of her visits he told me he needed to "de-drag" his apartment.

I once joined Stan on a drive to visit her. He offered to drop me in Connecticut, where I could spend a weekend with my brother and his family, and then pick me up on his way back. He had Tom Petty's new album in his tape deck, and the song "Free Falling" blasted gloriously as we drove across the Brooklyn Bridge. As soon as we were outside city limits Stan reached for a six-pack of beers under a jacket in the back seat and popped open a can. He offered me one and I told him no thanks. He took a foamy sip and nestled the can against his crotch, swigging from it occasionally as we talked. The sight of him drinking while driving alarmed me, but I didn't say anything. I prayed it would be the only beer he drank. It wasn't.

A lot went unspoken between Stan and me. For one thing, we hardly ever talked about dressing, or what it meant to us.

"It has its moments," is all he would say. (He said that about a lot of things.) I wondered about his ascetic style, the pageboy wig and shapeless frocks, the lack of makeup or female name. I was also curious about his experience in Vietnam, but other than acknowledging having been there, Stan didn't go into it.

I was most curious about his relationship to Jeri, the young Black woman he was handcuffed to when I first met him at the Fabric Factory. What was *their* deal? He was very fond of her—that's all he would say. He never spoke in physical terms, preferring to wax philosophical about BDSM, explaining that it extended to more of life than people suspected, and that most of it was mental. He described "financial domination" and other power plays, forcing people to do things against their will. I questioned if that could really give someone sexual pleasure. "It has its moments," he assured me.

One time Stan called to invite me to an event in lower Manhattan where a famous dominatrix was giving a demonstration of the finer points of flogging. Not wanting to be closed-minded or judgmental, I agreed to go. Afterward, when he asked how I liked it, I confessed that I found it painful to watch, and frequently had to turn away. He made no comment at the time, but he attempted, repeatedly, to get me to come to another BDSM event with him, despite knowing how much I disliked pain. I started to wonder if putting me in an uncomfortable place held the thrill of dominance for him.

ON A NIGHT when I stayed till closing at the Fabric Factory, Vicky, the DJ, invited me to ride with her to the Vault, an after-hours S&M club downtown. The Vault wasn't my favorite place, but crossdressers got in for free (men paid $30), and

I could go there to feel like a woman for an extra hour or two on a Saturday night when I didn't want to go home.

In her car Vicky told me something remarkable: she'd never worn women's clothes until she was fifty. That's when a girlfriend coaxed her to try on some of her lingerie during foreplay. "And that was it," she said, snapping her fingers. "I was hooked." She said that once her mother passed away, and her kid graduated college, she planned to be "a full-time sissy." She said "full-time sissy" like I was supposed to know what that meant.

Vicky seemed to be in her own private world. At the Fabric Factory, you couldn't really have a conversation with her because she was so preoccupied with handling the music. She needn't have been; her outdated playlist was on a single cassette, but she insisted on hitting stop after each song so she could get on the mic to announce a factoid about Tom Jones or Olivia Newton-John in a screechy falsetto that sounded like someone driving a nail through a parrot. In the couple of years that I'd known her, I'd watched Vicky's skirts rise higher, and her girlish mannerisms become more caricatured, until she was prancing around the bar with thong panties and saggy butt cheeks exposed. She appeared to be growing breasts, though that could have been ordinary flesh rearranged by a cincher, some duct tape, and a couple of push-up bras (a trick many of us knew). Her face looked like it had been cleared by electrolysis. I'd asked her once if she was on hormones. She batted her hand and said, "Aw c'mon. I know who I am."

The Vault was in the space where the Hellfire had been—where Sara's sister Rivka had bartended just a few years before, in what seemed like another lifetime. They didn't have a liquor license, but you could buy soft drinks in plastic cups to mix with whatever alcohol you brought with you. Each room had a different scene. There were men in black hoods on leashes shuffling behind dominatrixes, women splayed out on wooden tables getting candle wax poured onto their breasts. There were people handcuffed to exposed pipes high along the wall, or tied to cargo nets and getting flogged. The most haunting space of all was a small dark room with nothing but a bare mattress on a concrete floor. People wore shiny latex, fishnets, combat boots, spike heels, nipple clips, testicle clamps, gags, blindfolds, diapers, and lots of leather.

The only ones who freaked me out were the voyeurs—men naked from the waist down, standing near the walls, masturbating. Occasionally I was startled by one of them standing right next to me, working the meat of his penis. As when a water bug suddenly appears in the middle of your kitchen, you couldn't tell if the masturbator crept up on you, or if it was you who drifted toward him unaware. The sight of these men jerking off in public set me on edge, perhaps because I always felt ugly when I masturbated.

I mostly hung out near the bar, where I struck up a conversation with a short-haired Latina woman who said she danced with the Joffrey Ballet. Judging from her trim body and lack of extraneous movement, I didn't doubt she was a dancer. She was dressed simply, in jeans and a black turtleneck, which made her seem out of keeping with the club, though she assured me she belonged there. She said she was lesbian—"But you're gorgeous," she added, smiling. I returned her compliment, but said that I wasn't into pain. Her dark eyes gazed into mine with a hardness I couldn't read. "Perhaps we could negotiate something," I said. She nodded yes, slowly, keeping her eyes fixed on mine.

We moved to a table in a corner. "I'm not sure what you're into—" I began. The smack came out of nowhere, hard across my face, making one of my ears ring. She peered into my eyes, as if to study the results of her violence. I grabbed her hands and squeezed them, clamped down on them like a vise grip, harder and harder, until she grew terrified. So much for our negotiation.

On my way out of the Vault I saw Vicky kissing a man who had her pinned to a brick wall. Her mouth was wide open, her eyes were shut. The passion on her face shocked me. Her assertion—*I know who I am*—flashed through my head as I wondered: *What really happens when you put on a dress?*

Stuyvesant

1990

An Indian girl named Tanya stands in the front of the classroom reading a poem about smoking pot with her calculus
teacher in the porter's basement. After a few tokes the teacher
says, "Man, you got to subtract the curve from the curve to
get the curve." The poem is a hit, and Tanya calls on Wesley
to read next. Wesley, a small waifish white kid, reads a poem
entitled "My Black People," which at first provokes, then
strangely charms us.

It is Friday, reading day in my poetry-writing elective. At
the beginning of the period, those who wish to read the poem
they've been working on all week write their names on the
board, and cross themselves off when they're called up. Matthew reads a poem called "There Are No Girls," a rhymed
catalog of the girls he feels are missing from Stuyvesant High
School:

> There are no butch girls
> There are no flower girls
> There are no sweet girls
> There are no sour girls . . .

He's playing on a familiar theme, the lopsided male-to-female
ratio at Stuy (as the school is affectionately called). "There

are no girls *in the girls' bathroom,"* Matthew concludes, to applause, then turns to the board and selects a girl.

Emily, tall and bohemian with short platinum hair, delivers a sonnet about a girl defending her disabled brother from Clark Avery, a football player who slow rolls alongside them on his bicycle:

> He says to me why don't you ditch that loony
> I've got ten bucks let's cut and catch a movie
> his wheels don't touch the ground he seems to hover
> I say to him you watch it he's my brother

Emily calls up Tara, and there's nervous laughter. Lately Tara has been writing poems in which her poetry teacher (me) is being physically tortured. There is no motive given, and she is always polite to me outside the poems. This week she's got electrodes hooked up to my testicles.

"Thank you, Tara," I say. "I can't wait to grade this. Who's next?"

When the bell rings they turn in their poems as they file out of the room. At the top of the page they've indicated the kind of feedback they want. The choices are "light edit," "just checks," or "surgery." "Checks" are check marks indicating what I think are their best moments. "Surgery" means close editing from me, whom they nickname "the slasher." The better they get, the more they want surgery. All I ask is that they take writing seriously. I don't accept late poems, unless the poem is signed by a poet at a reading the student attended on their own. Sometimes there's a note: "Dear Mr. Goetsch, please allow Mike to turn in his poem late. Best wishes, Philip Levine."

There are forty students crammed into this class. I also teach three lit classes, the journalism elective, and advise the student paper. I get up before dawn to prep lessons. Stuyvesant kids can chew up and spit out a conventional forty-minute lesson plan in about five minutes, so I've learned to ask only hard questions, questions I'm not even sure I can answer: *Why would Oedipus, given what the oracle at Delphi says, ever marry a woman older than him? Why would Auden call* Romeo and Juliet *a play about the failure to love? If Jim is escaping slavery, why are he and Huck traveling south?*

IN THE FALL of 1987, the day before I first met the students, the principal summoned all new faculty to his office. "You're probably wondering if they're smarter than you," said Abraham Baumel. "The answer is yes, but it doesn't matter. Your job is to open doors for them." It was the only quotable thing I would ever hear that man say, and he was right: Stuyvesant kids were geniuses—and by charter. Each fall, this one school huddled on East Fifteenth Street was fed the top eight hundred out of twenty-five thousand eighth graders who sat for the Specialized High Schools Admissions Test the previous spring. Those numbers made Stuyvesant more selective than Harvard. I don't know why the other science high schools—Bronx Science and Brooklyn Tech—were left with our sloppy seconds, or why the City of New York deprived neighborhood schools of their most talented students, and I'm not about to defend it. Abe Baumel, however, loved the setup, and went breathless bragging about the number of Nobel laureates who'd come from Stuyvesant, or Westinghouse prize semi-finalists, or National Merit finalists, or Model UN delegates, or debate champions, or Ivy League acceptance rates, and on and on—as if he had anything to do with it.

One beautiful outcome from this concentration of brain-power was a place where it was cool to be a nerd, and typical to be an immigrant. Students sat in the halls reading literature, playing chess, and conversing in forty different languages. When I taught Shakespeare I could require late notes and requests to use the bathroom to be in iambic pentameter. Another beautiful outcome was that each Monday, after a weekend of chaos and loneliness, I could step back into this vibrant community, this hive of youth and talent.

I'd been hired the year after Frank McCourt retired, and was known for a time as "Frank's replacement." They gave me his classroom—room 205, just up the grand staircase and past the principal's office—with a closet full of Irish record albums. I came to know Frank, who subbed for teachers on maternity leave, and helped us grade Regents Exams at the ends of semesters. He joined us at department lunches and regaled us with his beautiful and hilarious "benedictions." In the years before he began writing *Angela's Ashes*, he couldn't quit us. "You're Frank's replacement, aren't you?" said the payroll secretary, said the attendance secretary, said the guidance counselors when I first walked into their offices. Technically, there were three other English hires that year, but I just answered yes out of exhaustion.

"How's it going, Doug?" Frank said from the door of the teachers' break room. I was surrounded by stacks of student papers, and hadn't noticed him there.

"I know," I said, beholding the mess and quoting Thoreau: "Simplify, simplify."

"It's too late for that," Frank said. *"Organize, organize."*

I learned to stagger due dates between classes so I wouldn't be so swamped. But with a student load of 170, all of whom showed up, I was never without grading. I graded papers in coffee shops, restaurants, train stations, laundromats. I graded when I woke up in the morning, on weekends, during school vacations and at lunch in the faculty cafeteria, trying to get their papers back to them before the next ones were due.

"What's this?" a student asked, pointing to a ketchup stain on her paper.

"That's love," I said.

As the new kid on faculty I mostly went ignored. Why get to know someone without tenure, who may get excessed in June? I saw a lot of veteran teachers set in their ways, and pickled in their eccentricities. I suppose you could call them colorful: the alcoholic department chair who set up office in a bar around the corner on First Avenue, where students lined up to get his signature on class-change forms; the grammar maven who browbeat freshmen with exams on Latin roots and predicate nominatives until they were petrified of writing their own language; the draconian math teacher who made students write "death" on their textbook receipts next to where it said "penalty for loss"; the old German history teacher who declared the room we shared "a John Dewey progressive pigpen!" each day when he entered, ordering my students to arrange the desks in military rows for his class; the French teacher who doused himself in cologne before class and gave notoriously low grades, to compensate for the inflated grades of the other French teacher, a disheveled old lady with dementia.

Grade-hungry students were sandwiched between teachers, many of whom presided over their classrooms like fiefdoms, and parents, many of whom saw their children as guided missiles aimed at Harvard. The faculty was overwhelmingly male, and year after year, kids on the student paper spoke of pervasive sexual harassment, but had no idea how to cover it. (Stuyvesant had only turned coed in 1969, and we were still a decade away from an arrest for molestation, three decades away from a lawsuit.)

There were also some brilliant and dedicated veterans on faculty, and students with character to spare, who were future giants of science, technology, medicine, politics, diplomacy, education, the arts. We plucked them from their neighborhood schools, so we couldn't take credit for them—but still, they were wonderful.

AFTER SCHOOL I often took a ballet or jazz class on Broadway with renowned teachers such as Finis Jhung, Ronnie De-Marco, or Douglas Wassell. A cast member from *Cats* used Douglas's four o'clock ballet class as his preshow warm-up. He'd take barre with us, reel off a few quintuple pirouettes, then stroll across the street to the Winter Garden Theatre. In the elevator to the Broadway Dance Center someone had graffitied a note: "Advice to fags: don't look for a home in the theater." I'd never quite understood that message; was it bigotry, or was it tough love from one gay man to another?

Personally, I wasn't looking for a home in the theater (nor was I a "fag"). I'd performed in some small companies, and took class seriously, though mostly I danced to stay in shape. I also loved being around ballerinas, their strange and magnificent bodies, flexible and fluid, pointing their toes like bird claws. I noticed everything about them. This one wore tights under her leotard, that one wore them on the outside and folded the waistband down onto her hips, this other rolled them halfway up her calves. After class, they flopped on the floor in the hall, gossiping with one another. Some let their hair unravel spectacularly, or removed their shoes, revealing battered, chewed-up toes wholly incongruous with their porcelain faces. Just a few moments to rest and socialize, then they were up and gone. I might have been the only one in those classes not waiting tables between rehearsals or auditions.

Sometimes I'd shoot pool with Lou Gaglia at Julian's Billiards on Fourteenth Street. Lou was two years older than me and from my hometown of Northport, though we hadn't really known each other growing up. We both studied Tai Chi Chuan with the noted master Sophia Delza at Carnegie Hall Studios every Thursday. Lou was a teacher at a Catholic grade school in Chinatown, where nuns warned the children not to masturbate. He was shy and witty. We both loved sports and literature. We watched the Mets and ate Chinese takeout, but we never grew close, no matter how much time we spent together. We confined ourselves to a narrow set of subjects, as if by agreement. I didn't dare tell him what I did on Saturday nights, and I didn't know much about the burden he was carrying, just that he needed heart pills at a very young age.

Every so often I'd wander into Times Square porn shops to check on their selection of transgender magazines. These magazines were usually laid out in a few dedicated stacks on tables, beside other stacks dedicated to every conceivable proclivity—straight, gay, Black, Asian, fat, shaved, hairy, in uniform, tied up, urinating, etc. The T magazines had their own fairly wide range, from triple-X she-male porn (*Transsexual Climax, She-Males in Heat, Hung TV*), to naked posing (*Les Girls—Boys Will Be Girls*), to single-issue story porn (*Girl By Night, She's a He!*). Less raunchy magazines such as

Les Femmes focused on models and performers. My favorite of these was *F.M.I.* (*Female Mimics International*), which dubbed itself "a fantastic magazine for all the sisters out there who enjoy dressing as women to those who hope one day to actually become a real woman thru hormones and surgery." It featured incredibly beautiful transsexuals on the cover, articles on "transvestite world capitals," and photo spreads of female impersonators onstage, or half naked in their dressing rooms, or signing autographs in a doorway.

Several magazines published feminization fantasy tales. ("Her femme nephew had loved the feel and smell of satin and lace, and she felt it her duty to open his eyes to the fact he was different from the rest of the boys!") Others mixed in some journalism. *En Femme* reviewed books on people who transitioned, and reported on efforts to change marriage laws in various countries. *Tapestry* and *Transvestia* were tamer magazines geared to more conservative and closeted readers. They presented older transvestites in high-necked dresses and lace and pearls, and gave tips on posture and walking, breast forms and beard cover. They were like the *Ladies' Home Journals* of crossdressing—and yet I needed to go to a porn store on Forty-Second Street to find them. Most of these magazines didn't belong in a porn store.

Along the side or back of the stores was a wall of peepshow booths where men jacked off to videos, or to live performers behind glass. Every few minutes I could hear a woman moan, or say, "Yeah baby" or "Stroke it." There was always a guy mopping, not just the floors of the booths, but the whole store. The mop smelled of a sweet, slightly sickening disinfectant that, even though it was supposed to wipe away semen, might as well have been another kind of semen. And there was always a guy behind a register near the door reminding you to hold the magazines in both hands. He didn't care if you looked through them, as long as you didn't bend back the covers. Being forced to hold these magazines in both hands—like prayer books—exposed each customer's turn-ons all the more to the others, though none of us ever spoke. There was a feeling of vulnerability and shame about the place, like the shame on the faces of dogs shitting in public.

I usually purchased one or two of the magazines to add to my stack at home. The guy at the register slipped them into a brown paper wrapper and Scotch-taped it closed, and I shoved it deep into my schoolbag. Once home, I would spend countless hours between the covers of what I bought, drinking in images, memorizing facial expressions, hairdos, outfits, the length of their nails, the shapes of their lips and smiles, stances and postures. The posed photos and the candid shots. The passable girls living full-time interested me most, the "ladyboys" with sad wide eyes on the streets of Bangkok, glamorous transsexuals in their Miami Beach or San Francisco apartments (or whatever place they rented for the photo shoot). There was a black-and-white photo spread of the "legendary" showgirl Bambi that I could never get over. She was completely passable, thin and blond, wearing a full slip and ungartered nylons, leaning into her dressing room mirror; or bending forward in the bathtub while smiling sidelong at the camera, the point of a small breast brushing the surface of the water; or on a Paris street in a trench coat and kitten heels, talking with two other women or bending to greet a small dog on a leash.

There were features on classic female impersonators such as Danny La Rue and Craig Russell, conjuring fantasies of what it would be like to have a career dressed as a woman. I read about Les Ballets Trockadero de Monte Carlo, the drag ballerina troupe. I read about drag cabarets in their hey-days in Amsterdam, London, Berlin, New Orleans, Le Car-rousel in Paris, Finocchio's in San Francisco, the Jewel Box Revue in Miami.

Depending on the publication, the people in them were called T-girls, transvestites, she-males, trannies, impression-ists, vixens, temptresses, femmes fatales, or pageant queens. Also depending on the publication, the people in them referred to themselves as TV, TS, CD, transgenderist, closet queen, "my other half," gal, gurl, special girl, girl with something ex-tra, or lady. The one word I never saw used: "woman."

There were occasional articles purporting to explain "the growing transgender phenomenon." The preface to a pinup magazine declared transsexuals to be "psycho-sexual anom-alies" who must take "the lonely, but only road that has ever existed for them." An unnamed armchair historian in *Les Girls* ascribed the "explosion" in "transvestitic inclinations" to changing gender roles brought about by the sexual revolu-tion. Another called "transgenderism" a "bizarre evolutionary leap." I perused these brief, shoddy, typically unsigned arti-cles, then turned right back to the photos and dreamed, and touched myself.

I WAS GOING to therapy for depression, lying on Dr. Katz's couch for forty minutes every Monday. (I sensed exactly when she'd end each session because high school classes were also forty minutes.) When I first came to her office I told her I was a basket case and needed to lie down for "the full treatment," as though ordering a burger with everything on it. Maybe she was indulging me, or maybe she thought I was only capable of facing a ceiling.

Dr. Katz was an older woman, short, bespectacled, and formal. The only time I used her first name (Edith) was on the payment checks at the end of each month. When referring to my crossdressing, she used the terms "ladies' garments" and "attire," which made women's clothes seem clinical, like car parts, and not the supercharged talismans I experienced them to be. Dr. Katz had trained at the Psychoanalytic Institute, and I was familiar with the Freudian take on "object fetishes," which are regarded as perversions from "appropriate" erotic objects. Not that we ever discussed psychological theories—"Is that what 'the book' says?" she shot back, the one time I tried.

But Freud's view of fetishes rang somewhat true for me. Wearing women's clothes carried a sexual charge that seemed to be fueled by transgression and shame. I projected these feelings onto gorgeously dressed women (no shortage of them in New York), as though their own clothes and appearance were an electric current of sexual pleasure, but also a minefield of shame—the shame of lipstick, the shame of skirts and stockings, shame of heels and bras and panties. I marveled at the boldness of their presentation, the way a junior high bully might grudgingly admire the courage of a flamingly effeminate boy.

There was a glamorous short-haired woman I saw a couple mornings each week on the subway to work. We both boarded the front of the train at Court Street. She favored tailored skirt suits, sheer hose, classic pumps, deep red lipstick, and stud earrings. Often I'd see her doing the *New York Times* crossword puzzle in pen. I wondered where she got the discipline to ignore her magnificent hand holding the pen, her slender fingers and bright red nails, to focus on a clue asking for a river in Central Asia. I had my puzzle and she had hers, then she stepped off at Wall Street to figure out the New York Stock Exchange.

I knew that I viewed women through a completely fucked-up lens, yet knowing this did not affect that view. It was like having two selves; the reasonable self that insisted, *You're a man, don't complain,* was unable to get through to the wild self that kept flying out of my body to inhabit passing women. And possibly there was a third self to eroticize the whole situation, a voyeuristic self that was as wretched as the half-naked masturbators at the Vault.

When the papers reported the suicide of a fashion model who threw herself off an Upper West Side balcony, it confounded me: why would a beautiful woman ever do that? Whatever her problems were, I would have changed places with her in a heartbeat. I fantasized a scenario where I'd rush into her apartment in time to save her. *I find her on the balcony and try to convince her not to jump. I tell her how beautiful she is, though she's tired of hearing that (and maybe it's what got her into this mess). I point to the amazing wardrobe in her closet, and drawers full of magnificent underthings. "Why would you want to give this up?" I plead. She looks at me funny—though I have bought some time! I try to tell her how lucky she is to be in her body, and praise her proportions and curves, her beautiful hair and smooth skin, the magnificent flatness of her crotch. "What kind of a sicko are you?" she says, throwing a second leg over the balcony rail. "Now get the fuck out of here so I can kill myself in peace!"*

SHE WAS SITTING on the steps outside an office building on West Fiftieth Street, her head buried in what looked to be a tour book. I was sitting a few steps above her and to the right, shirtless on a hot day, drinking a carton of orange juice after a dance class. She was circling some things with a pen, and kept re-tucking her long dark hair behind her ears.

"Do you need directions?" I asked.

"No thanks," she said. "I live here."

"Sorry, I thought you were looking at a map."

"It's *TV Guide*. I'm picking out movies to record."

She showed me some of the listings she'd circled—westerns, horror flicks, documentaries. She was tall and quite good-looking. She wore a white T-shirt, jeans, and expensive loafers. Her eyes were ringed raccoon-like in black liner, though she wasn't goth.

"How often do you record movies?"

"Oh it's what I do, but lately my VCR is giving me trouble."

"I'm Doug," I said.

"Zorja," she said, and offered her hand. She asked if I knew how to program a VCR. I told her I could give it a try.

She lived alone in a nearby high-rise. Her apartment was spacious and mostly empty. There was a TV, several stacks of unlabeled videocassettes, new leather couches. The kitchen gleamed with expensive appliances and three big bowls of fruit. It was like an apartment in a furniture store, though the fruit was real. She said she was on a quest to become a "fruitarian"—to live on nothing but fruit—and showed me a how-to book by a fruitarian she idolized.

She was from California, just out of college, where she'd been a competitive swimmer. She was now a kept woman; her rent and living expenses were being paid by a Japanese executive who visited a few times a year. (I didn't ask how the arrangement had come to be.)

"You want to see something?" she said. She led me into one of the bedrooms and opened the double doors to a closet stocked with expensive skirts, blazers, and monochrome dresses, a few of them in dry-cleaning bags. Neatly arranged on the floor below were many pairs of expensive shoes—slides, sling backs and square-toed pumps with unusual blocky heels. "I only wear this stuff when he's in town," she said. "He needs me to accompany him to corporate functions."

For all her strangeness she seemed honorable, with no discernible agenda or goals, outside of taping movies and becoming a fruitarian. She was also, in a way, living a crossdresser's dream—the closets, the beautiful clothes, the furtive life of a "kept" woman—all of which inspired me to come out to her. I told her that if it were me, I would be wearing those clothes every day, whereupon *she* became the curious one, and started asking questions. She squinted and looked at me again, saying it was hard for her to picture me as a woman.

"Where do you go?" she asked.

"Different places. One of them you could walk to from here."

"Can you take me?"

THAT SATURDAY I stuffed clothes, makeup, shoes, and a wig in the black canvas bag I used for school, and took the subway for Zorja's apartment.

"Yo Goetsch," said a teenage boy on the platform at Union Square, where I was transferring.

"Hey Carlos," I said, giving him a fist bump. Carlos was the quarterback of the Stuyvesant football team. I'd choreographed him in the school musical, *Hello Dolly*, the year before. He didn't want to do it, but he owed Señor Diaz, his Spanish teacher, who was in charge of costumes, a favor. He and his offensive line agreed to be our dancing waiters—on one condition: Carlos had veto rights on all choreography, in case a step I gave them was too "faggy." Now here we were, two dudes out on a Saturday night, headed to wherever we were headed. The longer we spoke, the more I feared some telltale feminine garment was protruding from my bag, but I didn't dare look down to check.

"WOULD THIS FIT you?" Zorja said. She held up a little white dress with red polka dots and fluted skirt. *Wow!* I could fit into it, but there were cutouts in the bodice, and I didn't have the right bra. I also had to shave more of my chest hair. Zorja gave me a nude half-cup French lace underwire bra. It was snug, but it worked. I filled the cups with my homemade breast forms (bird seed poured into the cut-off feet of nylons, then knotted up).

Striding down Eighth Avenue, decked out beside Zorja, felt like the culmination of a lifelong vision, one that had its origin in an episode of the cheesy 1970s TV detective show *Vegas*. In the episode, three glamorous women conspire to rob a casino, resulting in a showdown on the airport tarmac. The lady criminals are strutting three abreast toward their getaway plane, when Detective Dan Tanna pulls up in his red sports car and shouts, "Stop!" The woman in the middle tells the other two to keep walking, then turns to fend off Tanna with an impressive series of martial arts kicks. But when her wig comes off someone shouts, "A man!," and Tanna pummels the crap out of her, or him. But I always came back to those three women sashaying toward the jet that would whisk them safely to Mexico. It was, for me, a vision of heaven. I contemplated it from every angle—including the experience of the actors themselves. How did the two female actresses relate to their crossdressing colleague? Were they warm toward him, or coldly polite? Did they share the same dressing room? And what about his experience? Was this just another job, or was he thrilled to be a tall pretty woman walking beside his gorgeous partners in crime—as I was, walking with Zorja, the two of us in heels and party dresses, turning heads on Eighth Avenue?

As soon as we entered the Fabric Factory all the crossdressers were checking out Zorja. She became engrossed in a conversation with a tall young CD I'd never seen before or since. She—I almost want to say he—wore a dollar-store rainbow tube dress and high-top basketball sneakers. She hadn't bothered to shave her legs, and her makeup was atrocious. She looked like a frat boy who'd lost a bet, or else someone out to satirize us. The whole time, the two of them were oblivious to everything else in that bar. It was as though Zorja had switched from me to another TV channel. I saw them exchange numbers. *There goes that,* I thought.

At least I knew I'd be walking out with her, if only to give back her dress. When we got back to her apartment, she immediately kicked off her shoes and changed into sweatpants and a T-shirt. She was completely indifferent toward me, though not unkind. She welcomed me to sleep in the guest room, which I did, alone. I called her the next week, but she didn't return my message, and I never saw her again.

Was I insane for wanting to date a kept woman who spent her days pirating movies and aspiring to an all-fruit diet? Probably. But I was starved for intimacy, and what were the odds of finding a woman, a beautiful one at that, who was OK with my dressing? Zorja had loaned me a dress, and stepped out into the night with me, and maybe, just maybe, we were each defective enough to belong together—a classic transvestite-meets-fruitarian love story.

Alas, no.

MOST FRIDAYS AFTER school I did research with my two favorite colleagues. "Research" was code for drinking martinis and talking about our week at a quiet Irish pub ten blocks north of Stuyvesant. "Will we be doing research later?" one of us could say to another of us if there were students around. Or we might get a note, delivered by a monitor in the middle of class, containing the single word "Research?"

All three of us loved literature and teaching and kids. We loved them differently, in different rooms all week, which made for interesting research. Michael Levine was a well-dressed gay man with prematurely gray hair. He had come to Stuyvesant the year I did, though he'd already taught in the system for fourteen years. Students would do just about anything for him. At his previous school in the Bronx he directed an all-Black cast in *Fiddler on the Roof*. He was the best classroom teacher I'd ever seen, though he never seemed like he was teaching. He'd stand off to the side in his suit and tie as the students self-conducted literary discussions that were at once rollicking and scholarly.

Grace Purcell was in her late forties and a bit of a femme fatale. She was short, blond, curvy, and liked short skirts and high heels. She spoke slowly, invitingly, making you slow down and travel her sentences with her. She had a flair for what Michael called pronouncements. "Listen to me," she once said to a class. "I'm getting a lot of 'my parents don't understand me' stories. If your parents don't understand you, why don't you try telling them who you are? My god, it's getting to be like the Dead Poets Society in here." When a second-term senior admitted she'd never once cut a class at Stuy, Grace opened the door and ordered her out. "Where will I go?" the girl asked, panicked. "Out," said Grace.

I was the young scholar in the trio, known for my range and rigor. By my third year I'd taught the entire English core curriculum, as well as electives in Shakespeare, African American lit, and fiction writing. A social studies teacher had nicknamed me "Real English," and the principal often sent visitors to observe my class. I was surprised to learn that students who didn't know me tended to fear me, while students I'd taught took pride in meeting the challenges I gave them. I didn't have my friends' charisma, though whenever a girl gave me a hard time Grace said, "I think she's in love with you."

It was Michael's idea to order martinis the first time we did research, and we stayed with that. "So Dr. Levine," Grace said after we toasted one another, "tell us something that happened this week," whereupon Michael treated us to some morsel of student misadventure, such as Rudolph Eliopoulos scaling the wall of the Central Park Zoo in order to fulfill the "one with nature" essay Michael assigned his juniors reading *Walden*.

"Tell Grace what Rudy said to you in the hall yesterday."

"Do I have to?"

"Yes," said Grace.

"Kid walks up to me, pats my belly with the back of his hand, leans in and whispers 'sit-ups.' Then he walks off."

"Sit-ups?!"

"Fuckin' kids—they know *exactly* how to get you."

Grace told us she was getting fed up with girls talking about "having it all." So finally she dismissed the boys from the room, shut the door, turned, and said, "Listen bitches," and delivered a lecture on female survival. Grace had grown up in rural Pennsylvania, and had just become a grandmother. Neither she nor her daughter were married.

I usually had news about a kid on the edge, such as Patty Incardo who'd turned in a scene where three friends sit on a stoop passing a bottle of vodka. Not much seems to be going on, until the speaker tells us why she's positioned herself in the middle: that way, as the bottle gets passed, she gets twice as many swigs. Suddenly it's a story about alcoholism.

"*The speaker*," said Michael.

The dirty secret of Stuyvesant was that our high-achieving students had the same problems as any other kids, and often it was an English teacher they told about it. We often alerted the guidance counselors to students with addictions and eating disorders, students who were homeless or in dangerous homes. The guidance counselors told us to stay in dialogue with such kids, since they already trusted us. We didn't always contact Child Welfare, even though by law we were required to report, because the foster system was a horror show. Cameron, a boy we'd all taught, was sleeping on friends' couches, and had perfect attendance. He wore cloth Chinese shoes all winter, and walked right past his father, who lived on a bench in Stuyvesant Park, each day on the way to school. Cameron wrote the best essay on Emerson's "Self-Reliance" I'd ever received. We were pretty sure he was going to make it to graduation, and then college, where he'd have a level playing field.

The dirtier secret of Stuyvesant involved male teachers and female students. I'd been working late and stopped for takeout at a local Chinese restaurant, where I saw a young girl dining with a math teacher. The girl was tall, wore heels, ripped stockings, and a lot of makeup. She was my student,

and had been cutting my class for weeks. The math teacher
came over as soon as I spotted them, and invited me to join
them. I told him no thanks.

"Jesus," said Grace.

"Should I report it?"

"Who are you going to report it to?" said Michael. He was
right, our administration was an old boys' network.

"What if I talked to *her*?"

"She's probably trading sex for grades," said Grace. She
grabbed her bag and walked off to the ladies' room.

"What we need is a plaintiff," I said to Michael.

He ordered another round.

"**YOU KNOW WHAT** they say about martinis?"

"No, tell us."

"One is fine, two is too many, and three"—Michael took a
sip—"is just right."

After five o'clock the bar began to fill. I noticed the women
coming from work, and what they were wearing. Perhaps later
I'd shave again, put on a dress, and go out.

It was on the third martini that our research turned to
one another. The week of Grace's birthday she returned from
the ladies' room looking dumbfounded, pointed a finger to her
face, almost like a pistol, and said, quite drunk, "This is what
it looks like to be fifty." She kept repeating that—"This is
what it looks like to be fifty"—as Michael held her hand. On
another Friday she revealed she was having an affair with her
sister's ex-husband, a machine parts salesman in Sarasota.
No one in her family would speak to her.

On another Friday, Michael turned to me and said, "So
we've been wondering about you."

"What about me?"

"You're a single man, and we never hear about your dates."

"I go on dates."

"We never hear about *second* dates," Grace corrected him. "And you're always noticing women's clothes."

"So you think I'm gay?"

"No," said Michael. They looked at each other, deciding who would say it.

"We think," Grace said, "you're either a virgin or a crossdresser."

I had feared this moment would come, feared it would threaten my professional life, as it had ruined my personal life. The two of them, sitting across from me in a booth, looked like my friends, but what did I know about friendship? I thought hard, trying to determine if this inquisition was a good thing or a bad thing. But I was drunk, and my mind couldn't land anywhere.

"Both," I said.

"I knew it," Grace said, turning to Michael.

We spoke for a while—not long—and only about my crossdressing. I answered their questions. *How often? Where do you go? What bathroom do you use?* Each sentence out of my mouth I immediately wanted back. Then again, maybe it was time to let some people into my life.

"Last week," Michael said, "a transvestite was beaten to death two blocks from me in Carl Schurz Park."

"I know," I said. "She was a prostitute. I don't go walking in parks at night."

"But you use the subway."

"I do."

"Well," he said, "I worry about you."

He got up from our booth to use the men's room, leaving

Grace and me alone. There was an awkward silence, then she put her feet up—shoes and all—across the seat. She had on a short skirt. "So," she said, in her femme fatale voice. "How do you like my stockings? They're Hanes."

Someday there would be language for this weird gesture (i.e., "fragile cis female guarding her habitat"), but at the time, in the martini swirl of my fear and confusion, the only thing clear was her intent to shame me. Staring down at her shiny calves, pressed and fattened against the seat of the restaurant booth, I immediately regretted coming out to Grace.

AFTER 1992, WHEN Stuyvesant relocated to Battery Park City, we conducted our research at a bar called riverrun in Tribeca. It was a fitting place for English teachers—"riverrun" being the first and last word of *Finnegans Wake*. I never spoke of crossdressing again, and they didn't bring it up. We met for research less and less often, until Michael confessed, glass in hand, that all this time he'd been off the wagon, and he needed to stop drinking. He was an alcoholic.

Jeri
1991

She was quiet, slender, plainly dressed in jeans and flats, free of makeup, a Black woman who kept her hair close-cropped. We had sandwiches in a café on Montague Street. I asked about her interests, where she grew up. "Brooklyn," she replied. She barely spoke—I couldn't tell you what her voice sounded like.

She was in her early twenties, maybe five years younger than me, and twenty-five years younger than Stan, whom she was handcuffed to at the Fabric Factory the night I met her. I couldn't imagine what kind of sex they were having, unless what I saw—the handcuffs, his shapeless dress, her silence—*was* their sex.

When Stan called to ask if I found Jeri attractive, I told him yes, half out of politeness. Then he gave me her number. I supposed Stan was now focused on Linda and their baby—though he didn't say. Everything went unspoken. I figured Jeri would explain the situation. She didn't. Perhaps she was under some role-play orders not to speak.

We walked back to my place. While I was in the bathroom she switched on my little Panasonic TV and turned to a cooking show on PBS called *The Frugal Gourmet*.

"Oh I *love* this show!" she cried.

"You do?" I said, coming in and sitting beside her. The

frugal gourmet was a grandfatherly white man with wire-rim glasses, a white goatee, and a nebbishy voice.

"He turns you on," I said.

"Shh!" Jeri said. Her eyes had come to life.

When *The Frugal Gourmet* was over, I asked, "Were you attracted to me as Tina?" (Tina was the name I used for going out.) "Do you prefer me as a man?"

She stared down. The life was back out of her.

"Did you ask to see me, or was this Stan's suggestion?"

No reply. She looked around and asked, "Where do you sleep?"

"We're sitting on a sofa bed."

"Can I see?"

SO THIS WAS IT. This was how I would lose my virginity. It was about time—no, long past time—to get it over with, even if I wasn't particularly turned on. Maybe it would shake something up.

After I'd removed the cushions and unfolded the bed I said, "I don't have any condoms." She made no reply—I was getting used to that. I put on a sweater, told her I'd be back in a bit, and walked down Court Street looking for a store open on a Sunday that would sell condoms. It was drizzling, a heavy mist that soaked my sweater. The inseams of my jeans chafed against my shaved thighs. The day was weirdly bright, and something about the rain and the light lent a cinematic feel to things. Though I was not desperate to have sex with Jeri, I suddenly felt like a character in a movie who is hell-bent for sex with a woman he knows nothing about, other than the fact that she is partial to older white men in dresses or kitchen aprons. Maybe she'd be gone by the time I got back, I thought, turning on Atlantic Avenue. Maybe I wouldn't find a condom. I half hoped I wouldn't, and yet I was moving like a man on a mission.

THE SEX WAS as barren as our conversation. After minimal foreplay (no kissing) she pushed me down and climbed on top. She impaled herself on my penis, and started bouncing up and down. I was in an awkward position; my head hung off a corner of the sofa bed, which creaked as she bounced. I feared the bed would collapse and I'd break my neck. As she rocked herself on top of me, the base of my penis began to chafe (more chafing). I was in pain, but somehow unable to speak. I looked for her eyes. They were half shut, and tilted up toward a high corner of the wall. I lay catatonic and frightened while she crashed down on my hips, harder and harder, until she came.

NOT LONG AFTER, I stood on the stoop of the brownstone watching her walk up the block. Presumably she was headed toward the neighborhood where she lived, though she could have taken a right on Court Street and gone to Stan's place. I didn't wait to see. I turned around, went back inside.

So I lost my virginity—but did I? Does it count if you don't come? If you feel no pleasure? If it feels like rape?

Straight Pool
1991

I am shooting pool into the morning at Mammoth Billiards on West Twenty-Sixth Street. I've been here since school let out on Friday, so I am in work clothes—chinos, loafers, a lifeless polo shirt. I can shoot pool for twelve hours straight and never get tired.

The billiard table is a perfect world, where geometry tells the whole truth and nothing but the truth. There's no doubt about solid spheres and straight rails, as you plant three fingers like the tripod of a lunar module on clothed slate, loop the other two into an OK sign, through which you slide a stick smooth as glass. There's no changing the laws of impact, spin, speed, and friction, as the ball you called, its unique color like jockey silks, hits the pocket hard, or taxis slowly to a precipice and plunges out of existence. And if you miss, the table shows you why and how badly—that, too, is exact.

Free will resides in the white cue ball, which must be controlled. A shot starts with a theory of where that ball will land, the theory becomes a vision, then the vision must be executed. Good players, after pocketing an object ball, can draw the cue ball back like a yo-yo on a string, with English— sidespin—to coax it across two rails and down to the other end of a nine-foot tournament table. Still better players can stun an object ball, causing the cue ball to slide laterally to a new spot in a crowd. At first the movement seems like the drift of a cloud. When you see where it's parked—straight on for the next shot—it can seem like luck. Getting shape it's called, and when it happens time after time, and the player has run the table without leaving himself one hard shot, it is like the cracking of a safe.

The jukebox at Mammoth is trash. It's 1991, and to be fair, we haven't yet recovered from the 1980s, a deplorable time to own a pair of ears. The Friday-night drinkers and daters who suck at pool also suck at music. They never tire of Paula Abdul and Milli Vanilli, unless it's Phil Collins and Michael Bolton, or Guns N' Roses screaming "Welcome to the Jungle," signaling the end of intelligent life. The best thing by far in that jukebox is Sinéad O'Connor's cover of "Nothing Compares 2 U," which makes me feel beautifully wrecked, and completely in sync with Sinéad, whom I am certain I could rescue, and who could rescue me, if only she knew I was here at Mammoth Billiards wasting my life.

My opponent tonight is a huge country boy who likes to pick fights with Black people. He tells everyone to call him Big Tex, but I call him Ron. Ron wants us to think he's a hit man. ("Ah do favors fer paiple," is the way he puts it.) We are playing straight pool to 300 for twenty bucks and the time. The time on the table, by the time we get done, will cost forty or fifty bucks. Long about dawn, as I'm crouching to shoot, Ron's massive hand appears before my face.

"See this?" he says, displaying a gold ring. "Ah got married today."

I STARTED SHOOTING more pool when I decided to stop dressing—a decision brought about by several concerning events, one of which was having my wig ripped off on a

Manhattan-bound C train. I was headed to Manhattan on a Saturday night. I'd gotten on at Jay Street and was seated next to the open doors while the train idled in the station. I heard some boys laughing on the platform behind me. Normally I'd have asked someone how long the train had been idling, but I tried to avoid speaking when I was out as a woman. I crossed a leg and opened a book.

A hand reached in, yanked my wig off, and deposited it on the subway platform, just outside the car. I don't think I've ever seen anything as out of place as that wig on the subway platform. I jumped out, snatched it up, jumped back on the train, jammed the wig back onto my head, and kept my hand pressed there until the doors closed. I kept looking straight ahead, frozen. Probably people were staring at me. I stayed small, like a lady, my legs tightly crossed. Eventually I opened the book again and read it until I reached my stop, then stepped off to begin my evening out.

There are moments, when you look back at them, that make you wonder how you ever lived through them. The answer is you didn't. Part of me will always be on that platform with that wig, hearing those boys laughing. I suppose it could have been worse. The kid could have snatched the wig and run off with it just as the door closed. I could have been stuck riding the train in a dress, full makeup, and a receding hairline. Then again, that would have only been a different kind of death.

Something else happened, in another subway station, that was even more disturbing. I had just come from work, and was standing on the platform at Union Square when a beautiful woman walked by and I felt . . . nothing. I looked around at other attractive women, and similarly had no reaction inside. It wasn't like I was now attracted to men. Seeing men had always been like watching TV in black and white, whereas women were in Technicolor. But now they weren't. Had crossdressing deadened my attraction to women? Was it messing with my sexuality?

The weekly ritual of transformation, the shaving and makeup and dressing, had begun to feel rote. I first realized this while putting on a burgundy dress, a simple work dress I'd found at the clearance rack at A&S. As I slipped it over my head, I suddenly felt . . . nothing. Beneath the dress I had on panties, pantyhose, and a bra, yet nothing turned me on about that either. And doing my makeup, which I'd always taken pleasure in, felt like a chore that evening.

Then, in a flash, I trampolined off the nothing into a new excitement, thinking, *This must be what women feel as they dress and make themselves presentable to the world: nothing! This nothing could be it!* The boredom I felt in the burgundy dress became a turn-on—*because* it was boredom. Though it only lasted a moment. All evening I tried to bounce off my boredom, but mental gymnastics could only get me so far. I came home to the chore of washing off my makeup, the mud swirl of foundation, blush, shadow, and mascara in the grease of cold cream. My eyes were bloodshot and irritated. Blowing my nose brought up fields of snot reeking of cigarette smoke. I unfolded the sofa bed and hit the mattress exhausted. Curling up to sleep, I still liked the feeling of one shaved thigh against the other, though the slightest move brought the scratch of stubble already growing in.

Mornings after going out were hardest of all. I lay in bed late, feeling depressed and paralyzed. I thought of Odysseus, half dead and washed up on the shore of some Aegean island. Only he was discovered by a king's daughter and her handmaidens, who massaged him with oil and nursed him back to health, whereas I lay washed up alone in a no-man's-land. Something inside me needed to reassemble itself before I could be upright.

On one such comatose morning I was startled by a series of loud bumps, then a final crash at the foot of the stairs just outside my door. Then nothing. Half a minute later, I heard the heavy footsteps of Pat, the landlady's nephew, coming up the stairs from the ground floor. Not long after, the bleating of an arriving ambulance, the EMTs coming through the front door, their brief questions, Pat's brief answers, pops of static on a radio in the vestibule, a coordinated lift of what had to be a body, onto what had to be a gurney, and they were gone. The whole time, I lay in bed motionless, appalled by my depravity, my failure to get up and help another human being just a few feet away. Though had I opened my door, anyone could have seen the remnants of eye makeup on my face from the night before, and glimpsed behind me the women's clothes strewn about my apartment.

Eventually I arose. I stared out the kitchen window, as if there were something to see in Mrs. Caruso's tiny fenced-in backyard. I opened the refrigerator and stared into that for a while. I stared at my face in the bathroom mirror, removing the remaining gunk from my swollen lids with a Q-tip. Slowly, I began to straighten the place, which never felt quite straight. I'd long run out of space for my women's things, which had become a second wardrobe. Even though I had no special plans for Sunday, I felt sad to have slept through a chunk of it. I had work to do, lessons to plan for the week ahead, a ton of grading. Maybe I'd sit around watching football, trying not to think about the Sundays other people in Brooklyn were having, playing softball, going to galleries, getting together, getting married. Maybe I'd take an afternoon ballet class on lower Broadway, walking out past where the man died. Did he die?

I was twenty-eight and severely depressed. I'd been depressed for a decade. Therapy, which I still attended weekly, had yielded no insight into my isolation. All I knew was that I did not want to live this way, and crossdressing only made me more isolated, so I stopped.

I STILL PAID occasional visits to TV bars, just to be in the atmosphere. The Fabric Factory was no more, but there was a new place where people went on Saturdays, run by Vicky, who'd convinced a German restaurant just off Park Avenue South to have a TV night. I came dressed "in drab"—as opposed to "in drag." (We really needed to elevate our slang.)

"So what's with the new look?" Adele asked.

"I'm taking a break."

"How come?"

"I need to figure some things out."

"Like what?"

I explained my fear that dressing might be fueling my depression. She told me I was overthinking it. "If you're going to come here anyway," she said, "just put on a fucking dress." Adele's hostility surprised me. Did she think I was pathologizing her along with myself?

"I want your shoes," said Vicky. Several girls asked for my clothes, fully expecting me to purge my wardrobe. That's what crossdressers do. We're outed, or we have a new girlfriend, or we make a New Year's resolution, or we just freak out and, overwhelmed with shame and loneliness, we purge. We fill a few Hefty bags, toss them in a dumpster, and walk off to have another go at manhood. Sooner or later we buy a pair of panties and it all starts again. But not me—I kept my clothes.

THE PREMIER POOL hall in New York at that time was Chelsea Billiards on Twenty-First Street (around the corner from the Limelight). It had the best equipment, hosted the big tournaments, and the top local shooters played for high stakes on Saturday nights, putting up their cash in advance—literally: they stashed the bills in the light fixture above the table. The iconic Julian's Billiards ("No Swearing, No Gambling") on East Fourteenth Street, above the entrance to the Palladium nightclub, was a smoke-filled dive frequented by old hustlers who looked and smelled like hobos. For ten bucks one of them would give you an insane spot at nine-ball, pull down a cue from the wall, roll it on the table to show you how warped it was, then beat you easily. Overpriced Amsterdam Billiards on the Upper West Side was for yuppies; Fat Cat's, in a basement below a Citibank on Christopher Street, was favored by club kids and had blue tables. At Steinway Billiards in Astoria they actually played billiards—three cushion billiards— which involved three heavy balls that traversed huge tables with no pockets. One ball struck another, rolled out to the Hamptons, got a coffee in Connecticut, and drifted back to Astoria to touch the third ball just before it ran out of gas.

As with the dance world, and countless other pastimes in New York City, pool had its own subculture. You knew who would be where on a given night, and if you stuck around you'd have access to the luminaries. I once racked balls for Tony Robles and Flaco Rodriguez at a tournament. I played nine-ball at Chelsea Billiards against Jeanette Lee, before she was a fixture on ESPN, where the announcers called her "the Black Widow." She wore a long black skirt with a deep slit. When she fell behind to a male opponent that slit would open, and her lovely thigh would make its appearance, to great distraction. I took a few lessons with Jim Burke, who'd played in three U.S. Opens. Jim was the one who showed me you could run a table with nothing but easy shots. He never looked like he was doing anything—I don't even know if he could *make* a hard shot.

Jim was the most unlikely of gurus. He had a very limited vocabulary, and sounded like Burgess Meredith in the movie *Rocky*. His lessons consisted of me playing a rack with him heckling. "Stay off the rail!" he'd bark, whenever I left the cue ball on the rail. "You're on the rail again!" he'd helpfully point out. There was also positive encouragement: "You stayed off the rail that time." Sometimes he'd even say, "Your game went up," though mostly it was to give himself credit. I paid him ten bucks a lesson. He was decrepit, probably malnourished, and probably not as old as he looked. "Can you loan me something until I cash this paycheck?" he'd ask, then show you a check in his wallet that looked like it had been refolded a hundred times. His wallet also contained an official-looking shield, which he'd flash from a distance to token booth clerks to get into the subway for free. I never got a good look at that shield. He was a terrible teacher, but I couldn't come near beating him. "You see?" he'd say, as he ran the table, "now I got shape on the four ball. That's what I'm trying to tell ya." I actually don't know what he was trying to tell me, but he indeed had shape on the four ball—and no, he wasn't on the rail.

I often played with Luke, a tall skinny native New Yorker around my age, who used to be a punk rock drummer, then went into the roofing business his dad owned. He had a one-bedroom place on Perry Street, and was so certain he'd never cook for himself he stacked newspapers on the stove and had Con Edison turn the gas off. Luke liked to laugh about the cast of characters around us. "I'll bet Jim Burke's been carrying that old paycheck in his wallet for fifteen years," he'd say.

Sometimes I played with Richard, a stylish Black man around fifty years old. Richard favored extravagant shots involving banks and combinations. He could generate amazing English, jump and masse the cue ball, sending it on adventures. Some of his shots took a while to develop, like a trick play in football. You thought you knew what a shot was doing, then he'd hold up two fingers and say, "Part two," and something else would go down.

Richard played a lot with a tall muscle-bound guy named Frederico, who spent many hours at Mammoth doing meticulous drills at a tight-pocket table downstairs. He was trying to perfect an alternative system of aiming, having to do with calculating the degree of eclipse where two balls meet. He wanted to go pro, but I thought taking the intuition out of pool would ultimately limit him. Luke was certain Frederico was gay, which hadn't occurred to me until he said it. I just thought he was gentle and kind, especially for a muscle-bound guy. I was surprised to see Frederico leaving Mammoth early on a Friday evening, just as I was arriving. I asked where he was going, and he said, "Home, to watch the war." The U.S. invasion of Kuwait—Operation Desert Storm—had begun. I hadn't realized it until Frederico said it: this was the first war you could watch on TV.

Shooting pool put me in an all-male world, which saddened me, and made me think of Hemingway's *Men Without*

Women. The only women at Mammoth were on dates with boyfriends who ogled them as they shot, or told them where to aim. The one exception was a nineteen-year-old Chinese girl named Jane, a beautiful tomboy who'd graduated from Brooklyn Tech High School. I wondered why a smart young woman would be hanging around alone at Mammoth. One night Jane showed up in a pair of hot pants, sheer nylons and high heels, instead of her usual jeans and oversize sweatshirt. It was a spectacular transformation. She also had a new cue she showed me. "Nice," I said, balancing it in my palm, lining it up for a shot. "You do realize," I said, handing it back to her, "this is a lefty cue." Her face panicked for a moment, then she realized I was joking, which earned me a kick in the shin with one of her high heels.

I bought my cue, a Meucci, from a Korean nine-ball player named Eddie Lam. It had an especially narrow shaft and ivory inlays at the butt end that reminded me of Morse code. He knew I liked his cue, and on a night when he was strapped for cash he sold it to me for a hundred bucks. Eddie was always playing against a young Polynesian guy named Andy who had one misshapen eye but was otherwise good-looking. The two were aggressive and freewheeling in their play, yet modest when you spoke to them. I don't know what they did in their non-pool life. They liked to gamble, and they'd bet on just about anything. Luke and I once saw them flipping dollars—like a coin toss, except with paper bills. One of them tossed the dollar in the air, it fluttered to the floor, they peered down at it, came to some determination, then Eddie handed it to Andy, or Andy handed it to Eddie. The loser pulled out another bill and they flipped for that, though mostly it was the same bill going back and forth between them. "That might be the most pathetic thing I've ever seen," Luke said to me.

At midnight Andy and Eddie stopped, shook hands, and wished each other a Happy New Year. Luke and I did the same.

THE JOURNEY HOME from Mammoth Billiards at four or five a.m. began with a long wait for the F train. As the rats frolicked on the deserted Twenty-Third Street platform, lines of poetry would float up to me. They weren't lines of Frost or Eliot or anyone else I'd read, so I guess they were mine—just fragments, more sound than meaning. When the train finally arrived, I sat among the homeless, slouched and sleeping, their worldly possessions in taped-up bundles beside them, while the lines of poetry continued to roll around my brain. I came up from the subway in Brooklyn, walked down Fulton Street under a few vague stars, across to Borough Hall, and into Brooklyn Heights. There were no lights on in the apartment towers of Cadman Plaza, or any of the brownstones, just the primordial neon of Queen Italian Restaurant on Court Street. I turned onto Schermerhorn, tree-lined and deserted, and heard the first peeps of morning birds.

Once inside, I poured a glass of milk and sat in my tiny kitchen with a notebook. I jotted down the lines that had come to me in the subway, then added some more and played with them. The lyric phrases started to take on the flesh of a narrative. These would become my first published poems.

It's a weird way to begin writing poetry: shoot pool for hours with fellow misfits, watch the rats play, ride the subway among the dispossessed, until something has been discharged, or otherwise exhausted, clearing the way for words. I think I also needed the feeling of being the only one awake among millions of sleeping people—affording me a strange and elevated privacy, as though I were standing watch over consciousness, or treading the afterlife—in order to write. In a few years I'd compose a line about my uncle, who'd gambled away his soldier's pay in Vegas, on his way home from Vietnam: "He'd fallen so far behind he was ahead, just by being alive." That's also how it felt when I began writing poetry.

I had replaced an addiction to crossdressing with an addiction to shooting pool, which I would soon replace with an addiction to poetry. That's not quite right, but that's the story I told myself. The other story I told myself was that I was one of Hemingway's "men without women," condemned somehow to being alone, wanting only a clean well-lighted place. That wasn't right either. It was an impostor narrative for the one I couldn't see, not even with that closet in the wall, full of dresses I wasn't throwing out.

URNotAlone
1994

I am watching the New York Knicks play the Houston Rock-
ets in Game 1 of the NBA finals. I have the TV muted because
I am also on the phone with my therapist, who called during
the first quarter. A month ago I told her I wanted to stop therapy. She had been redirecting our conversations to the subject
of a group she wanted to start. "Do you have any more feelings
about joining the group?" she would ask, halfway through a
session. I tried to drum up some feelings for this nonexistent
group—she often accused me of not expressing my feelings—
but it was hard to consider the group without first knowing
the fee, which she wouldn't tell me. When she finally did tell
me the price, one I could not afford, I was infuriated. I sat up
on the couch—the first time in seven years—looked her in
the eyes, and said, "You have wasted my time." At her urging,
we met three more times for "closure." The reason you need
closure with some people is the same as the reason you'll
never get it.

She has called—post-closure—to ask if I'm absolutely sure
I want to end treatment. I suppose I should shut off the TV,
but did I mention the Knicks were in the finals for the first
time in twenty-one years? Besides, she hadn't done *me* that
courtesy. When we first began working, she would take phone
calls during our sessions. The calls were often from her adult
daughter. After hanging up, the rest of the sessions were

spent in silence. Each week I'd ask her to unplug the phone, but she was reluctant, and wanted to explore "the phone issue." She wanted to know how the phone calls made me *feel*. It was important I connect with my *feelings*. I told her it felt like I was undergoing open heart surgery, during which my surgeon, with bloody gloves, talked on the phone. She told me that wasn't a feeling. ("For example, do you want to kill me?" she suggested at one point.) She finally agreed to unplug the phone, though if I forgot to remind her, it inevitably rang, and she'd answer it. When I did remind her, she made a big performance out of reaching low on the wall, grunting with effort to pull out the jack.

Yet some of the sessions had been cathartic. She was the only one who knew how depressed and afraid I was. I cried often. I'm not sure if that was worth seven years of therapy, but who knows: maybe Dr. Katz's function was simply to keep me alive. Then again, as Thoreau suggested, a Saint Bernard could save your life.

In our closure sessions, I confessed that I'd never gotten over the phone issue, and couldn't understand why she didn't just turn her phone off. "I could have easily done that," she said, "but I felt it would have been unwise to forfeit its therapeutic value." I said, "Don't you think there's already enough pain in the universe, without you intentionally adding to it?" I suppose it might have been therapeutic to smash her phone to bits and stomp out of there, but at the time I couldn't bear the thought of having to look for another therapist and begin all over again.

The final thing Dr. Katz said to me was, "All the answers you need are inside you." Even if she lifted that from a book, it was comforting to hear.

But it *wasn't* the final thing, because now she's on the

goddamn phone asking if I'm absolutely sure I want to stop seeing her, and I'm wondering whether she's calling out of financial concern, or if she fears I'm going to throw myself off a bridge. I'm missing a lot of her words because I'm trying to stay with the basketball game. Plus there are sirens outside my window. I moved to Manhattan last year, to an apartment near St. Vincent's Hospital, so I hear the occasional incoming ambulance. Though right now it sounds like all hell is breaking loose. "Are you sure, Mr. Goetsch?" Dr. Katz says one last time. "Yeah, I'm sure," I say, and we say goodbye yet again, and I hardly feel a thing.

THE HARDEST PART of leaving therapy was losing the sense that I was "doing something" about my chronic depression. By going to appointments, I felt like a responsible parent getting help for a troubled child. Now I was more like my own camp counselor, planning activities to keep myself busy. I made a list each morning, including even the most inconsequential things. The list was a rope bridge to get me across the day, and I'd cross off items (e.g., ~~nap~~) as though I were accomplishing things.

Summers were especially challenging, without the schedule and workload of teaching. I arranged trips to writing conferences and poetry workshops, which nourished my love of poetry, my hunger to learn craft. I studied with Marvin Bell and Judith Kitchen in Brockport, New York, and Stephen Dunn, who would become a mentor and friend, in Brunswick, Maine. Alvaro Cardona-Hine, another future friend and mentor, taught a haiku workshop at a teahouse on a pond in Taos, New Mexico. I went to Coos Bay, Oregon, and Dublin, Ireland, all for poetry.

One year I auditioned for summer stock in Albany, and landed the role of a featured Jet in a production of *West Side Story* that mounted Jerome Robbins's original choreography. I was thirty, older than most of the cast. We were friendly, though somehow I didn't make any friends. They were people who aspired to a life of performing, and several wound up on Broadway. For me it was just something to do. I bought a used bike to get around Albany, played a lot of pool at the Golden Cue on Central Avenue, out by the state university. I frequented the cafés and record stores on Lark Street, and noticed a lot of young queer people. I found a gay bar called the Queen, and saw some drag shows there.

Another summer I applied for and received a National Endowment for the Humanities fellowship to a seminar on Euclid and Plato at St. John's College in Santa Fe, New Mexico. There were a dozen schoolteachers in the group, and they were wonderful people. When the seminar ended, I wanted to see more of the Southwest, and I had an invitation to visit an old Northport friend who'd moved to L.A. One of the teachers knew a woman who was also heading to L.A., wanting to do some sightseeing on the way, and looking to share the driving.

If my life were a movie, and I were a character tasked with meeting one trustworthy and uncomplicated friend, that friend would be Beth Rigazio, my road buddy. Beth and I zigzagged through the American Southwest in her used Volkswagen Beetle convertible, as though driving into a hundred iconic movie posters. We ate chicken fried steak and shot pool in Durango, drove the scenic Million Dollar Highway (no guardrails!), came down, through Zion National Park and Monument Valley, to the Grand Canyon, where we slept by a campfire on the North Rim, then stopped for three days of hedonism in Las Vegas. We laughed and conversed, at ease with one another, staying in the present, neither of us saying much about our past. We shared single-bed motel rooms. We were not lovers—somehow there was no question of that— yet that didn't stop me from writing a love poem:

WITH BETH IN VEGAS

I thought money was love when you found me
at the nickel slots and told me you lost some,
admitted later you lost a lot, and that you wired
New York and lost that too. All in fifteen minutes.
We played your last $20 at black jack, where women
in togas served us Black Russians for free, like love,
which must be why I asked the dealer to hit us
when we already *had* 21, because love is wanting
what you already have, I explained, as you howled,
as we swayed down the desert to our motel
and hit the bed in one another's arms.

Beth had wit and openness, and something else I admired immensely: an aptitude for aimless wandering. She was originally from New Hampshire, had lived in New York City, then Santa Fe for several months, and was going to L.A. to try her hand at screenwriting, even though she had no training in it, or connections in the industry. If she was nervous, it didn't show. Beth knew something about life, something I needed to know, though I couldn't name it—other than to say she was at home in the world, while I was hiding out at the nickel slots.

I ALWAYS WOUND up back in New York for the doldrums of August. I'd wake up on hot summer days and write poetry all morning and into the afternoon, then shower and walk to Soho to take Zvi Gotheiner's advanced ballet class. In class, surrounded by women, I wondered—always, endlessly—what it was like to be them, to be configured like them, with long hair and soft skin and female blood running through female veins. There was a minority of males (as always) in class, though if I looked in the mirror from the waist down I saw something deeply pleasing: the long-muscled legs of dancers in tights, male and female, tended to resemble one another.

Zvi was an Israeli man with a low voice, who sounded a little like Henry Kissinger. He gave surgically precise hands-on corrections, adjusting your demi-plié until the slightest tucking or tipping of the pelvis felt like the listing of a ship at sea. "That is a beginning," he'd say, even to veteran performers. Barre and floor, Zvi had us repeat every routine twice. It was a long class, and for anyone who valued training and precision, it was heaven.

During grand allegro, the men moved to the back of the line to go across the floor together, and Mary, our pianist, slowed the tempo for us, affording more air time for leaps. Leaping—jetés—is maybe what our bodies did best, and the women gazed at us as we flew. I might have gotten dates with some of them if they hadn't assumed I was gay. The overwhelming preponderance of men in the dance world were gay, and I could never figure out how, without being a jerk, I could indicate to women I wasn't. *Dance badly? Wear a football jersey?* I remember an amazing ballet dancer named Gregory who wore a New York Jets jersey over white tights. He was six feet tall and women couldn't take their eyes from him, even if he was, as I heard one lament to another, "Gay as can be."

I did get to know one woman, Joanne, a tall, soft-spoken

novice dancer, who was also a flight attendant. She flew a route from New York to Rome to London, and had a boyfriend in Rome. She could only attend class occasionally, and when she did we would chat afterward, sometimes in Italian. Out of the blue, she invited me to a movie playing at Cinema Village. The movie was called *Strangers in Good Company*. It was about a group of elderly women on a bus trip across Canada. The bus breaks down in a remote place, and the women have to fend for themselves for a while. They find an abandoned house. There's not a lot of drama, perhaps because they're so close to the ends of their lives (or maybe because they're Canadian). One woman finds a nearby stream, jury-rigs a fishing net with her pantyhose, and smiles when she catches a fish. What I remember best is a series of suspended moments, when the camera freezes on one of their faces, then fades to a slow sequence of photographs of her at different ages—a girl, a teenager, a young wife, a mother with children, middle-aged with shorter hair, etc. The photos start to look more and more like her in the present moment, and then we're back to live action, where she is observing a moth, or walking in long grass. The changes in the photos were *more* than changes—it was as though she'd been a series of different women. Every so often, without warning, the camera froze on another woman, cross-faded to another series of photos, and each time it was breathtaking. The director had to have gathered actual life photographs of each actor, and that too seemed remarkable.

Afterward Joanne told me that her therapist had recommended she see the film, but she hadn't told her why. When I asked her why she was in therapy she grew quiet. "I've been suicidal," she finally said.

I wish I had told Joanne something—anything—equally true about myself. I wish I had half her bravery.

BALLET TOOK ME into the late afternoon, at which point I hoped I could get through the evening without plunging into depression. If I had a new poem maybe I'd bring it to an open mic, though open mics were also depressing. The same sad characters turned up each night in a different place with newly scribbled poems that were no different from all their others. I occasionally attended concerts at the Bottom Line and other venues with two writers I'd met in a workshop. We saw Richard Thompson, Steve Earle, Lucinda Williams, Townes Van Zandt, Rickie Lee Jones, Greg Brown, and on and on. I loved those concerts, but as soon as I came home, an intense loneliness descended on me immediately, as if reporting for duty.

Something not often said of depression is how time-consuming it is, how many hours are spent staring at the ceiling. Some evenings I'd wander the streets, singing a line from "Bridge Over Troubled Water" or a refrain from Pink Floyd's *Dark Side of the Moon*. The words comforted me, though if someone heard me singing *I'll see you on the dark side of the moon* over and over, they might have thought I was going insane. They might have been right.

I never did drugs, never drank much. It had little to do with character or willpower, and everything to do with control. I'd always known, since I was a child, that my body was all I had, and I would need it to cross deserts.

Each time school returned in September, I became somewhat of a workaholic—though if teaching isn't an all-encompassing job you're probably doing it wrong. Still, I invested way too much of my identity into that role, and even after a good day of teaching, I felt hollow. As evening came on, the hollowness sharpened into a sense of not having lived. My antidote for this was to stay up late to watch reruns of *Hill Street Blues*, escaping into its fictitious world of urban policing, and that lovable band of dedicated and dysfunctional cops. The show didn't come on until midnight and didn't end until 12:55, when the beautiful public defender and the smart police captain climbed into bed after a day at each other's throats to laugh and tease and touch like teenagers. I should have been getting my sleep, but I needed, once more, to see two people find a home in each other.

I woke up a few hours later to my radio alarm. By some alchemy of program formatting, that radio played "Kokomo," the late Beach Boys ode to tropical paradise, each morning at the same time, and I lay in bed wishing that gorgeous wall of sound could hold back the day. I don't know how I managed to peel off the covers, prep lessons, eat, shower, shave, and dress for work in the dark tunnel of a life so desolate.

THEN CAME THE INTERNET.

Like a lot of people, I wandered into cyberspace wide-eyed and stumbling like a toddler. I used it mostly for email at first, then discovered AOL Instant Messenger—or it discovered me. A little text bubble from *BiteMe* popped onto my screen late one night. "Hi Mr. Goetsch," it said. "Hello," I replied tentatively. *BiteMe* turned out to be a shy Stuyvesant student with a question about the homework (though maybe he wasn't so shy after all).

At first, surfing meant clicking from one link to another to another until you forgot where you started. Then, with the first search engines, I sensed the promise of unprecedented data at my fingertips. I also sensed the promise of anonymity. A popular *New Yorker* cartoon at the time depicted two dogs sitting before a computer screen, with one saying to the other, "On the Internet, nobody knows you're a dog." There was so much you could do and find out without anyone knowing who you were.

The first transgender website I found bore the ominous name "URNotAlone." It was a vast grid of photos against a black background suggesting interstellar space. Like aliens beamed aboard *Star Trek*'s *Enterprise*, each image took a while to download through the bottleneck of my phone modem. They materialized from top to bottom—first hair, then eyes, a face, shoulders, torso, maybe even legs—until I beheld a closeted individual from the privacy of my own closeted life. Some were pretty, some were homely, some were skilled with makeup, most weren't, some posed joyfully, many seemed nervous or scared. The photos were often poorly lit, off-center, out of focus (perhaps on purpose). Some had the disturbing aura of hostage photos, a sense of incipient danger on the other side of a door or a curtain, about to burst through. I felt anxious when the computer froze partway through a download, as if the person, unable to be beamed aboard, would be lost in space.

Another website displayed a map of the world with a number over each country. When you clicked on the number it opened up to fourteen "TGirls" in Italy, five in China, thirty-one in Brazil. Mexico, Ireland, Russia, India, New Zealand, Nigeria, Japan—nearly every country had a number on it. Some were transsexual call girls. Most were closeted crossdressers. There was space below each photo for a little blurb, and contact information. "Call me," said the call girls.

"Fe-mail me," said the crossdressers. I went country by country until there were no more countries, clicking on each and every "TGirl," imagining what her life was like.

Personal pages began springing up, many in the "West Hollywood" (gay) section of GeoCities.com, where people going through life as men published anonymous diaries (what we'd later call blogs) about their adventures as women. Some accounts were believable, and reminded me of nights I'd gone out dressed. Others were over-the-top fantasies. There were a lot of forced feminization stories, where a male gets into some predicament that makes it necessary to present as a female, not unlike the premise of the classic film *Some Like It Hot*. *Kenny would not stop bullying his sister, so Mother made him dress in his sister's clothes all summer, and by the start of school in the fall he wanted to keep wearing them.* The stories went on for many chapters, extending the predicament like a TV sitcom. *Burt lost a bet to his friend Francine and, because he's an Eagle Scout who always keeps his word, he now must pose as her sister for an upcoming cruise, with just one week to train!* In the world of forced feminization, real world dangers were reversed—you had to switch genders or else suffer the consequences.

I'd already seen the analog version of this in transgender magazines, but compared to the internet, my stack of magazines seemed like a counterfeit world. Many of the pictures in them were recycled—the same photo shoots, differently laid out and captioned, popped up in different places. Most of the magazines had no dates on the covers, rendering them perpetually salable, and for all you knew, the personal ads in the back could have been a decade old, and might all have been written by the same person.

But the websites were alive and multiplying. People controlled their own narratives, and showed up in chat rooms with the name and gender they preferred. I suppose I'd already experienced the analog version of this too, having gone out as a woman and gotten to know others like me. But the internet brought awareness of an uncountable number of crossdressers, many of whom resided nowhere near New York City—or *any* city—in places where it wouldn't be safe to venture out as female. Even in New York, we took on great risk in order to dress and travel and socialize as women in repurposed dives and drug and prostitution spots. On top of being dangerous, going out was exhausting. It was like we had to wrest our femininity, time and again, from some fiery maw in the earth's crust, and then forfeit it each time we made the transit back to daily life. On the internet you weren't going out—you were going in.

I was especially interested in the writings of those living full-time as women. Some were stage performers or sex workers, though most were attempting to live conventional lives, and a few were in stealth. Previously you'd never hear about people in stealth unless they died or were outed, but the internet allowed them to tell their stories with their stealth intact. There was a transsexual who worked as a bank teller, whose postings I pored over. No one suspected she was anything other than a typical woman, which I found compelling, though for her it was lonely. She was attracted to men, but avoided relationships, knowing that if she got involved with a man he was sure to inquire sooner or later about her past. He might notice an absence of childhood photos, or ask to see her high school yearbook. She'd have to weave a web of lies, including why he couldn't meet her family. In order to live in stealth, she had to move far from where she'd grown up, because in that town she had a history. She needed to live like an escaped felon just to be seen as a woman. She posted a few grainy black-and-white photos of herself. She was slender and quite pretty. Her hair was coiffed in a perm, the way a lot of middle-aged ladies wore their hair.

There were post-op transsexuals who told about medical experiences, and advised readers on the various steps to transitioning, and lessons learned. A lot of medical information was coming online. I read about hormones, dosages, benefits, side effects, who prescribed them legally, and where you could get them on the black market. I read about surgical procedures, nose jobs, breast implants, sex reassignment surgery, the costs and outcomes, and profiles of the surgeons themselves. The journey from male to female had always been the most amazing story I could imagine, and suddenly I had all this access to it.

WHAT IS PERHAPS equally amazing: I never stopped to consider if I was transsexual. I envied them, I said *If only* to myself a million times—*If only that were me*—while another voice replied, *No, that's not you.* I'd known many others, at the Fabric Factory and elsewhere, who said *I wish* at the sight of a pretty TS, or at the idea of living full-time, but were resigned to being mere TVs because that (so they thought) was who they were.

At that time there was a wide gap between TV and TS. Male to female transsexuals proclaimed themselves women who'd been "born in the wrong body," and often looked down on transvestites as fetishists. Transvestites resented having their "lifestyle" reduced to a fetish, and the vast majority of them identified as straight males. The 1975 song from *The Rocky Horror Picture Show* about a "sweet transvestite from transsexual Transylvania" was way ahead of its time; in the 1980s and '90s, transvestites were from one place, transsexuals from another.

What's more, the idea of transitioning would have been like choosing to reside in outer space, over living on this planet, which to me was no choice at all. Crossdressers could still function as straight men and partake in the institutions—marriage, family, career—that give life meaning. No one gives those up unless they're forced to.

And yet, except for a career, I *had* given those up. Or rather, I'd never managed to partake in them, even though I pined for community. I'd boycotted crossdressing three years before, for fear it was keeping me isolated, yet nothing had changed. At thirty-one, I wasn't having relationships or sex. I watched my peers date and move in with one another, travel together, marry and start families, while I spent nights, weekends, and vacations alone. I had friends I valued from the worlds of poetry, teaching, and dance, though I doubt any of them knew how alone I was—because I didn't tell them. I wouldn't have known what to say. My isolation felt like a curse, something I needed to hide. In the company of others I was upbeat and jovial, while inside I was panicked and confused. Everyone around me seemed to possess tickets to life's pageant, while I could only observe from afar.

Meanwhile, a tectonic shift in culture and gender was taking place. For millions of closeted people, the internet was the beginning of community, and the normalization of gender nonconformity. These also were things I'd longed for, though I didn't participate in this community either. I didn't go into chat rooms, or upload photos, or exchange emails, or write about my experiences, or advocate for rights. But I kept on reading. I couldn't stop. I was happy for them, happy that more and more of them got to be who they were.

Not me. Before I could join them, I needed to be sure I was one of them. I didn't want to lie to myself and live a false life. Despite all that I was finding out about the journeys of others, I had no access to the truth about myself. Was my problem really about gender, or was it something else, manifesting as gender confusion? All this time I was betting on something else—because then it might be fixed, without having to forfeit my dreams of love and marriage, a life of belonging and safety. And I knew exactly where to look for the something else.

Part

TWO

Accident
1968

I am five, sitting on a toilet seat lid, staring at a tiled bathroom floor. The tiles are small and pink, with blue and white specks. If I stare at them long enough the specks lift and float, then fly diagonally across the floor, crisscrossing from corner to corner, faster and faster like shooting stars. When I blink, it all goes away, and the specks are specks again.

The bathroom is on the first floor of our house, which is half underground. If I stand on the toilet lid I can look out the window and see our backyard at grass level, out to the power lines separating our backyard from the backyard of the Watts. The Watts have two TVs, and since Mrs. Watt is telephone friends with my mother (they talk for hours) I'm welcome to go over and watch them. I tune the TVs to the same channel and sprint back and forth between the bedroom and the living room, checking to see if they're actually showing the same thing at the same time. Here, all I do is sit. I'm not allowed to leave because I am in jail. Last week I lit the garage on fire because Carl told me to. That's what I kept telling Mom and Dad, and it's the truth, but they didn't care. We sat at the dining room table, them on one side, me on the other. It was a like a trial. Mom said I needed to name my own punishment.

"I don't care," I said.

"Well, we're going to sit here until you do care."

"Isn't punishment *your* job?"

"Don't worry, your father and I will decide if the punishment you choose is appropriate."

"But Carl told me to."

Carl is my older brother by a year (a year *and four days*, he always adds). We were in the garage playing with matches. Matchbooks are all over our house because Mom and Dad smoke—a lot. I hate cigarette smoke, but I like the smell of the match right after they shake the flame out. Mom and Dad light matches with a finger pressed to the matchhead and one swipe at the black strip. That's scary to do, but Carl showed me another way. He tore out a match and folded the flap of the book over it like a sandwich. When he pulled the match through it came out on fire. "You try," he said. He tore out another match, made the sandwich, and held it while I pulled. I shook out the flame right away, and we leaned in to smell the smoke.

"You should light something," he said. He looked around the garage. There were rakes, shovels, a mower, bags of garden supplies piled on shelves. Carl pointed to the corner of a bag of grass seed and said, "Why don't you light this little corner?"

So I did. It lit easily. The flame was quiet and pretty— before it spread down and across the bag, to the bag next to it, and up to the shelf above. I rushed back and forth trying to blow the fire out, huffing and puffing like the wolf in the story. The flames spread to the wall.

Mom appeared at the open end of the garage holding a garden hose. "Get back," she said, and used the spray nozzle to douse the fire. She sent me to my room, to wait until my father came home.

"You could have burned down the house," said Mom.

"Carl told me to."

"Nobody but you did this. Now what should be your punishment?"

"I don't care."

We sat.

"Setting fire to a house is a crime," Mom said after a while. "What do they do to people who commit crimes?"

"You're gonna send me to jail?"

"Well, do you think *that* should be your punishment?"

"I don't care."

My jail sentence, they decided, would be an hour a day for thirty days, served inside the downstairs bathroom. Actually, *they* didn't decide—Mom did. Dad didn't say a word the whole time. He hardly ever speaks.

THE HOUSE I set on fire (because Carl told me to) was at 23 Malvern Lane, in the heart of a brand-new suburb built on what had been potato fields in Stony Brook, Long Island. We moved to Stony Brook from Bayside, Queens, when I was five. Before that we lived in a Brooklyn apartment I was too young to recall. Malvern Lane was an upside-down U with our house at the top. It arced in one direction toward Manor and Manchester Lanes, in the other direction past Middle Lane and Millstream Lane, which fed onto Moss Hill Boulevard and Millbrook Drive. We were in the *M* section, which (for the record) contained no manor, no mill, no moss, no stream, no brook, and barely a hill.

Stony Brook was my mother's escape from the city. She'd grown up in Flatbush, Brooklyn, where every square foot had long been conquered and reconquered, with nowhere left for a little Jewish girl to make her mark. In Stony Brook she papered the sheetrock walls of our new house, planted spiny little trees in the garden beds, and bid good riddance to New York City, which she now referred to as "the Rotten Apple," even as it supplied our family, and all of the suburbs, with money.

Weekday mornings my father rose in the early dark to shave, dress, and scarf down fried eggs and coffee in time to catch a Long Island Railroad train which trundled him fifty-five miles west to a job in Manhattan. I frequently woke to his shouted curses—"Goddamn it!" "Son of a bitch!"— along with my mother's name—"Fran, where's my goddamn socks!"—hollered down to the kitchen, where she was fixing his breakfast. On many mornings his shouts jolted me out of a deep sleep, my heart pounding with terror.

One day, after he drove off, I asked my mother what he was yelling about. "What yelling?" she said. I kept asking, and she finally explained that he needed her to pick out his clothes. He was color-blind—that was all—and he couldn't go off to work with mismatched socks. "Your father's job is very important," she said.

I was never told what my father's job was. Mrs. DeSimone, my first-grade teacher, assigned us to find out what our fathers did, then report it to the class. I stood in front of the room the next day and said, "My mother said to tell you that my father is a businessman." Mrs. DeSimone chuckled. Other kids knew exactly what their fathers did, even their salaries.

Once on a dock at Port Jefferson Harbor, my mother asked him to hold me so I wouldn't stray. It was strange to be in my father's strong, hairy arms. Another time he wrestled Carl and me on the living room carpet. He got down on hands and knees and allowed us to push and tug and try to bring him down. We karate chopped and dive-bombed his back, growling in fun. He grabbed one of us in each arm, and lowered us to the ground with a much deeper growl of his own. After a couple minutes he said, "That's enough," and stood and peeled us off, we who hung on him like monkeys. For weeks we begged him to wrestle again, but he said, "Not right now" or "I'm not up to that," until we stopped asking.

Those were the only two times I remember him touching me—not counting spankings. Mostly Mom did the spanking, but every now and then, when we were making noise after bedtime, he grudgingly agreed to take a turn. I heard him stomping upstairs, the lights came on, and before I knew it I was upside down. One hand held me by the ankles, the other yanked down my pajama bottoms and whacked me so hard I was voiceless. A second whack, and I was tossed back in bed. He moved on to Carl, two whacks, then the lights went out, and he was gone.

AFTER MY MONTH of jail in the downstairs bathroom, my holding cell became the bedroom upstairs I shared with my brother.

"Go to your room," one of my parents would order.

"Why?"

"Because I said so," they explained.

I stopped asking, just stomped off and slammed the door. Soon I added a variation: "Good, I was going there anyway."

I didn't know what I did to deserve my frequent banishment, but it usually happened when we were watching TV. We were a TV family. After dinner each night we gathered around the huge Magnavox console, Dad in his recliner, Mom on the sofa, my brother and I somewhere on the other side of a massive and incongruous coffee table. We watched whatever

Dad wanted to watch, and Dad wanted to watch *Mission: Impossible* and *Columbo* and *Mannix* and *Cannon*—basically, white men in suits catching criminals. He loved Detective McGarrett saying, "Book 'em, Danno!" at the end of every episode of *Hawaii Five-0*. He also liked shows about the great outdoors: *The American Sportsman*, which had nothing to do with any recognizable sport, *The Undersea World of Jacques Cousteau*, and *Mutual of Omaha's Wild Kingdom*, where corny old Marlin Perkins was forever stapling orange tags to the ears of beasts that his strapping young assistant Jim had gunned down with tranquilizer darts. At the end of each show, as Marlin Perkins droned on about how he and Mutual of Omaha were saving the planet, I wondered what prevented Jim from shooting his boss with one last tranquilizer dart he'd saved. But more than anything, I wondered why we were watching all this bullshit in the first place. What made Dad the boss of the TV? Who set that up?

Was I sent to my room for asking if we could change the channel? For wanting us to talk? For being too slow to empty his ashtray, or get him a snack from the kitchen? Was I sent there for the thank-you I never received? "You're welcome," I said anyway. "Go to your room," he replied.

MY BROTHER LIKED to pick on me. Mom called it teasing— "He's only teasing," she said. I didn't like hearing that because it wasn't true. She said he only did it to get a rise out of me, and if I didn't get so angry, he would stop. I didn't think that was true either.

The truth is he bullied me. He called me "Dog" because he knew I hated it, and he loved to see me melt down. "Hey

Dog," he'd say. He'd try other words, searching for trip wires. He sang a jingle from a TV cartoon, changing the lyric to, "Here comes shitty Doggit Froggit," which drove me berserk. He sang it over and over. If any neighborhood kids were present, he'd get them to join in. "Watch him turn red," he'd say, and they'd all chant, "Here comes shitty Doggit Froggit." I lost friends this way.

I tried retaliating, but it didn't work. He was somehow immune to name-calling. I tried appealing to my mother. "Mom, Carl's calling me names!"

"Here comes shitty Doggit Froggit," sang Carl, under his breath.

"Mom, Carl won't stop calling me names!"

"Mom?"

"Carl," she called from another room, "stop calling your brother names."

"He's calling *me* names!" Carl shouted.

"Both of you stop calling each other names."

"I'm not calling him names!" I said.

"Can I *please* have some peace and quiet!" she said.

"Here comes shitty Doggit Froggit," sang Carl under his breath.

"Stop it!" I screamed.

"Doug," said Mom, "go to your room."

There was never a time stamp associated with my exile. It was left up to me when to come out, which was tricky. If it seemed to them that I emerged too soon I'd get sent back. I solved the problem by not coming out at all, not even for dinner. Carl was sent for me—"Hey Dog, dinnertime." Later, Mom would come to retrieve me, but I wasn't budging.

At a certain point she decided to have a talk with me. She

knocked on my door (something she never did) and asked to come in. I didn't answer. She came in, sat on the edge of my bed, and asked what was wrong. Why didn't I want to come out of my room? "You know," she said, "you can't keep everything bottled up inside." She spoke in a soft voice I'd never quite heard before, and kept repeating that phrase: "bottled up." I couldn't have cared less about the dangers of keeping things bottled up. (Hadn't I been sent to my room for *not* bottling myself up?) More than anything, I was wondering how the concerned woman before me could be the same person who let my brother bully me relentlessly. I wasn't going to speak until I figured this out.

Not long after that, my mother took a different approach. She marched into my room with a belt, ripped down my pants, and began whipping me.

"Say you're sorry," she ordered, between lashes.

"No."

Thwack.

"Now are you sorry?"

"No."

Thwack.

I can't honestly recall what she wanted me to apologize for—perhaps because the belt erased everything—but I do remember the moment it dawned on me, *She wants me dead.* That's when I instinctually knew, as bad as the belt was, I couldn't give in.

Thwack.

"I'm still not sorry."

"Have it your way." Thwack.

"Well?"

"Not sorry."

Thwack.

I sensed a growing reluctance in her. There was more time between lashes, even as she kept whipping me. She may have begun to wonder what she'd gotten herself into—and who, or what, was this willful little monster on the mattress beneath her? At some point she gave up and, without a word, left the room.

I lay in the bed facedown, motionless, feeling numb, as though inside a cocoon, while on the surface my skin throbbed, and the space around my body buzzed like neon.

BEFORE I WAS a difficult child, I was reportedly an impossible baby. The report came from my mother, who told me that after a difficult labor, in which she suffered a great deal, I was born with celiac disease, which caused me to be allergic to all food including breast milk. She said that I subsisted entirely on formula my first two years, but even formula went right through me. Each day there were copious diaper changes. My bottles needed to be boiled and sterilized, which monopolized the stovetop and turned the kitchen into a factory. My mother never tired of telling me these things. It was upsetting to hear, again and again, how sick a child I was, and what a hardship I was to her.

She also never tired of telling me how difficult I was as a toddler, due to tantrums and meltdowns. As I got older I noticed there was never a narrative to these reports, and I once tried asking her what I was angry about.

"You were just angry."

"But why? It had to be something."

"Beats me," she said. "You were impossible. All we could

do is put you in a room and shut the door until you stopped carrying on."

Celiac, to back up for a moment, is a centuries-old disease where gluten wreaks havoc on the small intestine. It is not an allergy to "all food," and certainly not to breast milk, and no doctor at the time would have said so. My mother explained that I eventually "grew out of it," and in fact I had a well-rounded diet as a child, but celiac has no known cure—no one grows out of it.

I would love to know what was actually going on with my body as an infant, and why my mother chose to tell me, repeatedly, a whopping medical lie. I learned early on that my mother lied a lot, though she may have been right about the tantrums. I have a memory of being lifted from a kitchen floor howling, and looking back over the shoulder of someone carrying me off down a narrow hall to another room, where I screamed even louder.

What I remember most clearly from that time was being put to bed long before dark, and lying in broad daylight for hours in a bottom bunk, staring out the window at the dirty white shingles of the house next door. How young is too young to feel your life is being wasted? I didn't know why I was made to spend all that time awake in bed. Later I'd hear my father come home, and the excitement of Medusa, our little white dog, greeting him at the door, and then my mother greeting him. Later, the rustle of newspaper pages when he settled into a nearby chair, then the two of them having dinner, then the TV going on. I heard them living their lives, on the other side of the door.

Above me, in the top bunk, lived my brother. At night he'd climb down and go pee in the hall closet. My parents said he was sleepwalking, though how would they know? Once he peed in broad daylight against the bedroom wall. The bunk above me creaked when he stood, and the stream of his piss trickled down past me.

"YOU WERE AN accident," my mother said, matter-of-factly. "Technically you weren't supposed to be here." We were alone in the car, stopped at a red light. "I think you're old enough to be told this," she added. I was eight.

I didn't quite get what she was saying. I had never heard the word "accident" used to describe a person. I thought about this, wondering who among us *wasn't* an accident? According to my third-grade teacher, Mr. Carpenter, life itself, on this or any planet, was against all odds.

When a boy in my grade named Alan lost his father and brother in a head-on collision on Nichols Road, *that* was an accident. I read about it in *Newsday,* which was delivered to our front stoop. It was the first time I knew someone with their name in the paper. Alan was in the back seat of the little white sports car, and emerged unscathed. Was *he* the accident?

Nichols Road ran beside the Little League field where I played catcher for the Central Federal Savings Mets. Three weeks after seeing Alan in the newspaper I was crouched behind home plate when he came up to bat. He had just lost half his family, yet there he was, beneath an oversize batting helmet, trying for a hit.

Was Jimmy Doak an accident? He pitched for the A's. "Wait till you see Jimmy Doak," kids on other teams said, but they didn't say anything else. We played the A's late in the season. Jimmy was a small kid, a lefty with a strong, accurate arm. His ball came whizzing past us from a weird angle. He struck out the side in the first inning, and when he got back to the dugout he took off his cap to reveal a pale veiny head that was completely bald. Jimmy Doak had cancer.

Not much happened in Stony Brook. A sixth grader named Mitchell blew his braces into his trumpet while playing "Georgy Girl" at the school talent show. Patrick Sims, who lived down the block, ran away from home and wasn't seen for several days, but then he came back. He and his little brother Curtis told the Aron boys next door to keep off their property, chanting *Cock-a-doodle-doo, you're a dirty Jew.* Jay Aron scoffed at the toy drill he got for his birthday, tried it out on his sneaker sole, and struck a blood geyser. Such accidents stopped me cold. But when I mentioned to people I was an accident, it stopped *them* cold. "Your mother *told* you this?" Mrs. Aron said. I didn't know why it weirded people out, but I learned to keep my accident to myself.

OFTEN MY MOTHER asked me to kiss her. "Come give me a kiss," she would say. "Just one kiss," she'd repeat, trying to coax me. She'd point to a spot on her cheek with her index finger, explaining that the spot was in dire need of a kiss. I didn't like it when she did this, and she did it habitually, for years, like smoking cigarettes, which I also didn't like her doing. We'd be alone in the same room. I could be playing in the corner, or looking into the refrigerator, and she'd say, "Why don't you come over here and give me a kiss?" The request always froze me inside. I'd mumble the word "no," or just shake my head, or I'd wander out of the room pretending I hadn't heard her.

Sometimes she did it in front of her friends. "Watch this," she'd say, then ask me to give her a kiss. I'd freeze and look away, or shake my head no. Her friends would laugh at how cute I was. "You won't kiss your own mother?" one of the ladies would tease. I'd shake my head no, and they'd laugh even harder.

But sometimes I did kiss her. It was when I wanted something, such as ice cream, or permission to go over a friend's house. "Only if you give me a kiss," she'd say. The kiss was payment. Often she grabbed me when I got near, and pulled me into a tight hug, and gave me extra kisses, even though she had promised not to. I fought to get away, and she laughed and laughed, like I was playing a game of hard-to-get.

It wasn't a game. It was just something that happened—though I never saw it happen to my brother. I knew of no physical intimacy in my family, other than this.

I started refusing to kiss my aunts hello when I saw them on holidays. Initially it was a source of puzzlement, then they laughed, as my mother's friends had, at how shy and cute I was. My aunts were pretty and I didn't dislike them (except for one), and though I hated being ridiculed, my refusal to kiss them solidified into a policy that lasted my whole childhood. At a certain point I thought it might be easy to resume kissing my aunts hello, yet I was unable break the policy. No one ever asked for my reason—not that I could have explained it if they did. My aunts still bring it up: my refusal to kiss them as a child. It became a family joke.

MY COUSIN PAMELA came to stay with us. She was enrolled in the grade behind mine at William Sidney Mount elementary school. Pam was shy and giggly, her plump cheeks were always flushed. Her mother was my aunt Patricia, the eldest of my father's three sisters. Aunt Patricia had recently divorced my uncle Dave, a carpenter, who was the reason Pam's last name was different from mine.

We put her up in my father's study, a small, shag-carpeted room that overlooked our front lawn. Hanging out with her there, I spotted her black patent-leather Mary Jane shoes radiating from the floor of the closet. I could hardly think in their presence. Sometimes I'd see Pam at school, walking through the hall in line with her class, wearing those Mary Janes. I imagined it must have felt like riding a flying carpet.

Other things about girls that stood me still were dresses, tights, and most of all, hair. I couldn't get over how lucky girls were to have long pretty hair cascading from their heads and caressing their shoulders. I tried to discern from their faces if they took pleasure in their hair, and it was hard to tell. Though in the hall, when they caught their reflections in a glass display case, I watched them linger longer than any boy would dare, adjusting their bangs or ponytails, or simply beholding themselves.

My mother kept her hair short, rarely wore dresses, and didn't use lipstick or nail polish. On Saturday nights, when Mr. and Mrs. Brewer came over to play bridge, she occasionally wore an unusual pair of polyester pants that came to her knees. They were blue, with white polka dots, tight like a girdle, with several tiers of frills. She walked differently in them, awkwardly, to make sure the frills fluttered. She wore the pants to be sexy, but the effect was clown-like and weird.

I loved that there was now an actual girl in the house, giggly, shy, feminine, with a pair of Mary Janes pulsing like a quasar on the floor of her closet. Sadly, I did not develop a bond with Pam. Carl and she were much closer. He often bullied me verbally in her presence, inviting her to join in. She mostly demurred, but he still caused a triangulation that felt painful and unsolvable, and I avoided the two of them.

Once in a while my aunt Patricia visited Pam on a Saturday or Sunday and drove off with her, delivering her back to our house a few hours later. On one occasion Pam's father visited—I remember Uncle Dave's van parked at the curb, his name painted on the side. I never knew why Pam needed to live with us, and I doubted she knew either. It was a household mystery that went undiscussed, taking its place beside other mysteries, such as what my father did for a living. At every turn, my parents chose secrecy over openness. I wasn't told the simplest things, such as where we were going in the car. "None of your business," was the default answer to questions. It was as though life itself were a crime, and to satisfy a child's curiosity would be to make them a material witness.

The code of silence seemed to be family-wide. My grandparents' house in eastern Long Island, where my father and his siblings dutifully journeyed each Thanksgiving and Easter, was a place of rectitude and frozenness. Pam had also lived there for long periods, which was hard for me to imagine. My father's mother divided children into two types: well-behaved, not well-behaved. Only adults were permitted to talk at the table, and the talk was stilted and formal. Though one time a lively conversation about silicone—whatever that was—broke out among my aunts and grandmother over after-dinner drinks. I never heard my father in conversation with his mother.

My grandfather was a large, barrel-shaped man who used to be a *bon vivant*, according to everyone who'd known him, but was stricken with a degenerative disease and became an incredibly slow-moving person, which was how I knew him. He walked by rocking side to side, like a ship. He listed to one side to allow the foot on the opposite side to shuffle a few inches forward, then tilted the other way. The quickest I'd ever seen him move was when he placed his hand on my head and rammed it into a coffee table. He'd come a long way, shuffling through the kitchen, past his chair in front of the TV, to where I was playing with my cousins on the living room rug. My aunt Nancy tried to console me as I cried. She explained that Grandpa had been down the hall trying to take a nap when he heard me laughing, and so he rammed my head into a table.

It's often said you can't understand people until you know what they've been through. But there was no knowing the Goetsches. If someone in the family had experienced profound grief, or taken a chance on love, or walked a picket line, or came out as gay, or had a spiritual epiphany, I never heard about it. It wasn't just that they were strangers—even with strangers, you could begin to get acquainted. We were *actively* estranged by some invisible force, like magnets reversed.

"You wrote a book?" my father said to me in 2008.

"I wrote six books, Dad."

"What are they about?"

"You."

I was kidding of course. I hardly know a thing about my father. Who were his friends growing up? Did he date? Did he have a car? What music did he listen to? Did he ever travel abroad? Was he political? What was college like? How did he meet my mother?

Once, in my twenties, I asked him to tell me some things about himself.

"Like what?" he said.

"Anything."

He couldn't think of anything to tell me, so he suggested I

ask him questions. But after a few simple questions he said, "I feel like I'm getting the third degree." So we stopped.

It was as if a previous generation of my family had witnessed a horrific crime that had to be kept secret, yet they passed it on anyway in the form of silence and tension. But I can't say if the Goetsch code of silence is a result of trauma or reticence. I can say that reticence is a trait I didn't share. Neither did my uncle Will, my father's younger brother. "There was no love in the house," he would tell me, decades later.

PAM STAYED WITH us for a year in Stony Brook. When she was about to leave, we gained another guest: Uncle Will. He returned from the war in Vietnam and slept for three days straight on our living room couch. The story was that, just before the end of his tour of duty, he'd received a letter from Aunt Theresa saying she was divorcing him. He flew from Saigon to Las Vegas, where he lost a lot of money, and used what he had left to buy a blue Camaro, which he drove to our house. There are other, more extravagant parts to this story, which was told to me by my mother—so I don't even know if the above is true.

But Uncle Will did have a blue Camaro. He took me to Jones Beach in that car, and we swam in the ocean. He put me on his back, and dove and surfaced like a porpoise. His back was huge, I had to hold tight to his neck and shoulders to avoid sliding off. Driving to and from the beach, I got to sit in the front of the car, which had bucket seats and a high dashboard, making it hard for me to see the road. It was just the two of us, alone for the day. Perhaps it was no big deal for him to say, "C'mon, kid, let's go to the beach," but it is astounding what a single day can mean to a kid. He resembled my father—a bit taller, with a higher forehead and lighter hair—but he was nothing like him. For one thing, I have never spent a day alone with my father.

Later in the summer, Uncle Will drove Mom and Carl and Pam and me to the Bronx Zoo. At the zoo I saw a person with a crew cut and large breasts walk out of a public bathroom. The sight perplexed me. Was this a man with women's breasts, or a woman with a man's head? If it was a man, I thought, *How disastrous to have breasts!* If it was a woman, I thought, *Why would you cut off all your hair?* The person had emerged from the women's bathroom, and was probably a woman, but my questions remained, and I couldn't shake the sight.

A few years before, while we were still in the city, I sat on a bus staring at a child whose gender I could not determine. The child, who was standing in the aisle waiting to get off, was bigger than me, maybe two years older. I glanced down and saw navy blue socks disappearing into pants—*or were they tights?* If they were tights they would go all the way up, and that would make her a girl. I had a consuming need to know. When the bus stopped, and the child stepped off and disappeared into a crowd, I stared through the window feeling desolate and somehow heartbroken.

When I was five, soon after we moved to Stony Brook, a woman with silky black hair that came to her shoulders visited my mother. She climbed the half flight of stairs from the front door to the living room, her hair caught the light, and something in the back of my brain exploded. It felt like a bolt of lightning had ravished me. I thought of the concussive force of that moment when I later learned of epiphanies—the Annunciation, God talking to Job through thunder, or Tiresias knocked unconscious by the sight of two snakes coupling. I came to regard that unknown woman's shiny hair as my annunciation—not that I understood it. No one can understand an epiphany, because the epiphany is what understands us.

My fixations grew as I did, and seemed to have lives of their own. Like cards shuffled to the top of a deck, they changed, from hair to shoes to tights to dresses. More than anything it was nylons, which few girls wore, though women often did. From my school desk I'd stare at my teacher's legs, feeling thrilled and ashamed. I tried to picture her putting them on in the morning, but the picture soon dissolved; the idea of touching nylons was too overwhelming to imagine.

I knew if I were to suddenly appear in girls' clothes it would be a catastrophe. That's what happened in an episode of *I Dream of Jeannie*, the show I watched each night just before my father got home. When Jeannie showed up at Cape Canaveral in a yellow skirt suit, and Major Nelson complimented her outfit, she said, "Do you really like it, Master?" He said yes, and so she folded her arms and blinked and voilà: there he was in an identical yellow skirt and jacket. He looked down at himself mortified and demanded to be changed back into his uniform. I understood his feeling, yet I also shared Jeannie's innocence: how could you love clothing on someone else, and not on yourself? How could a skirt be marvelous for girls, but poisonous to boys?

It was like our worlds were upside down from one another. Girls hardly ever got into trouble, whereas boys seemed to be on a perpetual crime spree. You weren't allowed to hit a girl, but it was OK to hit boys. I resented this—not because I wanted to hit girls, but I was jealous of their protected status. It didn't seem fair that they should have that, in addition to their magical clothes and long hair. On the other hand, I was appalled at the misfortune of girls, who were weaker, couldn't run as fast (except for a tall girl in our class named Tracy), plus there seemed to be something scandalously wrong with their throwing arms. Most horrifying of all were their future prospects: breasts erupting to unpredictable shape and size, having to marry men, and change their names, and give birth. Yuck!

Yet every so often a desire shot through me: *If only I were a girl*. It came out of nowhere and blindsided me. I felt certain no boy on earth had ever thought that, and I knew I could never tell anyone. At night I dreamed of waking up as a girl and getting ready for school, standing for a long time before a closet full of dresses, then stepping to a mirror to do my hair. In the dream it felt like I possessed a superpower, yet I was only doing what every girl at school did each day—Deborah, Tracy, Linda, Meredith, and little Eileen. I had another dream of a limousine that had parked in our driveway. The limousine didn't go anywhere. Instead, a procession of people filed into it and out the other side. When it was my turn, I got in, closed the door, and came out the other side as a girl.

A THIRD DREAM, a recurring one, consisted simply of waking up in Grandma's house. Not the Lutheran ice woman in Hampton Bays, but rather my Jewish grandma, my mother's mother, who lived in an apartment in Hartsdale, having moved from Brooklyn around the time we did. How I loved to stay with her.

After she tucked me in at night, I'd sneak out to the plush feather-down love seat in the living room, where she'd find me curled up in the morning, and gently scold me. "Children need to grow in the night," she said, "and this chair gives you no room to grow." I couldn't tell how serious she was about the love seat stunting my growth. She may have been worried about my mother finding out where I slept, and never letting me visit her again. Grandma had a similar reaction to a sneeze, or the slightest of coughs.

"Uh-oh."

"What?"

"I don't like the sound of that."

"I was just clearing my throat, Grandma."

"Here, put on this sweater. We can't send you home sick."

I didn't know if my mother had threatened to keep me from her, or if Grandma was being paranoid (or just Jewish). I only got to visit her a couple times a year, yet I felt a bond with this woman I could neither explain nor live without. She wasn't particularly dynamic or pithy. She was neither funny nor stylish. She was in fact sickly, given to terrible coughing spells. Fluid was lodged deep in her respiratory system, which only grew worse over time, and she would eventually drown in her own lungs. But she seemed to live only for me. Maybe that's also typical of Jewish grandparents, though I had the feeling she loved me even before I was born. (She once told me she was sure I'd be a girl, and that she'd have a granddaughter. It secretly delighted me to have existed, if only in her mind, as female.)

On a rainy day she took Carl and me to the movies to see *The Adventures of Tom Sawyer*. "How did you like it?" she asked, as we walked out. We told her we loved it so much we could watch it again. That's all she needed to hear. She found a pay phone in the lobby, called Grandpa, and told him not to pick us up. She bought three more tickets, and *The Adventures of Tom Sawyer* was even better the second time.

She taught me hygiene. She made sure I brushed my teeth,

which I seldom did at home, and had a mouthful of cavities to show for it. Carl had even more cavities than me, and was strangely proud of them. It's embarrassing to admit, but I never knew to wash my hands after using the bathroom. Nobody had ever taught me to use a washcloth, or told me to shower. I came to Grandma unwashed and filthy. If she was shocked, she never let on, though she was adamant about washing and brushing and flossing. She spent time in the bathroom with me, teaching without shame. I think of her every time I'm in a public restroom stall, arranging a triangle of toilet paper over the seat.

But mainly she cooked. She filled the cupboards and refrigerator in anticipation of our visits. She used the whole kitchen—oven, broiler, mixer, blender, and all four burners of the stove. Everything but a cutting board; she chopped vegetables out of her hands with a paring knife, right into the pot. She made pot roast, meat loaf, lamb chops, cottage cheese lasagna (don't knock it till you've tried it), baked potatoes, corn on the cob, string beans and carrots in the pressure cooker, homemade cucumber salad and coleslaw. While dinner was cooking she brought us plates of sliced vegetables and bowls of grapes, cherries, apples, melon. *Who was this woman?*

GRANDPA BESTOWED ON us a different, and equally Jewish, abundance: kvetching. "Oy gevalt," he said from the other side of the morning paper, held before him like a movie screen. "What a buncha schmegegges!" He clucked his tongue and said, "I don't know what's gonna be." He sighed and said, "Oy yoy yoy." When he folded up the paper, and you asked what was going on in the world, he'd shrug and say, "Nothin' much."

He was a lifelong salesman who'd survived by his mouth, by trying to convince total strangers the two of them were connected through a friend, a cousin, an uncle, an in-law, the army, college, a housewares convention in Milwaukee. Most of his stories involved people he'd either befriended or out-smarted in some American city: Saul Winegar in Chicago, Mike Schramm in Dallas, Sid Farks in Albuquerque. Men were either morons or "very fine gentlemen." Women could be "honeys" or "chatterboxes" or "built like a brick outhouse." The stories never stopped. While eating, he tucked half-chewed food into a pouch of his cheek so he could keep telling them. I had no clue why he thought I needed to know that he once doubled his commission in Jacksonville, or that Betty Ogilvy from Eastern could get him on a flight anywhere. I just knew his job was to talk and mine was to listen. One day he im-parted to me his deepest truth: "Nobody I don't care who it is sells below wholesale."

My mother, an only child, had a complex relationship to this man, whom she faulted for treating her "like a son." The incident she most often cited in this regard was how he taught her to swim: he put her in a boat, rowed to the middle of a lake, and threw her overboard. (If true, that would have been a brutal way to treat a child of any gender.) Yet she often bragged about her swimming prowess, and having competed in water ballet. She skipped two grades of public school so she could enter an engineering college at age sixteen to be "the son he wanted." Yet she touted these accomplishments too, while ridiculing the conventional femininity of my grand-mother. Then again, she was inordinately proud of her sewing and her cooking (which were rudimentary). She married my father at eighteen, was pregnant immediately, and had two children by twenty.

It figures that a talented woman in a patriarchal culture might be conflicted about gender roles. My mother's far greater problem, however, was her own patriarch—Grandpa—in whose presence she became infantilized. Despite her being far more educated than her father, verbally he ran roughshod over her. His mouth was a fire hose of ignorance and revisionist history, which she struggled to correct, but she soon surrendered all hope, shriveling in red-faced silence. His death at age ninety-one came as no surprise—he'd been in hospice for days—yet she made sure not to show up until the day after he died, and she didn't lift a finger to help me arrange a memorial for him. I have no doubt he was far more brutal to her, and in more ways, than my mother will say.

It's equally true that Grandpa loved me a great deal. He took me to ball games and restaurants. He visited me several times after I'd moved to New York City. We saw Broadway shows, and walked his old neighborhood, visiting with friends who were still alive. He pointed out the grocery store on Flatbush Avenue where he worked his first job as a stock boy. He had a seventh-grade education and he put me through college, and never took credit for it. He wanted me to succeed and thrive—my brother too—and would have gladly laid down his life for ours. When the hospice nurse told me he'd stopped eating I said, "No he hasn't." I left and came back with a bowl of vanilla ice cream, and spoon-fed him his last meal. Abuse can skip a generation, so can healthy love, and there's nothing fair about it.

I DIDN'T KNOW why I dreamed recurrently of waking up in Grandma's house. I only knew that in my grandmother's presence my body relaxed, and the world around me opened.

Colors and sensations became more vibrant. The weather, and strangers, took on a deeper reality. I could not have said what that reality was, just that I saw people and things for who and what they were. Even my brother changed: in Grandma's house he didn't bully me. If we'd been allowed to visit her more often—who knows—we might have grown to love each other.

Once back home, the old patterns resumed. At school I was always on the verge of tears, and I didn't know why. If another child choked up and started to cry, I lost it too, no matter how hard I tried to hide my emotionality. My eyes were always red and swollen, and crusted with dandruff-like scales. A lunch lady spotted this and had me brought to the school nurse, who asked me what was wrong. "Nothing," I said, trying not to cry. She kept asking, but my mind drew a blank, and after a while she let me go.

A carnival came to the strip mall out by Nesconset Highway, a small caravan of trucks with trailers that unfolded into rides like Swiss Army knives. The rides were fun and fairly tame, except for one: a souped-up, flattened-out Ferris wheel that looked like a propeller. It slingshot you around at the top, and jerked you back up at the bottom, and top and bottom kept switching. The cars were enclosed cages that flipped independently on their own axes, multiplying the g-force and the fear. I think the ride was called the Zipper.

"Let's go on *that*," Carl said. I told him I didn't like all the flipping. "We'll get in one that doesn't flip," he said. "Don't be chicken."

I heard the heavy chain dangling against the outside of the cage when the carnival man slammed the door shut and locked it. There was no seat belt, just a wide bar to pull against your belly. Our cage rose and stopped with a jerk when they loaded the next cage. We began to tilt backward. I didn't like this one bit. We tilted more with each cage they loaded, in a slow-motion flip. Soon we were at the top of the ride, completely upside down. I was panicking. I looked upward at the parking lot below, fearing we would plunge and die. "Get me out of here!" I screamed. Carl laughed beside me. The ride started. We were in one of the cages that wouldn't stop flipping, and we whipped around with terrible force. I yelled and screamed, clutching the bar to me for dear life. The more I yelled, the louder Carl laughed. It wasn't a real laugh, but rather a fake "Ha, ha," like a bad actor. I thought that ride would never end. (In some ways it never has.)

When we finally got off I was speechless and devastated. That's when Carl told me, smirking, how it worked: the bar I'd clung to was the thing that made us flip. All I had to do was stop pulling it. "What an idiot," he said. He didn't say this to me, but rather off to the side, as if speaking to a Greek chorus in agreement with him.

My brother's hatred was as mysterious to me as my grandmother's love. Later, when I grew strong enough to fight him, I did. (My mother once brought us to the emergency room with lead pencils stabbed so deep in each other's backs they needed to be surgically removed.) I didn't want to hate him, but the alternative was to accept that I was the worthless dog he kept calling me. It wasn't much of a choice.

WHAT STAYS WITH me most from Stony Brook is a moment at age seven when I watched my mother and brother drive off together, from the window of my room, where I'd been sent earlier that day. I don't recall their destination, just that I had asked to go with them. They left the house without telling me. I heard the car doors slam and the engine start, looked out the window, and began to scream as Mom backed out of the driveway. When she shifted into drive and headed off down Malvern Lane, the screams took on a purpose—as though, like some superhero, I could achieve a volume loud enough for them to hear, turn around, and come back for me. When the car made a left onto Middle Lane and disappeared behind the Plotkins' house, I screamed still louder, as if to shatter the sky and bring it crashing down.

What happened that day was nothing new; the dynamics had been there all along. But this time I snapped. It was as though a veil had been ripped away, and now I saw—plainly, nakedly—just how unwanted I was. I fell into a leaden silence.

The moment would leave a deep imprint on my life. Whenever I felt excluded or forgotten—even the *anticipation* of being forgotten—the offending party became my mother and brother driving off without me. Minor breaches of connection, the unreturned call, a friend letting me down, would humiliate and infuriate me. Rather than admit to others (or myself) how worthless such slights made me feel, I would cut off friendships. I cultivated enormous pride and independence, to compensate for my inability to trust or forgive others. My declarations of independence only added to my isolation, which felt punishing and unsolvable. This in turn distorted my judgment. Like Rapunzel in her prison tower, I pined for someone—it almost didn't matter who—to rescue me from my loneliness. I became *too* trusting of new people. Bullies and narcissists sniff out such vulnerability, and I regularly welcomed malignant people into my life. And no wonder: the people I was calling from the window, to turn around and come back for me, were the very ones who'd left me for damned. Calling to them was the essence of insanity, and the whole world would wear their faces.

And of course, I *was* Rapunzel in more ways than one. My brother, after all, was bullying a sister, my parents were trashing a daughter. Nobody saw this, but that didn't mean it wasn't happening.

I knew, at age seven, I was in serious trouble. *Who the hell are these people?* I wondered, as though I were a change-ling, and the family I'd been given the result of some cosmic bureaucratic error. I was completely on my own, even though I *couldn't* be on my own because I was also a child, depen-dent and defenseless.

I came away from the window, opened the door to my room, and wandered the empty house, staring at the walls, the furniture, the space itself, as though I were walking underwater, surveying a wreck. When the people in the car returned, and the man got home from work, the house would go back to being 23 Malvern Lane, and I'd have no choice but to resume living in it.

MOST OF THE time I told myself I had the best of all possible mothers, on account of: she was smart; she was a teacher and her students liked her; she wasn't racist; she had nice hand-writing; she liked big dogs; she drove me to Little League games and watched some of them; she touched her forehead to mine to check for fever; there were Christmas presents under the tree each year, including a new bike, which I would ride through the *M* section past houses containing mothers who couldn't possibly be as good as mine.

I had no need to square these feelings with any others. In

fact, I needed *not* to. I had come into this world on business, the business of every child: to live life. And life itself was good—how could it not be? In Stony Brook, where I lived from age five to ten, I learned to read and write my language. I memorized the planets, the times table, the presidents. I sang "Michael Row the Boat Ashore" and "Leaving on a Jet Plane" with the rest of the class. My best friend Kevin had lots of freckles and the two of us played chess in our heads. I played jacks with girls, and jump rope, and hopscotch. I played football on front lawns, going long and catching every pass Patrick Sims threw my way.

Each summer we spent my father's three-week vacation in Rangeley Lake, Maine. We stayed in a cabin at Pickford Camps, where I learned to dive off a dock, and swim, and catch nightcrawlers by flashlight, which we used as bait for trout. I met other kids from other cities, including the Hobarts, who rooted for the Philadelphia Phillies, which was weird. Greg Hobart played "Both Sides Now" on his saxophone, Randy played the drums, Danny bet us he could drink his own piss using the water purifier from his camping kit, Keith and I tied towels around our necks and ran into the wind, pretending those towels were flapping capes and we were superheroes. Their father, Marv, let me work the stick shift of his fuel-injection Mercedes, calling out the next gear as he stepped on the clutch. In the rec hall we watched Bobby Fischer play Boris Spassky in the Match of the Century on a grainy black-and-white TV. We went to a drive-in and saw *Take the Money and Run* by a young director named Woody Allen and I never knew I could laugh so hard. My birthday was July 4th and I half believed everyone when they said the fireworks over Rangeley Lake were for me.

My family tried its best—it really did—to be a family.

We left in the middle of the night for the four-hundred-mile drive to Maine. Carl and I lay head to foot under blankets in the back seat of our Buick LeSabre and woke up in daylight, somewhere in Connecticut, to the best music ever to play on AM radio: Bob Dylan, Carole King, Joni Mitchell, the Beatles, Creedence Clearwater Revival, Janis Joplin, Marvin Gaye, Smokey Robinson, Rod Stewart, the Jackson Five, the Rolling Stones, Crosby, Stills, Nash & Young. Coming through the White Mountains of New Hampshire, Mom cried, "Oh *isn't* that beautiful!" whenever a turn in the road revealed a sheer rock face. "*Isn't* that beautiful!"—when she saw a moose, a covered bridge, a river through birches. We mimicked her from the back seat in falsetto—"Oh *isn't* that beautiful!" Dad, one hand on the wheel, the other holding a cigarette, said, "Don't make fun of your mother."

It would be easy to tell a story of a happy childhood. It's what I told myself. Everything in it would be true—except for the whole thing.

Northport
1981

I am sitting on the orange couch in what my parents call the family room. The couch is an ungainly dual-reclining contraption, in which two people each get their own angle and footrest. It has grown old, rickety, and comfortable.

Out the big picture window to my left is Northport Bay, an undramatic body of water leading to what F. Scott Fitzgerald called the great wet barnyard of the Long Island Sound. To the west, across the mouth of Northport Harbor, is Little Neck, where the red Spanish roof tiles of the Vanderbilt mansion and museum are visible in winter through bare trees. The beach at low tide smells rank, due to a wide stripe of exposed muck and mussel beds. In the wind, which is constant, seagulls hoist up mussels and drop them on stones to crack their shells while screaming at other seagulls to stay the fuck away. Electric horseshoe crabs hunch like land mines, while hermit crabs in borrowed shells make sidelong dashes across tide pools like old men in bath towels scampering down hotel corridors.

But what I'm looking at is the ceiling. Each day after school I sit here staring up, fingers woven behind my head, trying to envision my future, and each day I draw a total blank. I am about to graduate high school, near the top of a class of over eight hundred. I have never done drugs or been arrested, never broken a bone or started a fight. But I am worried that something is very wrong with my life. I love art and sports and theater, which keep me after school each day for hours, but all of that has ended. I have no date for the prom and have given up trying. Despite being madly attracted to girls, I have never gone steady with one.

I didn't kiss a girl until ninth grade. Her name was Dawn Lyle. She played the lead in the school musical, and Frank Forte, who played male lead, kissed her at the edge of the orchestra pit, right above where I played clarinet. When the curtain came down on the final performance, the girls in the cast were devastated that it was all over, and threw themselves into the arms of boys, who were generally OK with the fact that it was over, and even more OK with girls throwing themselves at boys. I finally went backstage and kissed Dawn. "What took you so long?" she said. It was like the end of a corny black-and-white movie.

Dawn was only in eighth grade, and might have had the biggest breasts in the junior high, but that's not what attracted me to her. She was feminine and talented and kind. Her mother, a single mom who was a lot older than other moms, offered me sweet iced tea when I came over, but she kept a close watch on us. I never walked with Dawn down Main Street, or took her to a movie, though one day we French-kissed on her porch. It was scary and strange at first. Then it became warm and comfortable. Our tongues liked visiting each other's mouth. Then I touched her breast, slipping three fingers past the border of her bra. I had never felt anything so soft. Dawn closed her eyes, inhaling deeply. When she opened them again and met mine, it felt like we were in a new place.

The next time I called her house her mother said she couldn't come to the phone. Dawn didn't call back, and when

I tried again, her mother told me to stop calling. I joined the high school marching band that summer, and met a ton of new people. In the fall, when I began tenth grade, there was a rumor that Dawn Lyle had gotten pregnant, and that her mother had sent her away to have the child. (The rumor didn't say where, or who'd gotten her pregnant.) *How could any of that be true?* I wondered. Yet she was never seen in Northport again.

High school, meanwhile, was teeming with beautiful girls I'd never met; girls in tight disco jeans who feathered back their hair; girls who smoked pot and were into Zeppelin and the Grateful Dead; rich preppy girls who lived in huge houses and looked down at you as though they were on horseback; hippies in clogs and peasant skirts who sang James Taylor tunes; tomboys who, with the slightest nod to femininity— stud earrings, an exposed bra strap—could send you over the moon.

THE SMELL OF dog piss wafts up from the shag carpet. Despite all the time she spends outside, Dolly, our Dalmatian, prefers to pee in the corner. There's a basic stench, and occasional waves of it hit you like failure. I'm embarrassed to have friends over. The living room, on the other side of the kitchen, is where Dolly shits at night. For years, my mother woke up a few minutes before my father to rush around with big wads of toilet paper, lifting soft piles from the carpet, flushing them in the hall lavatory before Dad came marching through on his way to the kitchen for breakfast. It was like the dog was making a statement for my mother, shitting and pissing all over the house she never wanted to be a housewife in.

We moved to Northport when I was ten to shorten Dad's

commute to New York City. In Stony Brook Mom had begun a career as a high school math teacher, but was fired after receiving unsatisfactory evaluations. She claimed it was an administration scheme to save money, by replacing teachers up for tenure with rookies. The only thing clear is my mother is always fighting, demanding to see store managers, threatening small claims suits. She once protested a mistaken decimal on a supermarket price tag, until the manager let her have a gallon of milk for seventeen cents.

My father's goal in life was to retire by age forty. He spent most weekends alone in his study at the other end of the house, poring over stock market data in thick binders called *The Value Line*, which were delivered each month. Other times he just sat with his elbows on his desk, cigarette in hand, staring out the window at the bay. His other goal in life was to have a house on the water—that's also why we moved here.

For a while Mom ran a consignment jewelry business for my father. She drove around to drugstores and beauty parlors all over Long Island replacing costume jewelry in cheap display cases and collecting our share of what sold. Later they added cheap pantyhose called "Lollypops" in little red-and-white cartons. When all of that failed, they purchased a yarn store in Merrick, on the south shore. My mother drove there each day to supply rug-hooking enthusiasts with all their rug-hooking needs. It was a dusty, depressing place.

Each morning before leaving for the train, Dad used to give her a list of tasks, such as renewing the car registration, or retrieving his dry cleaning. He'd say, "Now if you don't do anything else today, do this," and point to one of the items. When he got home from work, after they kissed hello, she'd go on and on about her day. Then he asked about the list, and her posture sank. She'd say she didn't get a chance to do any of the things on it, whereupon Dad would go apeshit. "What the hell is wrong with you!" he'd scream. He wouldn't hit her, but he'd get pretty irate, which scared Dolly. All Mom could say was, "Yes, dear," and look down with a weepy face, like she wanted to crawl under the table with the dog.

Once I went into his study and found a yellow legal pad open to a page with the heading "Rules for Talking" in his scribbly handwriting. It was a list of things Mom was and wasn't supposed to say, which boiled down to sticking to the point, and saying 50% less. (He actually wrote a percentage sign.) I'd noticed they'd been having long discussions, Mom in the chair beside Dad's desk facing him, while he faced the window and the bay. Later I'd find her alone on the orange couch with a *Reader's Digest,* though she wasn't reading. She was taking heavy drags of her cigarette and staring into space.

SOMETIMES WHEN I get home from school I take off my jeans and socks and put on a pair of pantyhose, then put the jeans and socks back on. I started doing this at sixteen. The pantyhose come from the hall closet, which has stacks of leftover inventory from the failed consignment business. Sometimes I steal from my mother's dresser drawer (which is stuffed, though she hardly ever wears them). I took a pair of panties too. They were full pink panties with firm elastic fabric. Wearing the panties and pantyhose gives me a euphoric thrill, and an incredible hard-on, and then a deep comfort I don't understand.

I keep track, almost unconsciously, of the girls who come

to school in hosiery on a given day—the shade, the sheerness, whether they wear a skirt or dress, and the shoes. Sometimes I see a group of girls all wearing skirts on the same day, comparing outfits in the school commons. It's obvious they phoned each other the night before to coordinate, as though skirt-wearing were a risky undertaking requiring solidarity. The less-daring girls wear thick tights, while the brave ones wear clear nylons that make their legs look wet and naked and incredible. Bravest of all are the loners, who wear skirts and dresses whenever they please. They are like women already. I picture girls at home after school, wondering who keeps her pantyhose on, who takes them off and changes into jeans. I can't seem to get over the fact that girls can dress in clothes that make me breathless, and do so with impunity, any time they want. *What would it be like to be a girl?* is a question I ask nonstop.

I have a boy's body—a man's body—muscled and hairy. I played soccer all three years of high school, and this year we won the state championship. I trained hard all summer, running the formidable hills of Northport, the route of our town's famous 10K run that starts along the harbor, past old clapboard houses on Bayview Avenue, past Mariner's Inn restaurant, where I worked as a line cook. The turn up James Street, the hill that school buses labor to climb, which I took on a sprint. A left on Ocean Avenue, which runs along the rim of the Sand Pit, the housing development where we live. The Pit, as most call it, was a square mile gouged out of Long Island's north shore by Steers Sand and Gravel Company. From the rim above it you can see all of the bay and across the Sound to Connecticut. The right turn, down past the LILCO power plant, its four tall smoke stacks peeking intermittently through the surrounding woods. Another right onto

Waterside Drive, the gradual mile-long incline that drains your stamina if you're not aware of it. Then out briefly to 25A, a hard right at Pumpernickel's restaurant, onto Main Street, past the two churches, where the old trolley tracks begin, and back down to the harbor.

After the run I'd work on ball skills in the backyard, juggling, heading, dribbling, and shooting, blasting the ball low at the neighbors' split-rail fence, righty, lefty, top of the foot, outside of the foot, dropkick, volley, spinning it, bending it. Then some wind sprints, then some weight training in the basement.

I like working out, and I like what my body can do. I know that girls like boys with bodies like mine, yet I don't take advantage of it. I've had some dates, and we've held hands and kissed in the park at night. Sometimes we dated for a few weeks, but then they broke up with me, and didn't say why. I think they wanted to do more than kiss, and they gave up waiting. It's weird: I crave that physical pleasure and intimacy, but sex has always seemed surrounded by a high-voltage fence. When my male friends discuss sexual experiences I become quiet, and feel demoralized. It's like I'm depriving myself of the best thing ever.

Actually, the best thing ever is down the shore from our house, past the public beaches and the town boat launch, where the land curves out in a narrow spit called Asharoken, which leads out to Eaton's Neck. In the third house on the bay side of Asharoken lives a girl my age named Bridget Faulkner. She has a deep feminine voice, the voice already of a woman, to go with a curvy body and dirty-blond hair down to her shoulder blades.

She was a captain of the Tigerettes, the kick line that performed in front of the Northport Tigers marching band. I'd stood behind her in rehearsals for two years, buried in the ranks of the clarinets, unable to take my eyes off her. We finally met on the cast of the school show, *How to Succeed in Business Without Really Trying*. I was surprised she tried out for the show because she seemed way too cool for it. I'd heard a rumor she was dating a lighting designer in his twenties who lived in the city. Every now and then she came to school looking like a New York businesswoman in a gray skirt suit, silk blouse, heels, dark stockings, and her hair in a bun. Most days, though, she wore faded jeans and had her hair down, looking like a rock star's hippie girlfriend.

But the Bridget I finally met was so plainly kind, and warm, with such a charismatic laugh, that no rumor could survive her presence. All my ideas about her evaporated, except for the fact that she was out of my league. Then I found out where she lived. You can't quite see her house from ours because it's set back from the water. Still, I gazed at the beach in front of her property, much the way Gatsby gazed across Manhasset Bay at the green light at the end of Daisy Buchanan's dock.

One day after school I walked over to Bridget's house with no particular plan. That is the kind of thing you do when you're sixteen—you dream so hard you think you can knock on the doors of goddesses. "Hi!" she said, smiling. The arc of that single syllable from her lilting alto voice sent a charge through me. She'd come to the door in a yellow bathrobe, with a towel turbaned on her head. "Give me a minute to dry my hair," she said, letting me in. I watched her climb a wrought-iron spiral staircase and step around the atrium of a house that seemed like a film set, then disappear through a doorway. She hadn't even asked why I'd come over. (I'd said something epically idiotic, like "I was just walking.") Maybe she was used to this. How many other boys of Northport, and elsewhere, had randomly shown up at her door?

The Who's *Quadrophenia* poured out of four gigantic speakers in the sunken living room where she'd invited me to wait. I wondered if that was what *quadrophenia* meant—that it needed to be played on four speakers. The house was elegant and immaculate, with slate floors. There didn't seem to be anyone else home. *This is Bridget's house,* I said to myself ponderously. *Just before I was in my house, but now I'm here.*

She came down the stairs in soft faded jeans and a pink T-shirt, still towel-drying her hair, tilting her head to the side to clear her ears. She could have been in a photo feature in a magazine, a celebrity kicking back to Roger Daltrey in her downtime.

"Thanks for stopping in," she said.

"All these years, I didn't know we were neighbors."

"I know!"

We talked some about being in the chorus of the show— the only thing we had in common. We'd spent rehearsal that day wedged between tall flats that functioned as the company elevator, while the leads rehearsed a scene outside. The scene closed with the song "Been a Long Day," at the end of which the elevator doors were supposed to slide open and we, the chorus, would sing the last line of the song with them. But Mrs. Flanagan, the Napoleonic director, who was really just an English teacher, kept telling the actors to move to different spots and say their lines again. There were a lot of us packed inside that elevator. "Is that Give Hedy?" someone whispered, when the oversexed character Hedy LaRue spoke her line. "I'm having a company erection," someone else whispered, and we all lost it. "Shut up and act professional in there!" screamed Mrs. Flanagan, causing us to lose it even more.

It was easy to talk to Bridget Faulkner offstage at rehearsal, whereas being alone with her in her house was so surreal and overwhelming that afterward I could hardly recall a thing. Mostly I was trying to hold myself together. I don't think I stayed very long, and I can't say how we parted. (One of us may have said something corny, such as, "Well, it's been a long day.") I couldn't say if Bridget knew how in love with her I was, only that we didn't come within a mile of romance, or even friendship. I walked home feeling small and pathetic, past the boat landing and public beaches, past our neighbors' houses, up the slope, and onto our lawn full of weeds.

Bridget started dating the rehearsal pianist George Lyons, who was humble and witty. He and I had been friends since elementary school, and since most of male friendship in Northport centered around sports, he was usually the one envying me. I couldn't believe his luck in landing Bridget. Most remarkable of all, *she* seemed to have pursued *him*. One morning she stepped solemnly across the high school commons holding a single red rose. She stopped before George, looked up, and presented it to him. It was as if, with that rose, Bridget Faulkner was teaching the whole school that there was no such thing as anyone being out of anyone else's league. (That's bullshit of course. Bridget wasn't sending any social message, she was just into George, and hoping it was mutual. Even a girl who knows she's beautiful wants love and wants to be known. And I'm pretty sure, the day I walked over her house, she saw a kid wholly incapable of relating.) I was glad for George, and heartsick with jealousy. He and Bridget lasted several months, then broke up. They reunited briefly after a family tragedy, then broke up again.

I still feel heartsick, and Bridget still lives in that house on Asharoken, whose beach I can see out the window. But now that we're all about to graduate and go our separate ways, it feels too late to do anything about anything, except sit here staring at the ceiling.

FROM THAT SAME orange couch, at age fourteen, I watched Howard Cosell interview Renée Richards, "a man who became a woman," on *ABC's Wide World of Sports*. Richards had just won the right to play in the women's bracket at the US Open in Forest Hills. It was the first time I'd ever heard the word "transsexual." I stared hard at the TV screen, which seemed to be staring hard at me. Cosell, the iconic boxing announcer, spoke to her gently, in a voice I barely recognized, a voice maybe reserved for a daughter. Renée Richards was tall and thin, her voice was scratchy. They showed footage of her playing in a white tennis dress. She was surrounded by controversy, but whatever she went through, getting to wear that dress seemed worth it.

My family was also gathered around the TV watching the interview, and I felt naked. I feared that at any moment Mom or Dad or Carl—or all of them in unison—would turn to me, then back to the TV, then back to me again, and they'd know my secret. I wanted to bolt from the room, but I was riveted to the screen. *A man who became a woman.*

Prior to that, I'd only seen rough approximations of men becoming women. Flip Wilson's alter-ego Geraldine, and Milton Berle in drag, were ridiculous. Jim Bailey, a Judy Garland impersonator who sang "Get Happy" while dancing in a tuxedo jacket and a leotard, left me speechless. On *Gilligan's Island* a potion made Mary Ann's voice come out of Gilligan's mouth, which wasn't nearly as good as the formula that Grandpa on *The Munsters* concocted to turn himself into Marilyn

Munster. He emerged from the trapdoor of his basement laboratory as a glamorous blonde, and fooled everyone, until his old man's voice came out of Marilyn's pretty lips. But none of that could match Beverly on *All in the Family*, the woman Archie Bunker saved by administering mouth-to-mouth resuscitation in his cab. When she showed up later at the house to thank him, Beverly revealed she was a transvestite. (You actually couldn't tell until she removed her wig and dropped her voice an octave.) Here was a man who *lived* as a woman!

These TV sightings were rare, and I savored them, rerunning the images and story lines in my brain. They packed an intense sexual charge. My attraction to girls was powerful, yet clear and organized compared to *this*. Visions of becoming female blew my mind, like a drug that explodes your pleasure center with just one hit.

Nothing, on the other hand, felt sexy about being male. The penis sticking out of me looked ugly and embarrassing. Erections felt good enough, but were even uglier, and I was mortified when they arose "on their own" at school. I even found them embarrassing when I was alone. On mornings when I woke up hard and needed to pee, I would not walk out to the bathroom. *Who could possibly be OK with this situation?*, I thought, while waiting to get soft.

"You haven't *masturbated* yet?" Ross Flemmer said. I was sixteen, a junior at the time. Ross, a senior, made no secret of being gay, and wasn't shy about breaking into a Dolly Parton song at random. He was friends with several beautiful girls (including Bridget), who kissed him hello and goodbye on the lips because he was safe and pretty.

"I masturbate all the time," Ross said. "You must be going insane!"

"Not really."

"We should watch a porno."

"I doubt there would be one porno that would turn us both on."

"We should watch *Young Lady Chatterley*."

That's what we did. He was housesitting that Friday for a couple on James Street who had a VCR. *Young Lady Chatterley* was badly acted, which had the odd effect of making the sex parts more real. Ross and I sat on different couches. Out of the corner of my eye, I saw him start to touch himself, moving his cock from side to side beneath his tight jeans when Lady Chatterley was feigning disinterest in the hunk playing the gardener. I was identifying with Lady Chatterley in a different way, which had nothing to do with the man, a way that made me want to watch *Young Lady Chatterley* in private. Ross saw I wasn't touching myself, and out of consideration, he didn't unzip or go any further. He was a good guy. He informed me later, with a measure of excitement, that when I finally did jerk off I would explode. "Just make sure you use a lot of lube," he cautioned. He displayed zero shame or shyness around sex, which I admired.

I don't know why it had never occurred to me to touch myself. (I was beginning to learn that this was unheard of for a sixteen-year-old boy.) No one ever discussed sex in my family. As my friends, one by one, received the compulsory sex talk fathers give teenage boys, I became insulted by my father's failure. I would have felt embarrassed by the talk, as my friends did, but who sends a young person out into the world as if sex didn't exist? Carl and I had separately discovered a huge supply of condoms our father kept in his night table drawer—several boxes, each containing dozens of rubbers in foil sheets—so sex between our parents was taking place. They just didn't act like it.

A few weeks after talking to Ross, I took one of my father's condoms, along with a book, into the back bathroom to masturbate. No one was home, but I locked the bathroom door anyway. I brought the condom because I didn't want a mess on my hands. The book, loaned to me by another friend, was a novel by Robert Heinlein called *I Will Fear No Evil*. It was about a wealthy old man in the future named Johann Sebastian Bach Smith who invents a way to preserve his brain when he dies, so it can be transplanted into a newly brain-dead younger body, and he'd be immortal. The old man dies and comes to life in the body of a gorgeous young woman who turns out to be his loyal secretary—who'd been in a freak accident right around when he died. I was getting to a really good part, when he hears her voice speaking from inside her body, which is also his body, coaching and guiding him. He can't believe how much sexual pleasure there is in this female body, and she basically says, *Now you know*. I put down the book and lost control, exploding into the condom with a force more powerful and thrilling than even my wet dreams. (Ross was right.)

After masturbating to *I Will Fear No Evil*, I grew worried. Had this first-time experience hardwired me for a life of perversion? I'd had my first wet dream when I wore pantyhose to bed. The dream involved Linda Franco—my first crush, whom I thought I'd gotten over. Linda had straight dark hair, large eyes, and the sultry, stoic face of a silent film star. Though in the dream I didn't see her face. Instead, I was under her skirt (even though she never wore skirts) and I was tiny, as though aboard a lunar module about to touch down on her crotch, which was cased in nylon. I woke up with semen messing the pantyhose.

If it were ever to become known I slept in pantyhose,

I'd want to die. I kept them stuffed inside a leg of a pair of sweatpants in my bottom dresser drawer, where I was sure no one would find them. So when *I* found them, laundered and neatly rolled up, atop a pile of other folded clothes on my made bed, imagine my panic. I must have left the pantyhose buried in my sheets, and Felicia, the cleaning lady who came every two weeks, found them. My mind raced. Was this secret just between Felicia and me, or had she told my mother? Had my mother instructed her to leave the pantyhose on top of my laundry pile, as a signal? If so, to signal what? If Felicia had told my mother, whom had my mother told? My father? Had she asked for advice from my friend Eric Berglund's mother, who was a therapist, and who also employed Felicia? For once I was grateful my family never talked.

MY BROTHER CARL seemed to be having a lot of sex. He might even have been good at it, since he had older girls interested in him, girls emerging from his bedroom when our parents weren't home. The two of us were only a year apart, but we had zero friends in common. He joined the Smokeaters, who were supposedly youth volunteer firemen in training. They wore varsity-style leather jackets with the word "Smokeaters" in red-and-black flames on the back, which were pretty cool. But mostly what they did was sit around bonfires drinking hard liquor. Carl was also doing a lot of shoplifting. He was arrested at the mall with a stack of Beach Boys albums shoved into his pants. Then he drove Dad's train station car without a permit and hit something, destroying the front end.

Not long after he wrecked the car, I came home to find the living room packed with born-again Christian teens and two adult cult leaders. They were singing a guitar song called "Don't Depend on Mickey," about how Jesus, and not Mickey Mouse, is going to save you, and Carl was smack in the middle of the group. I had no idea where he found these people. Given the direction he was headed, maybe Jesus did save Carl, though now *we* needed saving from all his Jesus talk. His new thing was to quote the Bible to us and speak rapid-fire in a weird disembodied tone with his head at an odd angle. Once he hit that tone, all you could do was wait for it to run its course, or leave the room, or shoot him. Mom, who was atheist, teared up when he preached, like she was losing her son. Though I didn't see much change; he never treated me any differently. By then, we had our separate countries.

In my own social life, I was drifting away from the kids in a big mainstream clique I'd known since before high school, toward a smaller group of artistic kids. I often hung out in Mrs. Rowe's art room after school among introverted artists, most of whom were way more talented than me, drawing, painting, poring over art books, and talking to Doris Rowe, a provocative and eccentric woman who saw all of life as art. I was also hanging out with theater people I'd performed with. We'd often meet at the house of Dave Troup, a talented actor who lived with his widowed father, Stuart Troup, who was a jazz columnist for *Newsday*. We communicated through improv theater games and philosophical conversations, or danced with abandon to Stevie Wonder's *Hotter than July*, and "Turning Japanese" by the Vapors.

In the spring of my junior year, Eric Berglund wanted me to come to a picnic at Sunken Meadow State Park organized by the mainstream clique. Eric had been my best friend for years. I'd spent a lot of time at his house. His mom was a therapist, his dad an art history professor. Mrs. Berglund often said she regarded me as "a second son," and I often wished they were my parents. But I felt Eric had become shallow as we got older, and deeply manipulative—he'd lie for no reason other than to lie.

The picnic was to say goodbye to junior year, as if that were an occasion for nostalgia. I told Eric I wasn't interested, but he kept goading me to come. He said it would be a chance to reconnect. His parents were asking why they didn't see me as much anymore, and he didn't know what to tell them. On top of that, some kids were calling me a snob, which put him in the middle, and he was frankly getting tired of having to defend me. I told him he didn't have to defend me, and that I didn't have anything against these people. He said that if I had nothing against them, why not prove it by coming to the picnic? We could drive there together, and if I wasn't having a good time he promised to drive me home. I gave in.

There was a friendly game of soccer on the beach that turned unfriendly when a few boys attempted hard sliding tackles on me. "Break his legs," I heard one boy say to some others. I'd been in a lot of dirty soccer games, and these were mostly track team guys whose attempts to hurt me were easily sidestepped. But the vibe was nasty—especially the "break his legs" part—so I left the game.

I walked up the slope to where there were shade trees and barbecue grills. Eric was hanging out there with some girls. He took me aside and said, almost whispering, "I just wanted to let you know: in a while there's going to be an egg toss, and I overheard a few of them planning to throw their eggs at you."

Ordinarily you'd think this would be a good time to ask for the ride home you were promised if you weren't having fun. But I froze. I thanked him for the tip, and stood my ground—you might say. When someone said, "Go," several kids broke out of formation and ran toward me. The attack was fairly quiet. The eggs pelting my body sounded like hailstones hitting wet sand, though the ones that broke against my skull were louder. There was no shouting, no epithets, just a few laughs as they turned and jogged away.

I turned the other way and walked—slowly, deliberately—out of that park. I didn't wipe off the eggs, just let them dribble down my clothes and skin and dry in the sun, shells and all. My right ear was ringing, and would be for several days. By the time Eric pulled up in his father's Datsun to offer me a ride, I was walking the shoulder of 25A toward Northport. I ignored him. He slow rolled alongside me for a minute, but I didn't even turn my head. Finally he peeled away, leaving me alone for the six-mile walk home. The next day I took another walk, up the hill out of the Sand Pit to Eric's house, and left a note in his front door. The note said, "I will never speak to you again."

I never told anyone what happened to me at Sunken Meadow. I'm sure word got around, though it never got back to me. I was puzzled and surprised to be hated. When Eric mentioned that some people thought I was a snob, he didn't say who. The kid who said, "Break his legs," was Neil Donnelly, the lone senior at the picnic. His fellow seniors didn't accept him, partly because Neil was a braggart, so he hung out with juniors. Was he looking for a scapegoat?

I've often wondered if Eric orchestrated the whole thing, and he, more than anyone, considered me a snob for having drifted away from him. Worst of all, I feared he knew about the pantyhose somehow, through Felicia, the cleaning woman our mothers had in common. Or had my mother confided in Mrs. Berglund, asking for expert advice about her deviant son, and had Eric somehow gotten wind of it that way? If Eric knew, he would surely have told others.

DAD LEFT MOM in early June. He'd been having an affair right under her nose, with a woman named Mrs. Blau, his tournament bridge partner. (Mom had been his bridge partner up until some months before, when he told her he wanted to get more serious about bridge.) He left late at night (I was asleep), then returned the next day to retrieve his financial books and other stuff from his study. Each trip into the study took him through their bedroom, where Mom lay with the covers pulled over her head. She said she planned to lie there until she died.

After Dad left, everything seemed to speed up. I had my wisdom teeth out, turned seventeen, and began Drivers Ed that summer. Carl spent most days over his girlfriend's house in Kings Park. She was a quiet, verging on catatonic, girl named Gwen. They met playing Christian volleyball and would be married in a few years. Mom got out of bed after a week. "Look at all the weight I've lost!" she said, lifting her arms and turning before a mirror.

She brought me to her first meeting with a high-powered divorce lawyer in Nassau County named Jack Solerwitz, who promised to take Dad to the cleaners. "Are you sure you want him here for this?" Jack said, when the two of us got up from the waiting room couch to come into his office. "You don't know my son," Mom said—which I supposed was her way of indicating I was mature enough to be privy to her divorce planning.

Since Dad left she seemed to have become enamored of

me. She praised me constantly, admiring my intelligence and physical gifts. She said I was a better driver than she was, and often had me take the wheel. She began confiding in me, telling me intimate and sexual details about her marriage to my father. She told me he had always been paranoid and jealous, that he'd accused her of having an affair with Uncle Will, another with Mr. Brewer, his best friend in Stony Brook. She told me he'd had an affair with his secretary, early in the marriage, when I was still in diapers. She regaled me with nonstop complaints about him, such as how other couples dreaded eating out with them because "your father is a cheap tipper." (She referred to him exclusively as "your father"—as though he now belonged to me.) My mother was hardly a reliable narrator, and I regarded all she said as suspect. On top of that, it was awkward, not to mention covertly incestuous, to be used as her confidant. Still, I was fascinated to hear these things; she was breaking the Goetsch code of silence, and how could I not listen with interest?

Inside his office, Jack Solerwitz got around to asking about my parents' sex life. My mother assured Jack they'd had a good sex life. Jack asked how likely he was to remarry. "To that bitch?!" Mom howled. She then explained that my father only liked women with well-endowed posteriors, and that Mrs. Blau hardly fit the bill.

Mom quickly gained back all the weight she'd lost during her bedridden hunger strike. She joined a singles network called Parents Without Partners, and began dating a series of divorced men. She grew angry and bitter, and even started cursing (something she wasn't particularly good at). Carl left in August to begin his freshman year at SUNY Oswego. A month later I began my senior year at Northport High School. I stayed away from the house as much as possible. My mother's dependence on me faded, and instead we became free agents sharing a big house, eating meals on our own. In this new phase she was basically on strike as a mother, and she was just plain mean about it. She refused to give me rides or loan me the car. "You'll have to find your damn way yourself," she said, as though I were the enemy of her freedom. During our honeymoon phase, she'd confided that her therapist informed her she was frozen at the emotional age of a teenager. Maybe so, and maybe I caught the brunt of her teen rebellion. But it still would have been nice if she'd let me use the car every now and then.

DURING SENIOR YEAR I kept to myself a lot, and I got into writing. There was a teacher named Kathy Collins who taught a fiction-writing class that awarded us credits at Stony Brook University, even though we took it in high school. It didn't really seem like fiction writing, because she never asked us to make anything up. Though it wasn't like journal writing either. She had us writing in scenes, one scene after another, with dialogue and description, and sometimes third person narration—like literature. She was showing us models, exposing us to the craft of the great modern writers. It would never have occurred to me to *do* that—to write your own experience as though it were something out of Faulkner or Dos Passos. It felt exciting, and vaguely illegal. I began to dream of being a writer, and was never without a book.

Having no transportation, I walked the shoulders of the roads of Northport. I made it my pastime, and I walked great distances that year, at times refusing rides from friends, even when it was raining. I comforted myself by singing Neil Young tunes—"Heart of Gold," "Helpless," "After the Gold

Rush"—trying to imitate his sweet voice that was both deep and high. My favorite Neil Young song was "Thrasher," a long magnificent ballad about losing your friends, hitting the road, and heading for "the land of truth." I sang that song over and over, and may well have been singing it on a spring evening when I rounded the curve of Hawkins Drive and saw a police car in front of our house with lights flashing.

Two uniformed officers were talking to my mother at the curb. When I arrived they asked me if I had any enemies. They were trying to figure out who in Northport would throw a lit M-80—a quarter stick of dynamite—into our mailbox. I saw the blown-out piece of aluminum on the grass next to a headless post.

The cops stood ready to take down whatever name I said. Mom stood beside them, the lights from the squad car turning her cheeks red and blue. (Why do cops always keep their lights flashing?)

"I go to a big high school," I said. "It could be a lot of people. But also, I'm not the only one who lives here."

"Yeah, your mom can't think of anyone either."

"Could it be just a random prank?" Mom asked.

"Could be," the cop said. But he knew better. We were the only house in the entire Sand Pit that had been targeted. And it wasn't the first time: our previous mailbox had been blown up around Christmas.

I could have given them a lot of names, but then they would have asked about the motive, and I wouldn't have been able to answer. That would have raised suspicion, switching the focus to me, and to why Northport hated me.

War Is Hell
1981

I am standing behind the counter of the Wittenhagen Deli, drawing a self-portrait in my sketchbook and listening to jazz as evening comes on. I work the night shift four days a week. We don't get many customers.

Wittenhagen's is on upper Main Street, near where Laurel Avenue ends in a T. Up Laurel, just around a curve, is Northport Junior High, where a mural I painted for the bicentennial—three colonial musicians marching out of a postage stamp onto a giant American flag—still hangs in a stairwell. Across the corner of Laurel and Main is the Nolan Funeral Home, which is always quiet and always busy. For as long as anyone can remember, someone named Nolan has been the mayor of Northport. No one I know has ever met the mayor.

Next door is the Midway, a stationery and candy store that morphed into a head shop. Its display cases are full of colored bongs that look like psychedelic intestines. We get a lot of stoners coming in for Twinkies and Doritos. People seldom order a sandwich, even though this is a deli. Whenever someone does I happily swing into action. I make a good sandwich.

It is mid-October and the days are getting shorter. Just about everyone I graduated with last June is in their first semester of college—except me. I was rejected by every school I applied to. I thought I was a safe bet to get into one of them.

So did my guidance counselor, Mr. Clark, who glanced at my average and extracurriculars and told my mother and me we had nothing to worry about. But my application was a disaster. My personal essay, a catalog entitled "Things That I Like," is too embarrassing to talk about. Worst of all, I used a faculty recommendation from a gym teacher *in another school*. The teacher was Mr. Devaney, my friend Dan's dad. He coached me in summer league soccer, and when he offered to recommend me I accepted. The crazy thing is I had several great teachers at Northport who I knew would have been glad to recommend me, yet I didn't ask them. I have never been able to ask people for things, even if it meant not getting into college.

This deli is in trouble. Maria Wittenhagen puts out half trays of coleslaw and potato and macaroni salads and winds up tossing most of it. Each day her brother, Paul Wittenhagen, sniffs the meats in the case to make sure they're OK, and slices off the stale edges from the various loaves of cheese. Just before heading out, he counts the drawer and leaves forty dollars and a spare roll of quarters. Then he looks me in the eye and says, "War is hell." Paul fought in Vietnam, and he's a pretty deep guy.

Of the customers we get, it's amazing how few I recognize. I thought I knew Northport—I practically grew up on Main Street—but I'm finding there's another Northport, a tribe of twenty- or thirty-something stoners who wander in here like zombies, grab a six of Bud from the fridge, blurt out, "Pack a' Pall Malls," then head out to beat-up cars they left running at the curb. This other Northport pays rent, works dirty futureless jobs, has bloodshot eyes, and can't wait for Friday night— which is why they start partying on Wednesday.

Above the deli there's an abandoned apartment. I go up the back stairs and explore it sometimes. I can only visit for a couple minutes at a time, before I have to rush downstairs in case a customer wanders in. There's not much there, a mattress on a rusty bed frame, a ratty couch. The wallpaper is peeling, there are holes in the bathroom walls exposing the plumbing. There are some clothes strewn about, and stacks of biker magazines. It looks like the last tenants left in a hurry without taking all their stuff—unless they died here, and this was all they ever had. Some of the clothes are women's, cropped concert shirts and stiff cotton pant-ies stained in the crotch. I am starved for anything female. I thumb through the biker magazines and stop at the occasional photo of a redneck-type woman posed beside a "hog" in jeans and leather. I keep turning pages, hoping to see a woman in a skirt.

Every Tuesday I buy *The Village Voice* and devour it front to back while standing behind the counter. I read political columns by Stanley Crouch and Nat Hentoff, music reviews of Patti Smith and Lou Reed and the Ramones, reviews of films and gallery shows. I even read the classified ads in the back, for "dates" and "massages" and "escorts wanted." I want to believe that an "escort" is exactly that, and Manhattan is teeming with moneyed elders in need of a young tuxedoed companion for a night at the opera or Carnegie Hall. I feel I'd make an excellent escort for a rich lady holding my arm and strolling down a theater aisle, or waiting under the aw-ning of the Russian Tea Room while I hail a cab in the rain. Maybe the rich lady will have a daughter for me, or a room in a luxury apartment. Maybe she'll remember me in her will.

Someday, I promise myself, I will live in New York City.

In high school I started taking the train into Manhattan with my art and theater friends. We'd head uptown to galleries and museums, or downtown to hang out in Washington Square Park. We'd eat in Chinatown, or walk the streets of any neighborhood basking in New York's nonstop blitz of motion, sound, and color, the whispered promise that you could invent whoever you wish to be.

My self-portrait is turning out strange. I look intense, maybe angry. It could be due to the ballpoint pen and too much crosshatching, or the black digital panel on the register I'm using for a mirror. Or maybe I'm just not that good.

Thank God for WYRS (96.7 FM), which comes in clear across the water from Stamford, Connecticut. They play bebop, Charlie Parker, Miles, Coltrane, Mingus, Monk. Also contemporary jazz, Bill Evans, Chick Corea, Art Blakey and the Jazz Messengers, even some Steely Dan. They play Mark Murphy's amazing version of "Ballad of the Sad Young Men," which begins with Murphy reciting the last page of Kerouac's *On the Road*, while someone tickles the keys of a Hammond organ. Dean Moriarty walks off alone in a ragged overcoat, the sun goes down over New Jersey, and Kerouac imagines all the people in the vast continent huddled out of sight, and the inevitability of growing old. Then Murphy's voice launches into song—

> Sing a song of sad young men, glasses full of rye
> All the news is bad again, kiss your dreams goodbye

Jack Kerouac once lived in Northport, and it's easy to imagine him feeling what I feel, listening to jazz as the days get shorter and the town around us fades into cold unrecognizability. It's easy to slip into romance and delusion when you feel this young and old and alone.

I FOUND OUT about the college rejections all on the same day, during a visit to my grandparents in Delray Beach, Florida. They'd moved to Florida on doctor's orders, because the New York winters had become too hard on Grandma's lungs. My mother flew down a few days after me, and when she arrived she took me aside.

"You didn't get in anywhere," she said.

"What?"

"The decision letters came after you left. Yale, Cornell, Brown, Duke all rejected you."

"You opened my mail?"

My mother's face was solemn, like a newscaster on a terrible day.

"Wesleyan wait-listed you."

"Can I see the letters?"

"I didn't bring them. I'm sorry."

Not getting into college wasn't the worst news I received in Florida. When Grandpa picked me up from the airport, he was alone. He let me drive, and wept intermittently in the passenger seat. "How your grandma suffers," he kept saying. "I've never seen such suffering." When I walked into the condo she was seated slumped at the kitchen table. There was an oxygen feed in her nostrils. Two tubes strung over her ears led to a small wheeled tank at her feet beside a walker. She was bloated from medication. The swelling had erased the shape of her face. Her eyes were dull, her skin had taken on a yellow pall. Her thick hair was unkempt. She didn't speak, and didn't want to speak. If any of her was still there, it was at the bottom of a deep well. She lifted her head slowly to take me in, blinking a few times. Grandma was gone.

She spent most of each day slumped in that kitchen chair, like a fighter on a corner stool. I came in several times a day to sit with her. I'd report some mundane thing about the world outside, ducks I'd seen on the grass, or just the temperature. She'd nod slowly, then lower her head and leave it down. I'd sit beside her reading for a while, then ask if she needed anything, before wandering back out.

For most of my childhood she was the only one who sent me letters. I always wanted to get letters as a kid. My father received tons of mail, and even though it was mostly bills and advertising, I was envious. Each day I'd go out to the mailbox and look through the stack, and each day there was nothing for me. I don't know what I was expecting—why did I think the world owed me letters? Then one day, lo and behold, I'd see my name on an envelope. But when I saw Grandma's handwriting I thought, *It's only Grandma.* The letter, folded around a ten-dollar bill, was Grandma writing a lot of Grandma stuff. She hoped I was doing well at school. She reported on which vegetables were in season at the market. Maybe she'd write about a colorful bird she'd seen, or a shell she'd found, or she'd ask my favorite color (which meant she would be knitting me something). She told me to make sure I put the ten dollars in the bank "for a rainy day." The letters were nothing compared to her physical presence, but they were the only letters I ever got, from the only one in the world who was thinking of me. And now, watching her fade away, I would have given anything for one more of those letters, telling me which vegetables were in season.

I should have spent more time with her in that kitchen.

I should have held her hand all day and into the night. But I was numb, and had been for a while. All my friends were gone and I wasn't going anywhere, not even to college. I should have stayed in Florida with her, but instead I flew back to Northport with my mother, to the big empty house with the replaced mailbox.

AROUND THE TIME of graduation I befriended Tim Scofield, the teacher of a popular improv theater class at the high school. In the spring he'd gathered a bunch of students into a company, and we put on an unusual show of structured improvisations and theater of the absurd one-acts by Edward Albee and Sam Shepard. We had a run of nine performances, which was the talk of the high school. Nearly all of us in the company were seniors and Tim treated us like adults. We even had glossy headshots done by a photographer friend of his.

When the run was over, Tim invited us to his house for a pool party. He lived with a younger man named Keith Pinto on Sunken Meadow Road in a wing of a mansion they rented from a lady I never saw. There was a large circular driveway and a vast back lawn with a pool near some shade trees. The lawn gave way to a meadow, which led to an estuary, and the estuary extended all the way to the Sound. We all knew Tim was gay. He didn't talk about it, though he didn't *not* talk about it. Maybe that's why he treated us like adults: he hoped we might repay his respect for us. He was tall—about six two—with blond feathered-back hair and a deep voice. He was preppy and well-dressed. "Too bad he's gay," more than a few girls said.

I was surprised that most of the cast didn't show up for the party. Maybe I shouldn't have been. Another time, Tim invited a few of us to join him for a day at Robert Moses beach, but I was the only one who came. The two of us went several times to Robert Moses that summer. He'd pick me up in his Subaru. At the beach we talked and lay in the sun, listening to the radio. We'd people-watch, and share a quiet giggle at some of the bodies walking by. Every now and then he'd walk down to the water for a short dip, just to lower his body temperature, then resume lying in the sun. He was a true hedonist, happy to spend one day after another lounging in his Speedo on the beach.

That was the summer I lost the last of my friends. I'd call to see what people were doing on a Saturday night, and wouldn't hear back from anyone. At first the silence was annoying, then it got weird, then it hardened into a verdict, though I didn't understand it. In August they started leaving for college without saying goodbye. I valued having Tim for a friend at such a time. We talked about art and culture and shared some laughs. He might have been partly a father fig- ure. Before Tim came out as gay he'd had a wife and two sons, so he knew about sex with women. I admitted to him I was a virgin, and he kept checking in with me about it, as though my status could have switched any day—which I sup- pose it could have. "Why don't you just go out and fuck a girl and get it over with?" he suggested, squinting sidelong at me from his beach towel. Another time he taught me the term "fuck buddies," and quizzed me on what I thought of it. He made it sound like sex was the easiest thing in the world, and maybe it was for everyone but me. The techno hit "Don't You Want Me Baby," came on his transistor radio, and he sang along softly to the chorus, giggling a little.

After returning from the beach we'd hang out in his kitchen and have coffee. He excused himself often to use the bathroom (because of the coffee, I figured), and I'd look around his black-and-white-tiled kitchen, furnished impeccably with framed art photos, a vase on the windowsill, and the lawn and the meadow behind it. His place gave me a sense of possibility, a feeling that someday my entire life could be art, as beautifully composed as Tim's kitchen. A classic stainless-steel Farberware percolator perched on a gas stove, a small art deco radio positioned just so on a shelf, from which Willie Nelson crooned "Always on My Mind" in a voice of interstellar clarity.

I know what you're thinking: Tim had been my high school teacher, and was a man in his thirties, and gay—what kind of a friend is that? But friendship takes many forms, and Tim was easy to be around. The only times that felt strange were moments in his kitchen when a serious, somewhat puzzled, somewhat sad expression came over him as he peered into my eyes. His pupils seemed to collapse, like sand draining from an hourglass. But it only lasted a moment, and then the weirdness was gone.

WHAT WAS FAR more weird: I started getting hit on by a series of older guys. The first was Bill Sauer, who had graduated two years ahead of me. He'd also done theater and knew Tim. Now he was waiting tables at the Australian Country Inn in Fort Salonga, where I worked part-time as a busboy. While tipping me out after a shift, he offered me a ride home, and in the car he made a pass at me. Bill was the longtime boyfriend, now fiancé, of Leanne Swain, a girl my age, who had also been in that theater troupe. Yet here he was slowing down and pulling over to the side of the road, turning off the ignition, and asking if I wanted to kiss.

"I'm not gay," I told him.

"Neither am I," he said, and he leaned over and kissed me. His lips were dry and uninteresting. (I never did see what Leanne saw in him.)

"Bill, no thanks," I said, and he stopped.

Another guy who tried to pick me up was Archie LeMay. Archie had also done theater in high school. After graduating, he'd landed small roles in a few films. He had movie star looks, though he was becoming greasy and disheveled. He lived on somebody's yacht in Northport Harbor, which somehow was his job. He took a seat next to me at a bar on Main Street and tried to engage me in a philosophical conversation about the book I was carrying, *The Brothers Karamazov*. He hadn't read the book, but that didn't stop him from quizzing me on it, and challenging everything I said. He was my first sophist, and I hadn't yet figured out how to talk to someone that sidewinding and annoying. "Read the book for yourself," I finally said.

He put his hand on my shoulder, like some sort of commanding officer, peered into my eyes, and said, "I've got some pot on my boat. Let's go."

"I don't smoke."

"Do you actually *know* that? Or do you only *think* that?"

The encounter was strange on many levels: not just the revelation that Archie LeMay was gay, and had a unique approach to flirting (i.e., being a total dickhead), but also that he assumed *I* was gay. What had given him that idea?

Random guys were coming out of the woodwork to proposition me, and another underside of my town was being revealed: gay Northport. I suppose it was the same as gay Anytown, where gossip travels fast and meetings take place in the shadows, on the shoulders of roads, or on boats. And I suppose word got out that I was fresh meat: newly graduated, legal, and gay—even though I wasn't.

In Northport at that time, or any town on Long Island, the worst thing you could be was gay. Growing up, boys called each other "fag" all the time—*You fag.* It was a staple of our trash talk while playing stickball, street hockey, basketball. You heard it from the back of the bus. You heard it in locker rooms, where it could start fights. You heard it after someone dumped your books in the hall. *Faggot* graffitied onto bathroom stalls, scrawled across cars and houses in shaving cream on Halloween. But when it was seriously thought a boy was gay, the trash talk stopped and the whispering started. Nobody was calling me fag to my face, but looking back on high school, on my lack of a steady girlfriend, my drift away from the mainstream and toward the arts, my friendship with Ross Flemmer, and later with Tim Scofield—how could they have concluded otherwise?

In my mid-twenties, on a visit back to Northport, Ann Olsen and I were driving in her car to a party. Ann and I had known each other since fifth grade. She came from a broken home, was tough, and had a good sense of humor. She pulled the car over, saying she had something she wanted to tell me. But first she had something to ask, or rather confirm.

"You're gay, right?"

"No."

"You're not?"

"I'm not."

"Oh."

"What made you think I was gay?"

"Um . . . I guess I just assumed."

"Does it matter? You were going to tell me something."

She was nervous, and made me swear to secrecy. Then she took a deep breath and came out to me as lesbian. She'd broken up with her longtime boyfriend and now was involved with a woman, and she was flooded with all these new feelings. I congratulated her. She repeated that I had to keep this a secret. "Of course," I said.

At that point Ann and I were both living in Brooklyn. I thought that conversation might rekindle our friendship, at a time when I could have used a friend. But it had the opposite effect—she never spoke to me again. A few years later she married a wealthy man, moved to a huge house in Westchester, and started a family.

THE ONLY ONE who called me a fag to my face was me. I whispered it, alone in my room at night, while rubbing my legs against each other in pantyhose. I said it to feel like a girl, because girls were impervious to the shame of that word. If you called a girl a faggot for wearing a flowery skirt or being feminine, all she'd do is look at you funny. *You fag*, I whispered to myself, in the sweet cocoon of my privacy.

High school had been a daily feast of girls to look at. Now I looked through women's magazines just to see women. In *The New York Times Magazine*, Macy's ran multipage photo spreads of models in bras and panties. I gazed at each woman, wondering how she felt to have a body that filled a bra, to have panties wrap tight and smooth around her. Their eyes in makeup looked catlike, not quite human. Or was I, with my unsightly penis and hairy limbs, the nonhuman?

It's no wonder I wasn't close to anyone in high school. I knew a lot of people, and it felt like I had friends, but how could I possibly share who I was? Instead, I constructed a person for them to know, a facsimile composite of male-athlete-artist-scholar for them to either admire or hate, but never know. I cultivated a force field of cryptic speech and a sharp tongue to prevent my peers from seeing through this facsimile person. I confused people, I cut people without warning—surprising even myself.

I once told the president of the senior class she was completely superficial and always had been. Lynn Maranis had written me a note, wondering why I never spoke to her. "I can't believe you're actually asking that," I wrote back. She replied, begging to have a conversation. Two years before, when we were sophomores, I had a crush on Lynn, and asked her on a date. She showed up at the movies with her friend Melissa. *Who brings their friend Melissa on a date?* Twenty minutes into the movie (*Jaws II*), the two of them got up to go to the bathroom and never came back. After a while I got up and walked out—and on my way out I saw them standing, watching the movie from the back of the theater. Lynn explained that her back was hurting her. I stood next to her and Melissa for a few minutes, unable to figure the situation out. Feeling weird and humiliated, I left.

In our conversation two years later, Lynn swore she had no memory of that date, but she saw how much she'd hurt me, and felt horrible. To feel even more horrible, she insisted I tell her why I found her superficial, and I obliged with a rather thorough critique. (What kid in high school, let alone the president of the senior class, isn't superficial?)

"What the hell did you say to Lynn?" Ann Olsen called to ask later that night. "I just got off the phone with her and she wants to kill herself."

I didn't know it at the time, but people had learned to

steer clear of me. In June, when we signed each other's year-books, I was shocked to read what they wrote in mine:

> Getting to know you has probably been one
> of the most confusing experiences I've ever
> encountered . . . —Christine

> I have had many different perceptions of you
> over the last six years. At times you seemed
> arrogant, other times enigmatic. Most of the
> time, I found you confusing. —Paul

> You may anger many, but if you cause one
> bit of introspection perhaps we can justify the
> anger. —Roger

> We seem to have grown apart. I feel it's been a
> grave misunderstanding . . . —Kathy

> I wish you the richest blessings in life and highly
> praise the girl who is capable of figuring you out.
> Sorry pal, I couldn't. —Donna

Who *writes* such things in the hallowed space of a person's yearbook? Maybe, given how much venom and bullshit I put out, they were surprised I even asked them to sign. Though again, I had no idea what was going on, and that yearbook is the most painful thing I own. To this day, I can barely stand opening it. But when I do, I now see something else: the in-scriptions, taken together, form a portrait of a closeted trans person in a place and time where no such thing existed. Even if they'd put their heads together, they couldn't have figured me out. Their collective puzzlement was my closet. Nobody had access to me, not even me. I only knew I wanted to be a girl—I didn't know I already *was*.

The strangest inscription in that yearbook was this:

> Well our road together sure has been rocky. Tenth grade brought tensions between the two of us, then tennis brought us together somewhat. But through it all, I've gained an understanding of Douglas Goetsch that is full of respect and admiration . . . Through you I've grown a tremendous amount and knowing you has not for one minute been in vain. I hope everything you do will be successful and I also hope you don't close your heart to the world. There are many fantastic people out there, and I'm sure you will find them. Best of luck always. Love, Greg Bassano

Greg Bassano blew up my mailbox. There were four people total in the car, one of whom was Frank Forte, who confessed it to me late in our senior year. When he pulled me aside in the school commons, I didn't know what Frank wanted to tell me. He started and stopped many times. He was pretty choked up. He said it had been weighing on him for months. I grew still as I listened. Then I asked questions: Who drove? Where were you sitting? Who supplied the M-80? Who threw it?

Finally I asked, "Why?"

Frank looked away with teary eyes, shook his head, and said, "I don't know."

We'd been friends since elementary school, played soccer

together, performed on stage, crammed for Regents Exams, hung out on Main Street, gotten blisters digging clams side by side in the harbor. We'd never once fought or argued.

When you are bullied by the people you grew up with, for no reason they will say, when they throw eggs at you and try to break your legs, you might walk around angry, and close your heart to the world. There was an eloquence to Frank's inability to speak, for these deeds were unspeakable. It would take years for me to realize they were hate crimes.

I'VE OFTEN THOUGHT that if I ever wrote a novel, it would take place in the interlude when everyone left for college except for me, when I saw the underside of Northport, and worked shit jobs and was mysteriously propositioned by gay men, as the 1980s got underway. It would be my own *Chilly Scenes of Winter*, and the leading lady, emerging late in the book, would be Raye Gutman.

Raye lived with her alcoholic mother in an apartment on the second floor of a dilapidated house on Scudder Place, which ran like an alley behind Main Street, a block from Gunther's Tap Room, where Jack Kerouac used to get plastered. I knew Raye from English class in our junior year, when she moved to Northport from Georgia. She was short and curvy with a pug nose, red hair, and lots of freckles. I'd forgotten about her until I wandered into Dunkin' Donuts on 25A, where she was waitressing alone during the night shift. I liked her smile and Southern accent. I liked the sight of her freckled thighs through nylons under her khaki waitress dress.

Raye drove a used Ford Torino and took me to large dive bars in Islip where songs by the Doors droned on forever, and where she taught me to order hard liquor. One night we parked that Torino in an undeveloped section of the Sand Pit and started making out. I wasn't all that attracted to her, but when she undid my pants—"Let's just see what we got here," she said in a teasing clinical way—excitement shot through me. She leaned over and tasted me, and started giving me my first blow job. I couldn't believe the pleasure. She liked the fact that I was a virgin, but said I needed to be "trained" to stay hard for a long time. She licked and sucked and brought me to the edge. "Hmm, you've got potential," she said, "though I have to be careful with a virgin." I was about to come when the car was suddenly flooded with stark light: the high beams of a Northport police car that had pulled up behind us. We buttoned up just as the cop came to the driver's-side window, blinding us with his flashlight. "What are you doing here?" he said. Fucking idiot—what did he *think* we were doing?

Raye caught a cold as winter came on and couldn't get rid of it. To numb the pain of a hacking cough she kept spraying her throat with cherry Cepacol, which smelled gross when we tried to kiss. Her mom went on a drinking binge, and Raye fell into a deep depression. After the night she almost brought me to orgasm, we never had sex again. Raye Gutman was my invitation to join the underside of Northport. She'd nick-named me "Professor," and I think she knew I wasn't going to accept that invitation.

ON A NIGHT in mid-December, standing behind the deli counter, I watched Paul Wittenhagen march in carrying a jig-saw and a small industrial fan in an unopened box. He strung an extension cord into the walk-in refrigerator, and used the jigsaw to cut a hole in the outside wall, then mounted the fan over the hole—backward, to suck in winter air. He emerged from the walk-in, shut off the wall switch, and duct-taped over it, thereby eliminating his monthly refrigeration bill. On his way out he stopped, looked at me, and said, "War is hell."

I didn't know what he planned on doing when the weather turned warm in the spring, and I wouldn't be around to find out because I'd be in college by then. Wesleyan, the one school that had wait-listed me, later accepted me as a "January freshman." It was a strange invitation—*Come, though not for a while*—but I took it. I had enough AP credit to finish in seven semesters, so I saved on tuition. I took out the maximum in student loans and worked whatever jobs I could. (I had two other jobs that fall, besides the one at Wittenhagen's.) I left for college, too relieved and excited to realize how socially ill-equipped I was.

I would return to Northport the first couple summers of college. I'd reconnect with some friends, who weren't really friends. I'd see some of the teachers who mattered most to me, including Doris Rowe, the brilliant art teacher, and Kathy Collins, who'd inspired me to write.

And I'd see Tim Scofield, who also wasn't my friend. What thirty-four-year-old single gay teacher pursues a platonic friendship with a boy just about to graduate? Obviously, it was Tim who had sent gay men in Northport to hit on me. He was grooming me. (Keith, the man he lived with, was never at the house when I was.) He wrote letters to me in college, mentioning beautiful men. Richard Gere was starring in the play *Bent* on Broadway. He played a gay man in a concentration camp, the Nazis made him wear a pink triangle, and "Maybe," Tim suggested, "you might want to try on that triangle too."

The summer after my sophomore year at Wesleyan, Tim

and I drove to the New Community Cinema in Huntington to see *Ziggy Stardust and the Spiders from Mars*, the 1973 David Bowie concert film, which was newly released. Bowie was in full glam and wore tight spandex costumes. I don't think Tim realized we were looking at two different Bowies. He was fixated on gay masculinity. I knew better: Bowie, who wasn't gay, was exploring gender.

Later that summer I showed up at Tim's place in Sunken Meadow, freaked out after a verbal altercation with my mother. (I'd screamed at her with such fury she threatened to call the police.) No one was home, but I let myself in. Tim soon returned to find me curled up crying on his living room couch. "Lie down here," he said, pointing to the floor. He placed a pillow on the carpet for my head. I lay facedown and he massaged my back for a while. "Turn over," he said. He undid his pants and hovered over me, lowering himself— push-up style—to rub his hard dick up and down against me. He fondled my genitals with his hand, periodically, to check if I was hard.

I wasn't hard, I was paralyzed. I felt confused and guilty, like I owed him something I couldn't repay. He kissed me on the lips and said, "Tell me something." It felt like one of the theater games he'd taught us, where you weren't allowed to refuse an instruction.

I looked up at him and said, "I've always wanted to be a girl."

It was the first time I'd ever said that to another person, and it was to the teacher who molested me.

Part

THREE

Isle of Staten
2002

I am preparing a lesson in the teachers' room of Passages Academy. The room is small, about eight by twelve. There's a massive Xerox machine shoved against a wall, a computer workstation against another wall, with a narrow aisle between them. A plump middle-aged secretary in very high heels clomps in every couple of minutes to monitor an eBay auction on the computer. She has been bidding on a pink fur coat. Dan Shane, the history teacher typing a test on the computer, politely moves aside for her. We are good at sharing space— Passages Academy is housed within a maximum security juvenile jail. The rooms are small, and few computers connect to the internet.

The door to the school floor is heavy steel, like all the doors here. There's no getting around the ominous sound of the massive dead bolt. We hear the throw of that dead bolt now, as the guards arrive, one after another, each leading a line of boys in khaki jumpsuits. The faces of the boys are tired, annoyed, desultory. They don't like mornings, they don't like being locked up, and they are particularly unhappy about coming to school. For many of them the school floor is like a jail within a jail, school being the place where they felt the worst about themselves in the outside world. The counselors line the boys up against the wall and have them count off before bringing them into the classrooms. There are also girls at Passages—never more than a dozen or so. They wear blue jumpsuits and have school on the first floor in a room called the barber shop.

It's important for teachers to get into the classrooms first, so we can arrange the space. Space means everything here. If the kids sit where they want there will be fights. But there's a traffic jam at the doorway of the teachers' room. As I'm about to leave, the secretary comes rushing in to post a last-second bid on eBay. Then a long line of boys from G Hall ambles past, and the counselors don't like you to break a line, so I have to wait. The secretary cries, "I won!" and the boys in the hall look in with curiosity, as she high-fives us in celebration of her pink fur coat.

I rush out, arriving just before my class, drop my stuff, move some desks, and meet them at the door with a pencil and a pound.

"Yo, Goetsch."

"Good morning, Marcos.

"Good morning, Malik. Take your pencil."

"Nah man, ain't doing work today."

"You're on strike?"

"Feelin' tight."

I put his pencil on his desk.

"You bring your boom box?"

"Good morning, Luis. No boom box today.

"Good morning, Rafael."

"Man, when you gonna be absent?" he says with an exaggerated frown.

"Never."

Dashawn reaches for the pencil I offer, then executes a fake out, pulling his hand back to smooth his hair.

Their entrances tell me everything I need to know—it's going to be a pretty good day. On the whiteboard I write the "Do Now," which is to list the five senses. It's vital to get them busy right away. While they do the Do Now, I pull their work folders from a cabinet and distribute them.

"I ain't doing this," Luis says.

"You're not?" I say

"Nope."

"You can't list the five senses?"

"I ain't in fuckin' kindergarten."

"Yo mista," says Rafael, "what do you call it when you touch something?"

"That's touch," says Luis.

"I know that, but what's the *sense*?"

"Touch," says Luis. "It's touch, nigga."

"Oh yeah. Thanks."

"How the fuck he not know what touch is?" says Malik to the ceiling.

"Fuck you," says Rafael to the ceiling.

"OK guys," I say, "raise your hand when you've got all five, and I'll come give you two points. If you've got your hallwork you'll get two more points." I've got them on a ten-point system. They don't care about grades, but somehow they care about points. Homework is "hallwork" because the word "homework" upsets them—"We ain't *goin'* home!" they'll say, then go on strike.

"OK guys," I say, "today we're continuing with the five senses, and the sense for the day is smell."

"Yo, you talkin' to us like we're in fuckin' kindergarten," says Luis. He knocks on the plexiglass window beside him and waves in Mr. Emmanuel, the counselor stationed outside in the hall.

"This better be good," says Mr. Emmanuel, half inside the door, staring Luis down.

"This nigga talking to us like we're in kindergarten."

"First off, next time you say the n-word I'm gonna drop your level. You hear?"

"Word. But he's makin' us write the five senses like we're stupid."

"Yo Emmanuel, I got 'em all. Wanna see?"

"That's good, Rafael," says Mr. Emmanuel, stepping fully into the room. "Mr. Goetsch, is it OK if I address the group for a minute?"

"Be my guest."

"OK listen up, guys. This morning I was feeling *so good*, just lying in bed half asleep, against my wife's warm smooth legs."

"That's what's up!"

"And do you think I wanted to get up, get dressed, go out in the cold, and come up in here to be with you knuckleheads all day?"

"*Hell* no."

"Right, Malik. But I came in, and do you know why?"

"Money."

"Yeah, money. But check this out: I can make money doing something else, 'cause I graduated college. I come in here to let you clowns know that you're better than you think you are. And Mr. Goetsch comes in here for the same reason. He don't need to be here. He could be teaching in college. So whatever he's teaching you, you need to listen up. Don't be an ass, go to class. Don't be a jerk, do your work. Learn, so you can earn, and not burn." With that, Mr. Emmanuel exits, and resumes his post on the other side of the hall window.

"Yo, who you think is smarter," says Rafael to the group, "Goetsch or Emmanuel?"

"Goetsch, you think you're smarter than Emmanuel?" says Luis.

"Nobody is smarter than Mr. Emmanuel," I say. "But I've been waiting to ask you guys a question, and it's this: Suppose you could get with Beyoncé?"

"Fuck yeah, Beyoncé!" says Rafael, closing his eyes, grinding his hips.

"What the hell kinda question is that?" says Troy, a newcomer.

"Beyoncé?" says Dashawn. "I'd definitely hit that."

"Who the fuck *wouldn't* hit that?" says Malik.

"OK," I say, " but that's not the whole question. Suppose you could get with Beyoncé, but then you find out—"

"Ain't nothin' to find out," Malik says. "She *Beyoncé!*"

"Then you come to find out she smells."

"Aw *hell* naw!" says Marcos.

"*Hell* naw!" says Dashawn, waving his hand in front of his nose.

"Yo Goetsch," says Luis, "why you gotta always ruin everything?"

"He gay, that's why."

"I'm not gonna lie," says Malik, "I still might pipe. I mean we're talkin' *Beyoncé.*"

"Nigga," says Dashawn, his face scrunched, "didn't you hear? She smells!"

"For real, mista?" asks Rafael, looking up at me, almost pleading. "Beyoncé smells?"

"Look," I say, "I don't know if Beyoncé smells."

"She probably *do* smell," says Troy.

"But do you see how powerful smell is?" I say. "That's my point, and we can use that in our writing."

"Here we go, he gonna make us write."

"It's one thing to *see* Beyoncé, or *hear* Beyoncé."

"Oooh," says Rafael, "I want to *touch* Beyoncé!"

"Or touch Beyoncé. But smell is a whole other deal. Smell is the only one of the senses where the brain is directly exposed to the outside air."

"Seriously Goetsch," says Luis, "you need to stop saying fucked-up shit like that."

"He learned it in college."

IN 2001, AFTER fourteen years at Stuyvesant, I transferred to teach in the jail—a move that puzzled people in both places. I'd taken a hard look at the workload at Stuyvesant. No one in the administration was willing to address the unfair burden on English teachers, the only department that assigned and graded student writing, while other departments taught to tests. Plagiarism and cheating were rampant, everyone knew it, and the administration wasn't willing to address this either. We had a bumbling and inept new principal who'd been plucked from the Physics Department. Male teachers continued to prey on female students. In 1999, the Bio chairman was led out of the school in handcuffs, and later pleaded guilty to child molestation. In the spring of 2001, an administrator demanded I embezzle money from the student newspaper and give it to him. I refused. I also decided it was time to go.

Passages Academy, which was part of the New York City public school system, offered me a teaching day of four classes, each capped at twelve students, for the exact same salary.

I could do all my grading and planning on-site, leaving me more time to write. In my job interview, I offered to install a creative writing curriculum at the jail, in exchange for a program consisting of nothing but writing classes. "Deal," said Principal Sydney Blair.

Before I could teach them, I had to learn how to see them. When a kid you've never met steps into your classroom in a prison jumpsuit, they know in the first instant of eye contact if they're being seen as a person or a perp. The policy was never to ask about their charges, nor to allow them to tell you, which could make you a material witness. Despite that, kids often discussed their cases openly. Sometimes all you had to do was open a newspaper. Some boys tried to rob a man on 125th Street, the man fled into the street and was hit by a car. A few days later one of those boys showed up in my classroom. The following week his victim died in the hospital, and his charge was changed to murder. Another student had been arrested for setting a homeless man on fire, a story millions of New Yorkers watched on the six o'clock news.

The Department of Juvenile Justice had conducted an extensive mental health survey the year before I arrived. I don't recall the exact figures, just that the percentage of court-involved youths who'd been sexually abused was through the roof (and since the survey relied on self-reporting, the true number was bound to be higher). The same for physical abuse. I was meeting students at the end of a long arc of crimes, most of which had been done to them. Every day in class a boy named Anthony who'd been charged with rape worked on a love poem. He rapped the lines of his poem incessantly, but he was learning disabled, and could only add one or two lines a day. It took a couple of weeks to realize he was rapping about losing his virginity to a thirty-year-old woman in his building. He was sentenced and sent upstate before he could finish that poem.

There was little continuity. Students were being admitted, taken to court, sentenced, or released each day. Coming in each morning, you first needed to find out what went down overnight, who had beef, who was tight, whose meds had been changed, etc. But day by day, I figured out how to teach whoever was in front of me, and how to get them writing. I built a curriculum, held poetry festivals in the gym, and published their best writing in anthologies I had spiral-bound, with student art on the covers. Those books were stolen right and left—the highest possible compliment.

After a year, I'd successfully transitioned to a new job on a team of dedicated teachers. The trade-off for more writing time had worked out—I soon had a new full-length manuscript of poems entitled *The Job of Being Everybody*. And I had something else that was new: a girlfriend.

DEBRA WAS SMALL, kind, quick-witted and beautiful, a freelance technical writer, who had once taught high school English. A single mother, divorced. We connected on an internet dating site, then had a long phone conversation, then met for a drink at the South Street Seaport on a breezy day in mid-July. We couldn't believe we'd found each other—online, of all places. (It was still the days when, if a couple met online, they agreed to a cover story.)

She lived on Staten Island, which she sardonically referred to as the Isle of Staten. I liked taking the ferry to visit her (the Statue of Liberty always appearing sooner than expected), joining other Staten Islanders for a sacred half hour suspended from the noise and chaos of the city. A bus was always waiting at the terminal, the number 95, which climbed Victory Boulevard, then snaked up Castleton Avenue, depositing me a block from Silver Lake Road, where Debra resided with her six-year-old boy in a three-story—though somehow little—white house.

She'd moved into the house with a man named Victor who was now her ex-husband. She said the legal grounds for the divorce was "constructive abandonment." Translation: while she was alone in bed on the second floor, he was on the third floor masturbating to porn on his computer, night after night, week after week. He'd also been verbally abusive, and occasionally violent. It had taken a year of covert planning for Debra to get out of the marriage, which involved a lawyer, various documents pertaining to custody and property, and a locksmith. When she finally executed her plan he didn't know what hit him. She could have written a how-to guide for women escaping abusive marriages.

Debra seemed to possess the keys to my body. Each time we got into bed, I became instantly turned on. It was the same for her, and she was quite orgasmic. Yet she was also willing to go slow, which was something I knew to ask for by then.

I'd had a relationship a couple years before with a struggling actress named Shauna, who was my first girlfriend since freshman year of college. Shauna freely enjoyed sex, and helped me adjust to intimacy, though I didn't fully trust her, and she turned out to be a sex addict. Each night she'd call asking to come over, and was unable to fall asleep until she achieved orgasm. I started dissociating. It happened every time, but I didn't always bring it up because I knew it frustrated her. Also, it's hard to talk when you're frozen and numb.

I felt safe with Debra, and safety itself may have been an aphrodisiac. I was still aware that I might check out during sex, but with Debra, before the fog of dissociation rolled in, I could pull back and tell her. Often the sex was good all the way through, and it was during the good, loving sex that I began to experience bodily flashbacks of my mother violating me sexually. They were touch memories, hauntingly familiar sensations in my pelvis and upper thighs. The flashbacks were like facets of an object at the bottom of a well, now catching the light. There was no accompanying narrative, yet the sense each time was unmistakable: *I'd been here with my mother.*

I'D BROKEN OFF all contact with her when I was twenty-three, following a small family reunion at a Red Lobster restaurant in Deer Park, Long Island. My brother and his wife had driven down from Massachusetts. I drove out from the city. My mother was living in Commack, near the restaurant. At dinner she talked nonstop about frivolous things no one else cared about, preventing any meaningful interaction. This was not unusual. When the check arrived, she called the waiter back and demanded he bring her another check that included the total before tax. This was also typical. She was about to administer a math lecture to the waiter, regarding the actual price of a meal, and the inflating of tips—when the following words shot through me: *You will never be in a room with her again.*

I looked across at my brother, sitting beside his wife, wondering if he'd also heard the words. There was the buzz of conversation from other tables, the crash of dishes and silverware from the kitchen, louder each time the doors swung open. There was my mother lecturing the waiter. And there was also that strange declaration, like some oracle: *You will never be in a room with her again.*

I began to feel a great sense of relief. There had always been something oppressive about my mother's presence. Not just her behavior, but her body, the shape of her, her unwashed scent. Since I was a teenager, I felt a gnawing discomfort, at times a visceral revulsion, whenever she was near. It went way beyond teenage embarrassment, and overwhelmed whatever positivity or respect I may have also felt toward her.

Stepping out of the restaurant, I sensed the words I had heard taking root. I said goodbye undramatically in the parking lot and got in my car to drive back to New York City, certain I would never see her again. I made no formal announcement of this, to her or anyone else. I just stopped contacting her. The strangest thing of all was that she never tried to contact me, to ask what was going on. It was like she already knew the steps to this dance.

"I would be mortified if Malcolm ever cut me off," Debra said. "I'd call every month for the rest of his life to ask him what was wrong."

When I told her about the flashbacks I was having during sex, Debra hugged me so hard I had to tap her for air. She wanted to know what she could do, and I told her she was already doing it. "I could kill your mother," she said.

"HOW DID YOU get that?" she asked, touching a two-inch scar below my navel.

"I don't know."

"What about this?" she said, pointing to a smaller scar a few inches lower.

"I don't know about that one either. It's always been there."

"And this?" There were several scars on my lower abdomen and inner thighs. I knew they were there, but I never thought about them. In bed, in bright morning light, Debra couldn't miss them.

"I've got news for you," she said. "They weren't always there."

ON A WEEKEND when Malcolm was with his father, Debra asked if we could speak in her kitchen at noon. It was a strangely formal request. Then again, she had a thing for formality. She was a big fan of Victorian literature.

"All right," she said, when we were seated at the kitchen table. "Before I start, I need to advise you of the exits. There's a door behind you, leading to the backyard." She gestured like a flight attendant. "And behind me, through the living room, is the front door."

"Got it."

"So"—she took a deep breath—"before I was married to Victor, I had another husband." She told me the story of her previous marriage to an unhappy poet.

"You're still here," she said.

"Still here."

"Well, in that case, you should also know that before the husband I just told you about, there was another husband." She told me about what she called her "starter marriage," to a man in Indiana, where she'd grown up.

"So Victor was your third husband?"

"Yeah," she said with a pained smile. "I guess I really love marriage."

"I actually would say the opposite." We had a good laugh. She reached for a tissue, blew her nose, then tossed the tissue thoughtlessly behind her.

"Debra?"

"Doug?"

"Can I tell *you* something?"

"Absolutely."

"Before I do, I'd like to remind you of the exits . . ." Then I told her about my crossdressing. Even though it had been a decade since I'd dressed, I wasn't about to hide this part of myself from a girlfriend. When I'd told Shauna, she was rocked—literally. She closed her eyes, and swayed like she was going to fall over. "Any other bombshells I need to know about?" she said. But Shauna got over it. When she started sleeping over every night, she borrowed my skirts and blouses to wear to her day job. She literally wore out her fears.

When I told Debra—at our kitchen table summit, at high noon on the Isle of Staten—she gave me a beguiled look of *touché*. She had not expected a confession to rival hers. She asked me questions (the main one being *Why?*) and I gave answers (the main one being *I don't know*). Needless to say, no one broke for the exits. Instead the exchange brought us to a new place, and something strange happened to my visual field: my perception of Debra, along with the house and surroundings, grew more vivid, as though I'd lived with a lens over my eyes. I sensed a lifting of a primordial layer of tension.

At age thirty-nine, I was finally being offered a life of companionship. The thought of Debra, and of seeing her next, could smooth the jagged edges of any day. I felt this especially on Wednesdays, when, after leaving the jail, I bought a garlicky roast chicken in the South Bronx and brought it all the way to Staten Island, where Debra and I would eat, make love, and spend the night together. We hadn't been seeing enough of each other—we joked that we had a bicoastal relationship—so we decided to try a sleepover during the week. The logistics were formidable; I had to wake up at five the next morning, catch a bus to the ferry, catch a local train at the southern tip of Manhattan, switch to an express at Chambers Street to take me far uptown and across to the Bronx. By the time I met the kids for first period, I'd already been up for three hours. It was worth it, to have slept with the woman I loved.

Sometimes Debra would wake me up to tell me I was snoring. The first time it happened she informed me it was proper etiquette to wake your snoring partner instead of suffering alone. I loved that little lesson about partnership, which my life of solitude could not have taught me. I apologized for snoring. "You couldn't help it," she said. She asked what I was dreaming, and we stayed up talking. She told me stories of small town Indiana, of her days teaching high school in Queens and Staten Island, of her fondness for Allen Ginsberg, who'd been her professor at Brooklyn College. She told me about the popular romance novel she once attempted to write, according to a strict formula prescribed by the Red Dress Books division of Harlequin Romance, Inc. We told one another where we were during 9/11. (She'd seen the burning towers while driving down Victory Boulevard; I was teaching at the jail—it was just my second day.) We were so content to lie in bed spooning and talking, not caring about sleep. "I adore you," she said.

DEBRA'S SIX-YEAR-OLD SON Malcolm was a challenge. He was loud, anxious, excitable, a perpetual-motion machine. He was a cute boy, alert and bright. In rare moments of stillness, you might have thought him ordinary, but seconds later some core of instability inside him would erupt once more. He liked me, but it was hard to be close to him physically. He head-butted me every time I visited. The headbutts weren't playful gestures, but out-of-control, full-on collisions, quite painful, accompanied by enthusiastic shouting. Malcolm wasn't shy about giving orders, and issuing refusals. Debra tried desperately, via activity and redirection, to keep him out of dark moods. Once in the car, having fallen into a particularly deep funk, he told his mother, "Everything is no." He'd been diagnosed with a sensory processing disorder, but no one was sure. Weekly therapy sessions were having no effect on him. After a day of his relentless demands and physical wildness, Debra looked ready to collapse. There were moments when he was tugging on her that I saw the color drain from her face. Yet she never lost her patience or blew up at him.

Due to Malcolm, we generally spent our time on Staten Island. Once, for a change of pace, she arranged childcare for a couple of hours on a Sunday, which left her just enough time to hop in her car, drive to my place in Manhattan, have sex with me, throw her clothes back on, and race home. I could tell she liked the thrill, and perhaps the literary feeling of our assignation (did it meet the formula for a Red Dress Book?), not to mention the sex. What most enthralled me was watching her reassemble herself, slightly disoriented after being fucked, putting her nylons back on (no panties), throwing a tan sweater-dress over her head, refreshing her lipstick and heading out wearing practically nothing, as so many women do, even on chilly days, walking in public, on the street, in her clothes, in her body, in her life. I'd never been in quite this proximity to a woman's life, which I found more heart-stopping than sex.

The first time she was over my place, she'd asked to see my women's clothes. I opened the closet (one of my closets had nothing but women's things) and let her look. She tried not to show it, but I could tell she was startled by what was there, and how much of it there was. "You wore this?" she said, holding up a slinky dress. I nodded yes. She took out a couple other items, regarded them, and replaced them respectfully. She said it was hard to imagine me as a woman. She was genuinely bewildered. I reached in and pulled out a tan sweater-dress and offered it to her. It was too small for me.

Sometimes I'd find a pair of nylons lying about her bedroom, and slip one of my legs into them, where Debra's small alabaster leg had been, and feel nostalgic for my crossdressing days. Mostly she dressed casually, but I asked her, on a day she was wearing pantyhose, how they felt. We were sitting on her bed. She put a hand on her thigh, gave it some thought, and said, "They're OK."

In late winter, six months into our relationship, we engineered a weekend getaway. She managed to get her mother to come from Indiana to babysit Malcolm as part of a one-week visit. Our destination was one of those cheap couples resorts in the Poconos, the kind I'd seen advertised on local TV when I was a kid. The package deal included a stand-alone cabin with a round king-size bed and a raised Jacuzzi shaped like a champagne glass, with plumbing that was hard to fathom. In the morning, a teenager in work boots trudged across a field of snow like a footman in a Russian novel, bearing our breakfast on a silver tray. We lazed in bed, or gave the Jacuzzi a whirl. Debra felt a periodic thrill of liberation to be on furlough from her life in Staten Island. We roller-skated in the old gymnasium with other couples, then dressed up for dinner. I wore a jacket and tie, she wore a velvet dress and dangle earrings—and lovely underthings she knew would turn me on. We ate dinner at a table in the main lodge with three other couples, all of whom were newlyweds. We let them assume we were newlyweds too. Someone came around taking photos, which the resort printed and presented to us in a small cardboard album titled "Memories." We went back to our cabin, slowly undressed each other, and had sex.

"THE COURSE OF true love never did run smooth," said the sign I taped up in front of the girls' classroom.

"That bitch is right," said Demetra.

"You think so?"

"Yeah. Who she?"

"She's William Shakespeare," I said, pointing to the name below the quote.

Teachers weren't allowed to give the students books, because they could hide a shank between the pages, so I fed them literature one line at a time—in the form of a "Quote of the Week" on Monday, for which they'd receive a memorization test on Friday. I chose quotes about love, hardship, and freedom, from great writers and philosophers, with some rappers thrown in. Even for their age, the kids were surprisingly well versed in the trials of love. Kaleigh's haiku—

> *I really love him*
> *he makes me smile everyday*
> *I think he cheats*

was a typical sentiment, as was David's—

> *How come all the girls*
> *love you when you are locked up*
> *but not in the world?*

But they were also starved for love. When I played the boom box (as collateral for doing their writing) the boys occasionally asked for a soul station, over the defiant rap they usually favored. Sometimes during a love song a deep peace settled over the room.

"Mista," said Tyrone, a five-star general with the Bloods, "you fuck your girl to this?"

"Tyrone, how's your poem coming?"

"C'mon," he said, smiling and nodding, "you know you fuck your girl to this."

One time I handed out the lyrics to the Beach Boys' "Wouldn't It Be Nice," played it, and watched them try to hate it, until Tyrone said, "Yo, run that back," and I did. They were total goners for Brian Wilson's innocent yearning for love. Chris wrote:

WOULDN'T IT BE NICE

Wouldn't it be nice if there was peace on Earth
Wouldn't it be nice to be home
Wouldn't it be nice to go to heaven
Wouldn't it be nice to be dead
Wouldn't it be nice if the judge was my uncle
Wouldn't it be nice for you to be my wifey
Wouldn't it be nice if I had super powers
Wouldn't it be nice to be home together

DEBRA CALLED SAYING she had something she needed to tell me. She wanted to meet for lunch in Manhattan, and proposed we go to Ernie's, a popular and overpriced diner on Sixth Avenue. After our food came, she told me, nervously, that she and Victor were separated. I was confused. She explained her legal status, and the steps she was taking with her divorce attorney, but technically he was still her husband.

"But he's out of your life, right?"

"Absolutely."

"I guess I don't see what the big deal is."

"Oh my god I'm so relieved!" She was near tears. She explained that a lot of men didn't want anything to do with a woman who was separated. She added that, on the day she told me about her three marriages, technically she hadn't lied: she never said she had three divorces.

It wasn't until after she'd driven off that I started to see what the big deal was. She'd misled me, and she did it according to a carefully timed plan. Also, why Ernie's? She'd arranged to have that conversation in a public place.

"TELL ME ABOUT Victor's violence," I said, the next time I saw her. We spoke downstairs in her house, during one of the rare moments Malcolm was playing upstairs by himself.

She said Victor flew into rages, like a child. He screamed right in her face. Sometimes he shoved her into things, a wall, some furniture. "Just a few times," she said. "He's not that strong."

"Fuck."

"Now don't you go getting upset," she said. She told me she'd been way more concerned about the porn he was viewing on his computer each night, in the little room on the third floor. She searched the computer's files when he was at work, and most of it was anal sex. "The same square inch, over and over," she said, rolling her eyes. She also told me about a photo he emailed her when he was away on a business trip, a picture of him and a male coworker embracing at a Gay Pride march in San Francisco. When she asked him what the hell was going on, he said he was just supporting his friend, who had decided to come out.

"What was my husband doing in a Gay Pride march in San Francisco?"

"Since when do nighttime legal proofreaders go on business trips?"

"Right?"

"Can we go back to his porn? What was the rest of it?"

"The rest?"

"You said most of it was anal sex. What was the rest?"

She froze for a moment, then looked down and said, "Child pornography."

"Holy shit."

"You cursed!" said Malcolm. He was crouched behind the banister on the bottom step of the stairs. "Doug cursed!"

"Doug didn't curse," said Debra, walking over to him.

"He did, Mom! He said, 'holy shit.'"

"He was quoting someone."

"What's a quote? Hey, where are we going?"

"Come show me what you built with your LEGOs."

"What's a quote? Let go my hand! I wanna know what a quote is."

When Debra came back downstairs, I asked if she still had that hard drive.

"Yeah, but he erased everything."

"Of course he did. But there are people who salvage hard drives."

I wasn't telling her anything she didn't know.

• • •

"HE SHOULD BE behind bars," said Connie. Connie Fink was a retired attorney who taught criminal law at the jail. The kids loved her class.

"Instead," I said, "he has visitation rights, every other weekend, with his six-year-old son."

"Monstrous."

"What's the dividing line," I asked, "between giving someone your honest perspective, and judging them?"

"You must judge," she said.

"I must?"

"Do you want to spend the rest of your life with her? You would also be marrying her choices."

She advised me to list the facts Debra had told me about Victor, and then show Debra the list. "Let her see it in writing," Connie said. "Maybe then she'll take it to her lawyer."

The list I emailed Debra included Victor's instability, immaturity, drug use, physical abuse, lying, lying about his sexuality, along with the purchase and consumption of child pornography. Debra and I had both noticed that each time Victor dropped him off, Malcolm was especially off the rails. I put that down too.

She called that night to push back, in her polite way. She said that she needed me to trust that she was a good mother. I asked her which item on the list referred to her mothering. She said that, given my own past, she was concerned that this all might be too much for me. I acknowledged her point. Then I asked, "How do you know he's not raping Malcolm?"

She gave in. She spoke to her divorce attorney, who asked the court to order a hair-follicle drug test. Debra knew that Victor, who smoked pot, wouldn't pass. The test was all that was needed to legally mandate supervised visits. Victor called Debra to complain. He was furious. Who was he going to get to supervise the visits? He said he had no relatives available. Debra suggested getting a friend to do it. He said he didn't have any friends. In that case, she told him, he'd have to hire a social worker.

A few weeks later, she called to tell me she couldn't see me that weekend. Victor claimed he could no longer afford to pay for supervised visitations. He'd been working her over. Finally, Debra agreed to be their chaperone.

"Are you serious?"

"He accused me of trying to take his son away."

The problem was she *hadn't* taken his son away. Instead, she was now spending every other weekend—our only time to be alone—with her husband and child in another part of Staten Island.

Meanwhile, Debra was becoming concerned about my sex life. She was worried that I wasn't having enough orgasms. I told her I was fine—better than fine: I was finally having healthy loving sex. She'd never heard of a man being fine with not coming. Why this sudden concern? Did she fear the infrequency of my orgasms meant that we hadn't bonded, or that I didn't find her sufficiently desirable? Or was she trying to make my body the main problem in the relationship?

At a guesthouse in Ocean Grove, New Jersey, on a rare stolen night away together, Debra insisted we make a concerted effort to have mutually mind-blowing sex, and I went along with it. When I needed to back off, she kept pushing, until I dissociated and went catatonic. By the time I arrived home the next day I was filled with the same blind terror that had sabotaged my life. *Why had she done this?*

Not long after that night, Debra had her attorney release

Victor from supervised visits, restoring his full access to Malcolm. Legally she didn't have to—Victor continued to test positive for drugs. She said she was confident her boy was safe, and that I needed to trust her. Besides, this way we'd get our weekends back. Wasn't that wonderful?

ON A FRIDAY night in late October, I sat crying on a ferry headed for Manhattan. A few hours earlier, I'd taken the ferry the other way—my final crossing to Staten Island—and broken up with Debra.

The reason I gave was that I hadn't bonded with Malcolm. I told her I'd kept the issue to myself, hoping for things to change, but they hadn't, and it would be unfair to waste any more of her time. That was a lie. Malcolm was troubled, but I worked with troubled kids for a living. The truth was Debra had been right: the sexual issues were too much for me. I was dumbstruck by her choice to make Malcolm available to a pedophile, and I'd become numb and indifferent toward sex. (Beneath that numbness, I knew by now, was panic.) I didn't want to talk about it, I just wanted a clean break, so I gave her a reason no good mother could abide. It was cowardly and heartless of me.

Debra's tears came instantly. She mopped her face with one tissue after another, tossing them backward over her head like shuttlecocks. "What choice do I have?" she said. "You hate my kid."

After acknowledging we were finished, we asked each other, like old friends, what we were going to do (i.e., for the rest of our lives, without each other). There are no answers to such questions. We held each other for a long time, swearing our love, crying. All the pleasures of knowing Debra flashed before my eyes. *What the hell was I doing?*

ON THE FERRY there were revelers dressed in costumes, headed to clubs in Manhattan. I'd forgotten: it was Halloween.

There was a time when Halloween was the most important day of the year for me. Any crossdresser will tell you that. On Halloween you can go as a woman anywhere—parties, hotel bars, friends' apartments. You can ride public buses in broad daylight. Halloween is the day that most closely approximates the life you can only dream about. Some crossdressers plan for the day months in advance.

We had a gym teacher in elementary school named Mr. Reilly, who dressed as a woman every Halloween. He stood among the mothers and teachers cheering along the drive behind the school, where we children paraded in our animal and princess and superhero costumes. Mr. Reilly was young and muscular, and a bit of a showboat—he invited kids to ride his back when he did push-ups. But for Halloween he shaved his legs and thick blond moustache, and he made himself so womanly he could have been any kid's mother in that crowd. We wouldn't have noticed him had he not said hello to us as we walked by. That's what I thought about most: that hello. He wanted us to *see* him as a woman. I don't know anything about Mr. Reilly's life, but I have imagined it to be a painful one, except for Halloween.

A few months before we broke up, Debra had given me a strange birthday present: a black binder containing a manuscript. The title page read *In Search Of*, with her byline beneath. "I wrote a full-length play about us!" she said. She insisted I read the whole play then and there, in front of her.

(It was a feat she could have performed in under ten minutes; she was a speed-reader—an actual graduate of the Evelyn Wood speed reading program, which I'd previously thought was a hoax.) Not wanting to seem ungrateful, I began, but after a few pages of her watching me, I thanked her for the present, and promised to read it on my own.

The play was about a woman who goes on a dating site and meets a man who turns out to be a crossdresser. Debra had been writing it in secret for six months. She'd gone on some research expeditions to a Staten Island bar that had a weekly drag night, where she befriended some performers. The man in her play bore little resemblance to me. Debra had never seen me dressed, and I was not a drag performer. *In Search Of* was not a play about us. It was, rather, a play about the ordeal of being in a relationship with me, an ordeal she kept hidden, like the play.

And I was hiding my own ordeal. Even in my happiest moments with Debra, I'd felt a gaping emptiness. The joy of being with her wasn't just fleeting, it was haunting. From Silver Lake Road you could hear the distant horn of the Staten Island Ferry. The horn felt like a reminder, every half hour, that my true life was elsewhere, and I'd missed another chance to embark for it. This made me incredibly sad, yet in my sadness I could conceive of no destination, other than my own empty apartment.

Several months after we broke up, Debra sent me a package with a note. She'd been cleaning her house and found a book I'd left behind, which she thought I might want back. The note was a relentlessly rosy update of her life, meticulously constructed (she was, after all, a technical writer). She had a new boyfriend, a police officer from a large Italian family that welcomed her with open arms. There were weddings, christenings, birthdays, holidays, a nonstop round of festive occasions to shop and dress up for. She'd grown out her hair, Malcolm was thriving, as was the stray kitten she'd adopted, the one we'd found on Delancey Street and named Della.

It was the first of several such updates she would send, every few years, almost always on the occasion of finding a new boyfriend or husband. She would first google me, in search of a pretense for writing, then segue into how happy she was with her new man. Receiving the notes felt weird, like she was somehow gloating. Though maybe she was mourning our love.

The title of that book I'd left behind bears mentioning: *Christine Jorgensen: A Personal Autobiography.* Christine Jorgensen, for those who don't know, was the first widely publicized transsexual in the United States. She began hormone replacement therapy in 1951, had sex reassignment surgery soon after, and died of natural causes in 1989.

Femme Fever
2007

John G. Angelet, Principal
Bayard Rustin Educational Complex
351 West 18th Street
New York, NY 10011

Dear Mr. Angelet,

I hereby resign, effective September 1, 2007.

Sincerely,
Douglas Goetsch
cc. Demos Triantafillou, A.P. for Organization

"What's this?" says Mr. Triantafillou.

"It's my resignation letter."

He looks it over. "It's not a letter."

"How is it not a letter?"

"A letter needs to have an introduction, a main body, and a conclusion."

"Mr. T," I say, "I'm an English teacher, and I'm telling you it's a letter."

"It is?"

"Yes."

"Come with me," he says.

Mr. T, who looks vaguely like Albert Einstein and speaks with a Greek accent, is pulling a wagon containing a large coffee urn. He needs to fill the urn at a bodega around the corner, then wheel it into the auditorium for an administrative conference.

"You're really resigning?" he says as we walk. He tells me he's thinking of leaving too, and asks me about the process. I can't answer his questions because he has enough years to retire, whereas I'm just resigning. He asks how many years I have.

"Twenty-one."

"You look young."

We're in the bodega now and Mr. T, feeling moved, tells me to pick out anything I want and he will buy it for me as a gift.

I glance briefly around the store. There's a tall rack of potato chips and Doritos, beer in the case, some beef jerky in thick plastic, coated in dust.

"Anything you want," Mr. T says.

"That's OK," I say.

"How about a cup of coffee? I'll buy you a coffee."

"You know what, I'd love a cup of coffee."

THE PREVIOUS WINTER, I'd left Passages Academy after five and a half years. I'd fallen under the purview of a transferred supervisor who was known for targeting one teacher in every building she was transferred to, and I was her new target.

It had been a brutal semester, and I was thinking of leaving teaching altogether, then opted to work one more semester before deciding. I found an opening, replacing someone on maternity leave at a balkanized school building on Eighteenth Street (which used to be Humanities High School). I was given a program teaching media studies and reading to a student population with historically low attendance. My classes were commandeered for a week in March by a team of proctors from a standardized testing company the principal had hired. I was required to be present, while forlorn students looked up at me from exam booklets wondering what had happened to our class. In May, the corporate proctors returned for another week of testing, and I knew it was time to get out of public school teaching.

Not that I had any idea of what to do next. There was poetry—I'd won several awards and book prizes by then—but poetry didn't pay, and I'd write poems no matter what else I did. My plan was to take a year off, collect twenty thousand dollars owed to me by the Department of Education for unused sick days, and say yes to invitations I couldn't have accepted while teaching. That took me to Niagara Falls and Marin County, where I did readings and led workshops, while indulging in the feeling of playing hooky. In the winter I began applying for college jobs teaching poetry.

ON A TRIP to Raleigh, North Carolina, I decided to call my father, who lived with my stepmother in Wilmington, and ask him to lunch. It was the first time we'd spoken in twenty years. He sounded reluctant, a little frightened. He questioned the logistics. There were 120 miles between us—how could we possibly do this? I said I had a rental car and we could meet halfway. He said there might not be a restaurant around there. "Dad," I finally said, "I'm proposing lunch. Are you interested?" He thought about it a moment, then said OK. I called back shortly with the name and location of a restaurant halfway between us.

A couple years after he'd left my mother, my father and I started talking again, and he came to my graduation at Wesleyan. When I moved to Brooklyn we fell into a pattern of monthly visits, where I was expected to drive to his house in Westchester. I'd arrive at the house, he'd come downstairs from his study, shake my hand, talk to me for a few minutes, then disappear upstairs to work on his stamps. (My father was a stamp collector. When he was fired from his last job as an insurance executive, he decided to turn his collection into a mail-order business.) I'd spend the afternoon talking with my stepmother, Sylvia. Then he'd come down for dinner, after which he'd shake my hand again, and I'd drive back home. This continued for many months, until I told him on the phone that I wanted us to spend time together. He didn't understand what I meant. I told him we could play tennis or golf, or see a Knicks game, or just take a walk somewhere. "So you refuse to set foot in my house?" he said. He accused me of insulting his family. I told him Sylvia and I were fine with each other, but he was using her to avoid me. He said that I resented her, and that I'd always been too close to my mother. I said that all I wanted was to spend time together. "You're shitting on me," he said. That's when I hung up. Neither of us had picked up the phone since.

What people didn't understand about my father and me was that we were no more cut off during those twenty years than we were before. If anything, the relationship was more honest.

THE RESTAURANT TURNED out to be a chicken shack just off the interstate. We arrived within ten minutes of one another. It was raining, we ordered directly from the cook and ate under an awning. We were the only ones there. Dad couldn't get over how rustic the place was. He seemed both appalled and giddy to be eating in a roadside chicken shack. Imagine that!

He tried to make small talk. The Giants had just beaten the undefeated Patriots in the Super Bowl. "What a game," he said. I agreed, great game.

"Dad," I said, "just so you know, I have no agenda here, other than lunch."

"I appreciate that," he said. He asked what I was doing for a job. I told him I'd left teaching, and was taking a year to decide what's next. He asked what I was doing for income. I told him I was OK, and asked what he was doing. He was a day trader, waking up early and spending each morning executing sophisticated trades. He liked to design ways to derive "income" from the stock market without having to pay tax.

He kept coming back to the subject of money, and my employment. "What about financial security?" he said. I thought of his divorce settlement with my mother, in which no money had been set aside for college tuition. I told him that there were things that mattered more than financial security, that you could even be happy and poor. He pondered that for a moment, then shook his head.

We said goodbye under umbrellas in the parking lot. "Do you come to North Carolina often?" he said.

"Who knows, Dad," I replied, "maybe we can do this again in another twenty years."

We shook hands and drove off in opposite directions. I rounded a bend and started weeping. *Do you come to North Carolina often?* Not *Keep in touch*, not *Let's not have this happen again*. But I was no longer angry at him. Maybe that's what the lunch was for, to show him that.

I would in fact return to North Carolina in two years, and pay him a visit in Wilmington, where I would see just how much of a recluse my father was. He rarely left his house, which was located on a golf course in a gated community. He didn't even play the golf course, which he could have done for free. My stepmother flew across the country to visit her grandchildren, and he wouldn't even drive her to the local airport. His sixty-mile journey to see me at the chicken shack must have felt like a moonshot.

I'd grown up confused and angry over why my father didn't want to know me. He wouldn't come to a single Little League game. Now I knew that whatever phobia or disorder he had, he'd always had it. It wasn't personal, it was just incredibly sad.

IN NEW YORK I went on a string of Match.com dates, the last of which was with Amy, an adorable, geeky, and self-effacing graphic designer who lived in Windsor Terrace, Brooklyn. Our first morning in bed together she told me she'd never in her life had an orgasm, and I revealed to her that I was a crossdresser. I didn't understand crossdressing, and she didn't know why she didn't have orgasms. It could have been medical or psychological. When she was little, her mother would get drunk and barge into her bedroom at night, wake Amy up, and rail about her father's inability to satisfy her sexually.

After a few months of dating, we took a casino bus down to Atlantic City for a weekend. We planned to dress up on Saturday night to see *42nd Street* at the Tropicana. Amy had recently purchased an expensive red dress and had it tailored. She was not a formal person, but something had gotten ahold of her. The dress was an elegant dual-fabric design, with a wool skirt and satin bodice that showed off her petite frame. I put on slacks, a blazer, and a tie, and sat reading in our hotel bedroom while she did her makeup in the bathroom—or tried to. It was taking some time.

When I went to check on her she was doubled over crying. I held her in my arms until she finally caught her breath, enough to explain, through mascara tears, her trauma at the mirror. Amy, who hardly ever wore makeup, had become more and more nervous applying it, until she started having flashbacks of her mother. Not the drunken visits to her bedroom, but another recurring episode: every time Amy tried to break out of her tomboy phase, experimenting with clothes or hair or makeup, her mother ridiculed her. As an adult, the slightest tint of blush or lipstick made Amy feel like a clown. I hadn't known it, but getting dolled up to go out in dumpy old Atlantic City had been weighing on her all day.

What a couple we were: two people who weren't allowed to be women. Huddled with Amy on the bathroom floor in that Atlantic City hotel room, I asked if she still wanted to go to the show. She nodded her head yes, stood up, blew her nose, washed her face, and changed into jeans. "You look great," I said, as we stepped out.

"HOW ABOUT A do-over?" I wrote a few days later, after we'd returned to New York. My email included a link to the

Femme Fever Gala Ball scheduled for the following Saturday in Lake Ronkonkoma, Long Island. Femme Fever was part of an underground circuit of crossdressing "holidays" held in hermetically sealed hotels across the country. The holidays were a facet of the crossdressing scene I'd only read about. Closeted husbands, fathers, and grandfathers made pilgrimages to these Meccas, having circled the dates on calendars months in advance.

"OMG!" Amy replied. "I'd love to, but will I be welcome?" I assured her that wasn't going to be a problem. Crossdressers love having women around. Suggesting Femme Fever could have easily backfired—I didn't want to rub Amy's trauma in her face. On the other hand, what could be safer for her than an entire event devoted to people exploring their femininity? It would also mean a return to dressing for me, only now I had a mission. Like the superheroes I loved as a child, who changed into capes and tights in phone booths or while sliding down the bat-pole, I would swing into action as female me in order to defeat the barbarians of wrongdoing—otherwise known as Amy's mother.

THIS TIME IT was Amy waiting in a hotel bedroom while I put on makeup in the bathroom. I had never changed in front of a woman, or anyone else, before, and I brought everything in there—bra, hosiery, dress, shoes, wig, and jewelry—so that I could emerge fully transformed.

"Are you ready?" I called.

"I'm nervous," she confessed.

I walked out. We didn't say anything for a while, and we were a little afraid to touch.

"You walk better in heels than me," she said in the hall. We were headed across the highway to an Applebee's, where some of the Femme Fever guests were having a first drink.

At the bar, Amy began to really take me in. "You're completely different," she said, "yet you're still *you*."

"I'm still me."

"How you sit, and move your hands . . . you're feminine, yet natural."

"I know," I said. "It's pretty weird."

"It's weird that it's *not* weird."

When we crossed back over the highway, guests were in the hotel driveway snapping photos of one another in the good light just before dusk. They had the excitement of girls before a prom. The posing and snapshots would go on all night, intensifying with each change of clothes. People brought one outfit for cocktails, another for dinner, still another for dancing at the hotel "disco" afterward, an ensemble for brunch the next day, not to mention sleepwear.

I was surprised to see several girls I recognized from my crossdressing years in the 1990s. After the adventure of being out in New York City, why did they need to come to Femme Fever? One girl I'd known as a crossdresser had grown out her hair and started on hormones. She brought a boyfriend to the ball—they looked like a happy sixty-year-old couple. Other girls were in "T4T" sexual relationships with one another, something I hadn't seen in the 1990s. Times were changing.

But the crew at the table where Amy and I sat was fairly homogeneous, and quite closeted. Some dressed like street whores in miniskirts, garters, and stockings, others like debutantes in pastel and floral. I had on a sleeveless green print dress with a high collar and chocolate Mary Jane pumps.

Amy, the only "GG" at the table, finally debuted her tailored red dress. She had on very little makeup, and she looked radiant.

At different points in the evening, people at the table came over to confess their envy of Amy and me. They told of angry, devastated wives confronting them with a suspicious item on a credit card bill, or a hidden trove of lurid photos, a pair of huge pumps, a clip-on earring, or one of their own stretched-out bras. A few had managed to keep their crossdressing hidden from their wives—or so they thought. Some carried enormous guilt about the pain they were causing their families. They commiserated with each other about the fear of losing custody of their children. They drank a lot. A few got up the courage to hit the dance floor, gingerly two-stepping in high heels.

AFTER FEMME FEVER, I started crossdressing again. I wanted to see if I could dress and not have it take over my life. I had a new rule: it needed to be fun. If I approached it as play, dressing might be safe. And unlike before, I had a supportive partner.

Actually, Amy was more than supportive. "Can Tina come out tonight?" she started asking. At first this delighted me, and Tina obliged. We'd go out for dinner or drinks. Once we attended a "Prom" at the Gay and Lesbian Center. I wore a polka-dot sleeveless sheath dress that felt better than it looked. When we posed for a picture to be made into a souvenir button, I was startled by how hideously masculine I looked beside Amy.

For a short while our sex life got more interesting, though our dynamic was shifting. In bars, Amy caressed my thighs under my skirt, and sometimes kept her hand plastered there.

That made me extremely uncomfortable, though I didn't say anything. I didn't think I had a right to complain to a girlfriend who accepted me. But I didn't like what was happening. We'd attended Femme Fever so that Amy could explore her femininity. The result was the opposite: after seeing me as Tina, she outsourced that project to me, taking vicarious pleasure in my femininity. The arrangement was unspoken, and I hadn't signed on to it. More and more, she asked if Tina could come out, which made crossdressing feel like a job.

Worst of all, my attraction to her was fading. I kept this to myself for fear of insulting her, while praying for my interest to return. There hadn't been much passion between us in the first place, but I loved Amy, and was scared of losing her.

In late spring I received a phone call from David Macey, the English Department chair at the University of Central Oklahoma, telling me I was their choice for a one-year poet-in-residence position starting in August. David asked if I needed time to think it over. I told him no, I was coming.

The next night I took Amy out to dinner.

"To the Broncos," I said, raising a glass.

"Who are the Broncos?" she said.

"The University of Central Oklahoma Broncos."

"YOU MADE THAT decision without even speaking to me," she said on the phone the next day. She was devastated. I was astonished at the selfishness and ignorance of my toast the night before, which may have been the cruelest thing I'd ever said to anyone. What the hell was wrong with me?

Yet she forgave me. She knew I'd been applying for college teaching positions. She didn't want to stand opposed to my happiness, so she waited a day to remind me of her existence.

"I'm visiting you," she said. "Once a month I'm flying out there, unless you fly here."

"Yes," I agreed. She was fighting for our relationship, which moved me, even though it was me—or something in me—she was fighting against.

Poet-in-Captivity
2008

I drove a 1992 Honda Civic fifteen hundred miles to Ed-
mond, Oklahoma, to assume my post as poet-in-residence.
Like leaving Stuyvesant to teach in the jail, this was another
move that puzzled people around me. All anyone in New
York City knew about Oklahoma was tornadoes and the title song to the musical, which they kept singing in my presence. My friend the writer William Zinsser referred to me as
a poet-in-captivity.

They gave me a two-bedroom corner apartment on the second floor of a sprawling dorm complex. My windows looked
out on a vast parking lot, on the other side of which was a football stadium. I'd come for the inaugural year of the first creative writing MFA program in the state of Oklahoma. I, who
possessed no MFA, would be teaching all the poetry classes.

I was in charge of a ragtag group of eight lovable students
who regarded my exotic accent as a mark of literary cachet—
since New York was where books came from. I appreciated the
unearned respect, and diagnosed them with low geographic
self-esteem. I set out to convince them that fine poems can
grow perfectly well in the red dirt of Oklahoma, though first
we had to forget we were on a college campus. I pointed to the
seminar table and said, "This might as well be a pool table in
outer space." I told them I was no professor, but rather a fellow
writer. I would be doing all assignments with them, and in

addition to my standard office hours in the English Department, I'd hold office hours twice a week at Java Dave's over on Broadway.

Two of those eight students were gender nonconforming. One was a small, smooth-faced, soft-spoken man named Craig. He wrote gritty, hard-nosed narratives of rural poverty and family violence. He was extremely well-read, though he stuck to his own hardscrabble subjects when writing. Every now and then there was a hiccup in clarity regarding gender or pronouns. In one poem he showed us, a boy gets arrested with his mother, and is relieved and grateful not to be held in a jail cell with her—though it's unclear why the boy is so relieved, or why it would occur to the police to put him in a woman's cell. Craig never self-identified as transgender, or anything else, and people were too polite to ask. He quietly thanked us for our comments on the poem.

I also taught a transgender woman named Paula Schonaeur, who was a Desert Storm veteran and a police officer. She was also an ordained deacon in the Episcopal Church. Her poems tended to be long surreal salvation allegories. Paula was six foot four, and quite well-known. Several years before I arrived, she sued the Oklahoma City Police Department for sexual harassment, took her fight to the newspapers, and settled out of court. Now she patrolled a beat alone—a rather dangerous one in the Capital District—because nobody was willing to be her partner.

She invited me to join her on patrol for a day, and I took her up on it. We walked the streets of the economically depressed area across the river from downtown. She checked in on shopkeepers and made her presence known. She told me stories of policing, of a knack she seemed to possess for getting confessions out of criminals, which saved the city the cost of a trial. "I just ask them what happened," she said, in her soft easygoing voice, "and a lot of times they confess." Toward the end of her shift she received a dispatch call to deal with a public drunkenness situation in another district. We circled back to her police van, drove over, and found two old Choctaw women drunk on mouthwash in a Walgreens parking lot. Gently, she coaxed them into a van and delivered them to detox.

Paula talked openly about her life ordeals, how hard she'd tried to prove she was a man, how much she didn't want to fail her family, and the wife she wound up losing when she transitioned. She knew, given her size, she'd forever be misgendered, but it didn't matter, compared to being her authentic self. I didn't tell her about my own interest in trans people, or the fact that I crossdressed. Not that I couldn't have safely outed myself to her; I just wouldn't have known what to say, where to begin or end.

THERE WERE POCKETS of queer community in central Oklahoma, and a measure of tolerance. Oklahoma City was twenty minutes south of the university, and every week or two I'd drive to an area where it was safe to be crossdressed. Going out was surprisingly easy. The trickiest part was getting from my door to my car, though even that wasn't so harrowing. The university was predominantly a commuter school, and the dorms were fairly deserted.

North of downtown lay a small cluster of gay bars and loud clubs, along with an "adults only gay resort" called the Hotel Habana. A mile west of those was a sort of country western lesbian bar called Partners. My favorite place was the HiLo Club, a dive bar with cheap drinks, an eclectic crowd, and drag shows on Saturdays. Everyone felt at home there. They played a lot of Lady Gaga. I rarely saw another cross-dresser, but that didn't seem to matter, and I got to know some of the regulars.

A blond woman approached me at the HiLo one night and offered to buy me a drink. She was young and heavy with a pretty face. She asked if she could talk to me, and we took a table. She told me about a long distance relationship she'd had with a man in Florida who was just beginning to cross-dress. She had fallen for him, and was open-minded about the dressing, but he was spiraling out of control. He began to binge drink, and question whether he was a man. Soon he cut off the relationship, but she was still worried sick about him.

"You seem like a well-adjusted person," she said, and asked if I could shed light on her ex. I didn't think I could. "If you talked to a hundred of us," I said, "you'd get a hundred different stories." But I was sad to hear he cut her off. I told her the thing he needed most was supportive people in his life, especially in the beginning.

Amy flew in to visit me a couple of times, and I picked her up at the Will Rogers Airport. We drove to the Wichita Mountains in southwest Oklahoma, and up to the pictur-esque town of Guthrie. We had dinner out as girlfriends in Oklahoma City on a night the Oklahoma Sooners were play-ing a home football game. The city was deserted.

My absence of desire for her hadn't changed, and I finally confessed this over the phone after she flew back. We hadn't been very physical on her visits, but if I forced myself to be intimate I was certain I would dissociate. It was another hor-rible thing to say to her—telling her I felt no desire. Amy accepted it quietly. I flew back once to see her in New York and, on a tearful walk by the Hudson River, we broke up. "I used to dream of a future," she said, "where you'd be Tina and we'd grow old having kinky sex." It might have been the most romantic thing anyone's ever said to me.

We spent a couple of days together post-breakup at her place in Brooklyn. They were peaceful, loving days, and not at all awkward. On my last night before flying back to Oklahoma, we decided to get our ears pierced. We found a tattoo and piercing place in South Park Slope. The artist was finishing up with a client, and advised us to go next door to the bar and have a few shots to numb ourselves. We did as he said. When we returned the tattoo place was closed.

MY LIFE IN Oklahoma was as solitary as it had been in New York, though it felt less haunted—perhaps because I didn't have a past there. I liked driving the rolling prairies, listening to my car radio. Twice a week I drove to the Oklahoma City Animal Shelter, where I volunteered to walk dogs in a large adjacent field, then deliver them back to their cages. (I wrote a poem about walking those dogs, which became my first acceptance at *The New Yorker*.) I played in an illicit weekly poker game held after hours at a sandwich shop in a strip mall in El Reno. (It was fairly safe because one of the regulars was a cop.) They nicknamed me "New York." I played golf every week or two with a former FBI officer named Everitt who taught in the Criminal Justice Department. He'd flown aerial surveillance for the FBI and was amazingly good at spotting my ball in the weeds. I swam laps in a saltwater university pool hardly anyone else used. (Swimming was a pleasure with shaved legs.) I had dinner periodically with Connie Squires and Steve Garrison, the founders of the MFA program, who both taught fiction writing. We discussed literature and music, and compared notes about our students, and their chances of success as writers.

But mostly I stayed alone in my large apartment beside the vast empty parking lot, where I practiced Buddhist meditation several hours a day. I'd been meditating since college, using it to manage the chronic headaches I suffered from. I became more dedicated when I began working at the jail, waking up early to practice, which helped me manage the stress of that job. I started attending open meditations at the Shambhala Center on Twenty-Second Street. The shrine rooms were elegant, and I liked sitting quietly with others. I could settle so deeply into stillness that I forgot my name. Sometimes I felt emptied of all identity and gender, and saw myself as a human-shaped bump on the earth's surface.

In 2006 a dharma teacher came to that Shambhala Center to conduct a weekend program in Vajrayana Buddhism, which blew me away. The Vajrayana is an ancient system of practice designed to dismantle all ideas about our bodies, our lives, and reality itself. If ever there was anyone in need of a reality overhaul, it was me. Each winter, that same teacher taught a monthlong program called a *dathün*—or "month sit"—in Crestone, Colorado. I attended the dathün in 2007 (the year after I left teaching) and encountered some of the most intelligent, spacious, and colorful people I'd ever known. We worked together, roomed together, ate and celebrated together. We chanted in the mornings and evenings, and sat in noble silence nine hours a day in the shrine room as the sun made its transit over a vast cold valley. For me, Buddhism held out two huge promises: the promise of community, and the promise of the second noble truth—that I might finally "see into the causes" of my suffering.

I drove to the next year's dathün from Oklahoma, through

"no-man's-land," the dust bowl towns of the panhandle, into New Mexico, past Trinidad, Colorado—"The Sex Change Capital of the World," due to the pioneering surgeon Stanley Biber, who practiced there—then west over a mountain pass, and up the valley to Crestone. On the way I received a surprise call from Everitt, my golfing buddy in the Criminal Justice Department. "You can still turn around," he said. He was concerned about my soul, and affirmed "our only Lord Jesus Christ." There was great care in his voice. I tried to tell him you could be a Buddhist and also a Christian (even though I wasn't Christian). It was a sweet call.

At that program I took the Buddhist refuge vows, dedicating myself to dharma training and study. I also fell madly in love with a much younger woman. The power of my attraction to Lisa astounded me, though she wasn't so convinced we should be together. After the retreat I tried to love her in two cities. (You can attempt such things when you're a poet-in-residence.) She was moving around a lot, looking for home. She was driving from St. Louis to Boulder when she stopped to visit me in Oklahoma, which is where she threw herself at me. We swore our love, but by the time I visited her in Boulder a month later, she'd turned cold and cruel. She criticized everything I said, and behaved recklessly behind the wheel. She was drinking a lot, switching into ugly moods, and personalities I didn't recognize. Lisa was a child of two alcoholics, a victim of rape and bullying at school, who'd taken to self-mutilation. Someone suggested she was testing me, displaying the ugliest parts of her personality to see if I could love those. If so, I failed the test. I couldn't take the cruelty, she was incapable of apology, and I abandoned my quest. I wrote some of my best love poems about her, which I would have gladly forfeited for the real thing.

The strangest part about the relationship was the sex—how great it was. Something enabled each of us to sail past the sexual obstacles we'd known in our lives. Perhaps it was meditation, and the fact that both of us were practitioners, that allowed us to drop our stories and temporarily defy gravity. Perhaps our bodies had special receptors for each other's trauma. Though saying anything feels like saying too much. It might be best to regard Lisa as a gift—an act without remainder, as they say in Zen—that didn't need to solve or fit with anything else in my life, including my gender identity. Lisa didn't care about that when I told her. Neither did Buddhism.

AT THE END of my year as a poet-in-residence I was asked to stay in the post. I had nothing better to do, so I said yes to another year in Oklahoma, where I wrote a lot of dharma-inspired poetry.

WRITER IN RESIDENCE, CENTRAL STATE

I'm writing this from nowhere. Oklahoma
if you care. It's not south, not west, not really
Midwest. Think of a hairless Chihuahua
on the shoulder of Texas, make an X—
I'm in the middle, in an apartment
over the dumpsters, on a parking lot
across from a football stadium.

Sometimes the parking lot feels like a lake,
a lake with light towers and cars on top of it.
Sometimes I see an Indian burial ground under there.
You don't think of asphalt as earth, but

if they paved the entire prairie—which seems to be
the plan—it would still curve with the horizon
and shine in the sun. And no matter where you are,
if you let the world quiet down, you'll start to hear
the most terrible things about yourself.
But then, like a teenager, it'll tire of cursing
and deliver you into the silence of graves.
You'll look out on the world and see
yourself looking out. Now I know,
when monks retreat to the charnel ground
and stay long enough, the demons
simply tire of shouting. No battles, no spells:
you wait for them to cry themselves to sleep.

If everyone were healed and well
and all neuroses gone, would there be
anything left to write about? Maybe
just the weather and death. I'd like to die
on a mountain in winter in New Hampshire,
the one the old man climbed, having decided
his natural time was done. How alive
he must have been during that short series of lasts—
last step, last look around, bend of the waist,
head on the ground, the soundless
closing of his lids. How easy to be in love
with the earth, breathing the crystalline air
as he shivered and yawned
and let the night take him home.

Don't worry, said a woman last winter.
I can see you're worried. She had the wrinkled eyes
of an old Cherokee, and spoke of past lives

without a trace of contrivance.
The silence here on weekends is so total
it holds me. Even when the stadium is full,
I don't hear the people, just the PA
telling who tackled who—who in Oklahoma
was born and raised and fed and coached
to deliver a game-saving hit. I don't know
where I will be or what I will do next year,
but five miles underground, in the womb of the earth,
there is no money, no lack of money,
no decisions about dinner or weekends, no friends
or enemies, no stacks of unanswered mail.
I'm trying to live there, so I can live here.

The woman in the poem, who told me not to worry, was Lee Ray. She was one of the teachers at that first dathün. When we had our interview, and I told her about my gender confusion, she looked at me and said, "This is the first life-time in which you are a male."

Revisionist History
2012

I am in a bedroom on the second floor of a house in Chevy Chase, DC. The bedroom is inexpensively furnished and has windows on three sides that look out on nearby houses, each in stark architectural disagreement with its neighbors. The sunlight of a September afternoon filters through a canopy of trees into the west-facing window, across from where I am sitting on a bed with Vanessa Han. Vanessa is an adjudicating attorney for a federal agency involved in immigration matters. She is a mother of two and a widow. This is her house.

We are having a dispute that is partly sad and partly ridiculous. She is of the opinion that I am happier in our relationship than I say I am. Previously Vanessa was a litigating attorney, so she is trained in making strong cases. I am trained as a Buddhist and a poet, and as far as I'm concerned, as soon as you try to make a case for something you've lost it. When we argue it is like we are gazing out different windows while discussing two trees as if they are the same tree.

"What about that day last fall we spent in bed?" she says. "You were happy." We both glance across the room to where the bed we are sitting on used to be, against a wall the sun is hitting. I know the day she's talking about.

That morning she'd been working downstairs in her office on an asylum case and came up here where I was writing. "Take a look at this," she said, holding up a photo clipped to a stack of forms. I saw what looked like three Latino children clinging to their mother and smiling. "They're probably in a lot of danger," she said, "and I'm about to deny them asylum." Their cheap immigration lawyer had applied on the wrong grounds, leaving her no choice, she explained, tears in her eyes.

"You can't rubber stamp it?"

"It'll get reversed, and I'll get reviewed."

I knew that behind this case she had a stack of others. Each Monday, she asked me to lift that stack, zipped into a suitcase, into the back of her SUV. "Thanks baby," she'd say, and drive across DC to work—her one day in the office. Later she'd drive home with a new stack.

She went downstairs, came back twenty minutes later. "I'm taking the rest of the morning off," she said.

"Good idea."

"What are you doing?" She sat on my thigh, facing me, caressing my shaved head.

"Just working on a poem."

"Sexy man." She moved against my thigh, rubbing her clit beneath her jeans. We started making out, then we both took the rest of the morning off.

After sex, we lingered in bed, and the world seemed to slow down. I sensed Vanessa, for the first time since I'd known her, in a state of total release. I envied her passion during sex, and the peace that came with its discharge.

"That was a good day, but I wouldn't say I was happy."

"You were, but for some reason right now you want to deny that."

"No, *you* were happy, and I was happy for you, but that's different from me being happy."

"There's a word for this," she says, searching her mind. "Revisionist history—you're doing revisionist history!"

"And why would I want to do that?"

"I don't know, but I'm telling you we were both happy. We just need to get back there."

THE TWO OF us met at a speed-dating event in New York City. It was a Pavlovian affair where the men moved to different women every ten minutes at the ringing of a bell. I noticed Vanessa several rounds before we were to meet. When I finally arrived at her table, I was content to sit back and behold her as she held forth on the shortcomings of the U.S. penal code. She was quite sexy, with her long hair draped over one shoulder.

After a while I leaned in and whispered, "Can I tell you something?"

"What?"

"I don't want them to ring the bell."

She wasn't even supposed to be there. She'd come to New York to visit her childhood friend, who was single and depressed. She convinced the friend to try speed dating, and offered to join her in solidarity. Vanessa had speed dated to great success in DC. Ten guys turned in scorecards requesting her number.

I had just come back from my two years in Oklahoma, returning home rather ingloriously. On the way, I planned to visit Stephen Dunn, my friend and poetry mentor, who lived in western Maryland. But my old Honda blew a transmission on a long Appalachian incline outside of Morgantown, West Virginia. I spent the night in Morgantown, sold my car for parts, threw my stuff in a rental truck, and lumbered home. When I reached my building, NYU students were shooting a film in the doorway, the elevator was out of order, and the heat that day was stifling.

At age forty-seven, I had no job or clue about how to live. I applied for and received unemployment benefits, I enrolled in a low residency MFA program in Vermont (an MFA was quickly becoming a union card in order to teach), and I poured myself into dharma practice.

I was engaged in an extensive series of *ngöndro* (pronounced "nundro") practices, designed to put the ego out of business. The first ngöndro consisted of 108,000 full prostrations, done on a smooth board while chanting a mantra and visualizing. You were supposed to visualize an elaborate lineage tree before you—the heads of gurus, atop soft bodies, stacked on one another like produce at the market. Sometimes I did see them, and on one occasion they smiled, turned around, lifted their robes, and mooned me. More often when prostrating I visualized swimming back and forth across the Atlantic, passing by Greenland, watching for the appearance of the Continental Shelf, flip turning on the shore of Ireland or France, and swimming back across.

Practicing dharma felt like tying myself to the mast, the one thing I could cling to in a life where I was floundering. I let New York City swirl around me in a blur, and I suppose I was a blur to it. Then I met Vanessa.

A FEW WEEKS after our speed date, she came back to New York for the Labor Day weekend, staying again with her friend. We ate at a romantic restaurant in the West Village and kissed in the street. The next day we sat on the stoop of an Upper West Side brownstone, negotiating what, if anything, we were going to do. We lived in cities 230 miles apart. She was a widowed mother who worked for the government. She wanted to know why she shouldn't see other men in DC. I asked how she would feel about me seeing other women in New York. "I don't know," she said, pointing to her neck, "but could you kiss me here again?" I liked her neck, but each time she pulled back her hair and requested I kiss it, it felt off-putting in a way I couldn't place. But if I refused it would have ended the relationship before it started, so I obeyed, much to her pleasure. The afternoon drew on, the stoop hardened under our butts, and we finally agreed to a six-month trial. Neither of us would date outside the relationship, and I'd commit to visiting regularly.

On my first visit I stayed at a hotel in Bethesda a mile from her house. She put her kids to sleep, drove over, and came up to my room. Underneath her jeans she wore a black corset. It looked sexy, but the fabric felt rough and bulletproof. Her agenda was clear. Mine was less so—partly because she'd driven herself to urgent care the night before. She'd recently competed in a triathlon (DC lawyers, I would soon learn, tended to be either distance runners or heavy drinkers), after which she experienced mysterious abdominal pain and internal bleeding. The urgent care doctor couldn't diagnose the bleeding, and told her not to engage in strenuous activity for a while. My other concern was my own need to go slow. But that's a hard thing to say to a woman in a black corset who clearly considered this a conjugal visit. That corset quickly came off, and Vanessa was all over me.

"You're bleeding!"

"Don't worry," she said. "Just let me find a good position."

THE NEXT DAY I walked to her house for lunch and met her boys. Nate was seven, Austin was five. They were big for their ages, shy and polite—or else nervous and silent. I stayed quiet too. They didn't finish their food, asked to be excused, and went off to play.

The boys, it was clear to see, had total respect for their mother. They'd received a shock two nights before, when she had no choice but to wake them from their beds in the middle of the night and take them with her to urgent care. Three years earlier they'd lost their father, and now their mother was bleeding mysteriously on the inside.

That evening, after she put them to bed, Vanessa came downstairs and sat beside me on the living room couch. She told me about the boys' father, her late husband, Lloyd. The two met as undergraduates at Berkeley. He was African American, smart, nerdy, the son of two schoolteachers from Beaumont, Texas. As a teenager he practiced elocution, emulating the voice of Dan Rather and other newscasters, so that he wouldn't be stereotyped. He felt grateful to be dating Vanessa—the intellectual geek who lucked out with a former cheerleading captain. Lloyd spoke five languages fluently, and went on to a career at the State Department, often traveling abroad. When he met Vanessa's racist grandfather for the first time he spoke to him in fluent Mandarin, which solved a lot of problems. He loved his life in DC, his family, his job, and proudly wore a Washington Nationals baseball cap.

"The strangest thing about our marriage was we never argued."

"That *is* strange," I said. "Not even once?"

"No."

"But there had to be disagreements from time to time. How did you handle them?"

"Whenever something came up, one of us just saw that it mattered more to the other, and gave way."

She asked if I was OK talking about Lloyd like this. I told her it was fine, that I was glad she'd had someone so wonderful in her life. She switched the topic anyway.

"We need to talk about sex."

"What about it?"

"Do *we* have a problem?"

She said "we" while clearly meaning me. I explained that it always takes a while for me to acclimate to a new partner, and no, I didn't think there was a problem.

"Well," she said, "I'm a believer in medicine."

"Me too," I said, and I reminded her that she was bleeding internally. She said that wasn't what she was talking about. I told her that there was nothing wrong with my body.

"Why suffer, though, when there are options?"

"What are you saying?"

"I want you to try Viagra."

"You want me to put *drugs* in my body in order to have sex?"

"Just give it a try."

"Why don't we just do heroin together, and pass out on the bed?"

Vanessa squared her shoulders and stared me down. "You need to leave this house," she said.

I met her eyes. There was a look of primordial fury. It was like staring into a volcano. I stood up from the couch and stepped carefully—the living room was littered with toys—into the next room to retrieve my things.

"You have asked me to leave the premises," I said, stepping back in. "That turns this into a legal matter, so I will go." She was still glaring at me, motionless. "But this is senseless. You really want to end this, just like that?"

She consented to a few minutes of conversation. We somehow managed to keep our plan for the next day, a Monday, when she'd drive in to the office. I was to check out of the hotel and let myself into the house, where I'd do ngöndro practice until she came home. Then I'd spend the night and get on a bus on Tuesday.

But even as we restored our plan, the look on her face hadn't changed, and I walked back to the hotel still in shock from what had happened. I tried to sleep that night, but I couldn't get Vanessa's death stare out of my head. When morning came, I changed my ticket and caught a bus for New York.

I WAS MOST of the way home when she called.

"Where are you?" she said.

"New Jersey."

"You *left?*"

"You ordered me out of your house. I left your key in an envelope at the hotel front desk."

"I can't believe you left." She sounded like a completely different woman—heartbroken. "I did some thinking," she said, "and I was planning to tell you this when I got home today. I guess it doesn't matter now, but do you want to hear it?"

"If you want to say it."

"I was going to tell you that I'm willing to give you a relationship without sex. It seems like that's what you need, and sex doesn't matter that much to me. I love you."

"I love you too."

"Then get off that bus."

"I don't think I can."

"Then get on the next bus back here when you get to New York."

"Wait a second, we're slowing down."

The driver got on the intercom and announced we were pulling over at a rest stop for a bathroom break.

"Wait there," she said. "I'll come and get you."

EVEN WITH TWO and a half hours to contemplate it (at the Woodrow Wilson Service Area on the New Jersey Turnpike), I could not understand what caused me to blurt out "I love you" to Vanessa on the phone. It felt like a wild leap, like my life, independent of me, took a sharp turn. I tried to see it in terms of Buddhism. "Trust the unfolding situation," my crazy meditation teacher liked to say. Even the bus driver seemed part of the craziness. The same driver who had taken me to DC also happened to be driving me back. He liked to get on the PA and tell us he loved us, while explaining the rules for riding his bus. When he pulled off the road for a bathroom break, he announced that the bus would leave in fifteen minutes—whether we were on it or not. "Oh I'll still love you," he said, "but I'll have to love you from a distance."

When Vanessa arrived in her SUV it was like the world had cracked open. We hugged for a long time in the parking lot. Even though we'd barely known each other, it felt like a profound reunion. The space between us was tender the whole way home. More than tender: there's something quite sexy about a woman who'll hop in a car and run an errand this wild.

Back inside the Beltway, we stopped at the hotel in Bethesda to retrieve her house key from the front desk, then at her friend Claire's, who'd picked up the boys from school.

I SPLIT MY weeks between New York and DC. I wrote, and worked on my low residency MFA, on the bus back and forth. I wrote at a little desk upstairs in Vanessa's house, and in the coffee shops along Connecticut Avenue. I had good luck in the downstairs café at the famous Politics and Prose bookstore, and even better luck at a Starbucks farther uptown, where I drafted this poem:

UPSTAIRS

I am carrying a boy who fell asleep in the car
upstairs. This isn't in itself unusual—nothing
in itself is. I could be rushing downstairs
in another house cradling a Yorkshire Terrier,
but that's not how things have worked out.
The boy isn't mine—though for the moment
I guess he is. He's big for six. I need to grip
him tight. He has woolly hair and dark
alert eyes when he's awake. He can't stand girls
and likes a little of his mother's pink
polish on his toes. Earlier, at the rest stop,
he and his brother played rock, paper, scissors,
only it was rock, paper, scissors, black hole!
which they cried, crashing into each other,
or rock, paper, scissors, supernova! or atom bomb!—
whatever disaster they could think up to trump

all previous disasters, though nothing to match
their father collapsed dead on the back deck
in his barbecue apron, or them being whisked
from the sight, as John Kennedy's children
undoubtedly were, by some wise and quick-
thinking soul, perhaps to a room upstairs—*these*
stairs I'm walking up now, three years later
with a boy sleeping deeply. If you've never
done what I am doing and get the opportunity,
I would recommend it. You might find
you've never stepped quite so purposefully,
as though climbing out of life's trouble
into a cloud realm, and laying down
a body that could be anyone's.

That evening, Vanessa found me revising that poem and
asked what I was working on. I met her eyes and told her
it was a tough one. "I want to read it," she said, "but give
me a day." I'd written another poem mentioning the death
of Lloyd, who I felt strangely close to. Vanessa was eager to
read it, though his death still overwhelmed her. Just a glimpse
of someone crossing a street in a windbreaker similar to his
could put her in tears for half a day.

At other times she was brutal. One weekday morning after I'd taken the boys to school, the two of us lingered over
coffee and *The Washington Post*. She pointed to a story about
a woman who'd tossed her two-year-old granddaughter off a
sixth-floor walkway at a Virginia shopping center, killing the
girl. "Frankly, I can't blame her," Vanessa said. "It's horrible,
but what parent hasn't felt like doing that?" I was too shocked
by that statement to argue with her. I knew her to be a good

mother, but I'd also been taken aback a few times when she shouted at the boys in raw fury, which stiffened their bodies for a while. I didn't know if these explosions were part of her makeup, or bouts of PTSD in the wake of Lloyd's death.

His death, by her report, happened at the zenith of their contentment, when all the ingredients of a happy life—marriage, family, friendship, career—were in place. It was Vanessa herself who administered CPR, then held him in her arms and said goodbye, all in the space of minutes. Her nightmare was only beginning. The State Department suspected he may have been poisoned. The autopsy turned up something even more disturbing: Brugada syndrome, a heart disorder that typically goes undetected, until an acute myocardial infarction. People with Brugada rarely live past forty. (Lloyd was thirty-eight.) What's more, the disease is hereditary, and skews toward males, which meant the boys could have it.

Meanwhile, Vanessa was suddenly a single mother with two small children, a household to manage, and an all-consuming job that had been her dream career. Mornings getting Nate to school, and Austin to day care, were mad dashes. She was losing sleep, losing weight, showing up late to work. Her productivity was falling off. A counselor at work informed her that crying for more than thirty minutes was "counterproductive." She was having more and more wine with dinner, getting drunk in front of the boys (who, I noticed, didn't like sitting to eat, or staying at the table for long). The tragedy of Lloyd's death was about to compound itself.

Yet somehow she managed to hold it together. Her friends came through, she joined a grief counseling group, and wisely switched to a desk job she could work from home. The job was far from satisfying, but it preserved her income, and enabled her to manage the household. The boys loved and needed her desperately, and they were her reason for continuing on. The three had saved one another's lives, and now I was getting to know them.

Nate and Austin soon grew excited for my visits. They had lists of things to report to me when I arrived. We communicated in the language of males, which often meant sports. They loved to play football with me on a patch of lawn at the side of the house. They craved the physical contact of tackling and being tackled. Nate was amazingly fast for his age, and Austin wasn't far behind. Austin looked up to his older brother, though they had entirely different personalities. He was moody, inward, and strong-minded. He often said, "I know!" if you tried to explain something—even if he didn't know. He acknowledged me on his terms; he'd run into a room and say, "Hi Doug," then run out before I could turn to him. He wasn't interested in team sports. When we attended Nate's soccer or Little League games, he'd ask for Vanessa's iPhone, go off beyond the outfield, and come back with photographs of trees, or rocks, or close-ups of weeds at odd angles. He was beautiful. He often asked his mother to paint his toes for the weekend, and Vanessa obliged. He was outed at a water park when the jets shut off without warning. The water in the pool became still and clear, and his girl cousins pointed and cried, "Look! Austin's wearing nail polish!"

"I am not!" Austin argued in his defense.

"Yes you are!" said the merciless girls, which sent him running to his mother.

"Mommy, tell them I'm not wearing nail polish!"

"Oh sweetie," said Vanessa, laughing, "but you are."

Nate loved sports and was more social than his younger brother, with friends of both genders. He was big for age seven, had a superb throwing arm, and hit mammoth home runs in Little League, sprinting across home plate before the ball made it back to the infield. When Nate was invited to join a select team of mostly older players, I drove him to his first practice. He was scared, shy and sluggish going through warm-ups and drills. But when the coach gave him the ball and sent him out to the mound, he threw flames.

"The coach," I told Vanessa later, "turned to me and said, 'Kid's got an arm.'"

"Are you crying?"

"I think he thought I was Nate's father. All I could think of was how much Lloyd would have loved to see Nate pitch, and hear a coach say, 'Kid's got an arm.'"

Now she was crying. "It's OK," she said.

"No it's not."

"No it's not."

"IT'S JUST CLOTHES," Vanessa said, when I told her I was a crossdresser. That made me laugh. "Hey," she said, "I have some stuff in storage that might fit you." She went to her closet and climbed a little ladder that led to the attic.

She may have been the least prejudiced person I'd ever met, though I assured her it wasn't "just clothes," just as with Austin it wasn't just nail polish.

"You think?"

"Time will tell," I said.

"Whatever he is, he is," she said, with a shrug. I loved that shrug.

During sex we sometimes engaged in role-play, taking turns setting the scene. In her scenario we were strangers fucking behind a dive bar. She was shoved up against a brick wall and straddling my hips. In my scenario she was wearing a short dress, high heels, and nylons while presenting a case in court. I started feeling her up from behind, while she continued her argument before the jury. In her scenario she was a flight attendant coming up to the cockpit to ask what I needed, and I was the pilot who told her to shut the door and lock it. In my scenario she was the pilot, and I was the flight attendant. She reached under my skirt and—"What have we here!"

On a trip to New York, we went out as women to a rooftop hotel bar in the Meatpacking District. We had a couple of drinks, talked to some people on couches, got bored, then came back to my place and had sex. I kept some of my clothes on, trying for something I'd never managed: feeling turned on both by myself as a woman, and by a lover. (Considering all the devices and kink people engage in, it seemed fairly tame to use clothing as a turn-on with a partner.) But keeping the fantasy going, while being present to Vanessa, was like a cocktail that wouldn't stay mixed. Her sounds and responses, instead of turning me on, pulled me from my own female dreamscape. Or if I focused on her, and what turned her on, I felt stranded and ugly, pumping away in my maleness— unless I vicariously imagined I was her, but then who was I? It was a dizzying experience that, along with the drinks I'd had, soon exhausted me.

ON THAT FALL day in Chevy Chase when we took the morning off from work, had sex, and lingered in bed, I sensed that for Vanessa a burden had been lifted. After the nightmare of

Lloyd's death, and the turbulent aftermath, things were falling into place. Her job was intact, as was her household, and now she'd found a partner who bonded with the boys. I was nothing like Lloyd, but a good man (all her friends agreed), and she didn't have to give up sex after all. Her life was suturing itself back together.

But what I loved most was the *other* half of that day, when we put on clothes and walked out to retrieve the boys from afterschool. We spotted them from the gate, playing in the yard. They were both happy to see us. Austin came over right away; Nate took longer to detach from his friends. The four of us strolled home along the sidewalks of Chevy Chase, which buckled where the roots of old trees nudged up. We stopped to take turns on a tire swing hanging from a huge oak. Nate talked football, gloating about the success of his favorite team, the New England Patriots, whereas my New York Jets sucked. I challenged him to name five players on the Patriots, and he got stuck on the long Polish name of their kicker. He asked if I would make steak for dinner. Austin stopped to study a patch of weird-looking mushrooms growing in the crotch of a tree, and we each opined inexpertly on whether they were poisonous. Vanessa pointed out the house of a rising star in the Obama administration, whose kids played with Nate and Austin.

At home, Nate pitched to me on the front lawn, fastballs that made a pop in the glove. I called balls and strikes, pretending there was a batter. When he threw a curveball I dropped my mitt and walked back inside.

"Why is Nate crying?" Vanessa asked.

"Because he threw a curveball and he knows he's not allowed. His arm is too young."

I rubbed salt and fresh garlic into two steaks to tenderize them. I served them slightly pink on the inside, with steamed broccoli and homemade French fries. I said grace before dinner—my lone insertion of rules into the household, so that we'd at least begin meals together, before they wandered off.

"Boys," Vanessa ordered, "get in your chairs so Doug can say grace."

We bowed our heads. "We are thankful for this food, without which our bodies couldn't survive. Amen."

"Amen."

"I could survive without food," said Nate, cutting into his steak.

"You could?" I said.

"Yeah."

"So could I," said Austin.

"For how long?"

"Like two months."

"What would you eat?"

"Lots of things." Nate looked around. "I could eat this chair."

"No you couldn't," said Vanessa, while cutting Austin's steak.

"I could eat my sneakers," said Nate.

"I could eat my sneakers *too*," said Austin.

"But then you wouldn't have sneakers," I said.

"I could go barefoot."

"I'm not gonna let you walk around barefoot," said Vanessa.

"But Mom, I'd be setting the world record for going without food."

"Did you know," I said, "that I once tried to set the pogo stick record?"

"What happened?"

"The rubber tip at the bottom kept busting through every few hundred bounces. I tried replacing it with a crutch tip, but that didn't last either."

"I bet *I* could set the pogo stick record."

"Mom," said Austin, "can I be excused?"

"Not until you eat three more pieces of broccoli." And he did.

After dinner I helped the boys with their homework, a chore Vanessa loathed. She couldn't fathom why I enjoyed it— then she remembered I'd been a schoolteacher. After homework they played. Sometimes they found me upstairs meditating and asked for a lesson. They plopped down crisscross applesauce on the rug beside me, pressed their palms together, shut their eyes tight, and tried (unsuccessfully) to go sixty seconds without giggling. We bowed, and I said, "Who did we just meditate for?" and they said, "Other people," and I said "Good job." They said, "When are we gonna meditate again?" I said, "Next time," and they said, "OK!" and ran off.

Later, Vanessa told them to wash up for bed, and soon she and I did the same. Before lying down, she took a calendar from her dresser and jotted down the main events of the day. Not a diary entry, no feelings or thoughts, just a brief list of three or four objective things—the score of a Little League game, a school assembly, a friend she had lunch with. She'd been doing this for years, and I admired the practice. It is astonishing what we forget about our days. There was one day that was impossible for her to forget, when she took a sedative before bed, opened her calendar, and wrote, "Today I lost Lloyd Jerome Nelson."

. . .

THE PROBLEM WAS we fought, and over stupid things. It bothered her when I spoke to strangers—supermarket cashiers, dog owners, people seated next to us during the intermission of a play. I didn't care for her consumerism. She thought I was cheap for not wanting to upgrade to a phone plan with unlimited texting. I despised texting, and had little regard for the Supreme Court, which she idolized. And on and on. We managed to have a fight over her marathon time. When she told me it took her about four and a half hours, I told her I admired her stamina, and she thought I was calling her slow. But she kept her resentment to herself for several tense days, before unloading on me in bed. Sometimes her anger felt so toxic, I moved to the floor after she fell asleep. One night she woke me from a dead sleep and asked, "Are you still crazy about me?"

We fought over unimportant things because the underlying issue was too big: we didn't much like each other. We admired aspects of one another, there was physical attraction, maybe even love, but we were unable to work through a single problem. Yet we stayed together—Thanksgiving at her sister's, Christmas in Chevy Chase, skiing in Vermont on New Year's. We fulfilled the six months we'd agreed to, and continued on.

In August I'd be going to Colorado for a Buddhist training program. Vanessa knew about it months in advance, but as the summer approached she grew disgruntled. "Why does anyone need to meditate for a month?" she said. She wanted me to promise to call her daily, but I couldn't do that. Much of the program would be in silence, plus the cell reception was spotty. She told me to buy a better cell phone, though it wouldn't have helped.

Every few days I walked two miles from the retreat center,

out to where the road curved down toward the valley floor, found a couple bars of cell reception and called her. Our updates were chatty, until she said, "Why the fuck are you there?" I laughed. She told me about a vision she'd had while driving on the highway past the exit where her aunt lives. The aunt, who only speaks Chinese, always reminded Vanessa of her mother. (Her mother had suffered a severe stroke years before, and was unable to speak.) "I feel like I can tell you this," she said, "because you're a Buddhist."

"Tell me what?"

"I wanted to go to my aunt, cry in her arms, and say to her in Chinese, *He's not as good as Lloyd.*"

I KNEW, WHEN I returned to DC in September, we needed to have a serious conversation. (I didn't expect it to turn into a ludicrous dispute over whether or not I was happy.) "This is crazy," she said, "but I was hoping you'd come back from Colorado with a ring." That *was* crazy, though perhaps not as crazy as our decision to stay together. She wanted me to double my time in DC—two weeks there, one week in New York. I agreed. She also wanted me to teach her to meditate. I asked her why. She said she needed something to calm her down. "I see what it does for you," she said. "You're like the Dalai Lama."

When someone asks for meditation instruction you're not supposed to say yes. You're supposed to wait and see if they ask again. She did, and she asked if her friend Kathleen, another attorney where she worked, could join us. Kathleen was a soft-spoken, willowy blond woman who you wouldn't think was a lawyer. I began giving weekly meditation instruction to the two women. Later in the fall Vanessa asked if I would take care of the boys while she attended a weekend meditation retreat in Maryland. The boys and I had fun that weekend. When she returned Sunday evening, she said very little about the retreat—just that she liked it, and was given a mantra.

"That sounds great," I said.

"You don't seem so interested."

"I'm interested in whatever you want to tell me. I'm also glad you have teachers other than me."

A month later, over the phone, she told me she thought my teacher was full of shit, and that she couldn't take Buddhism seriously. I was calling from an MFA residency in Vermont. I asked how long she had felt that way. She admitted that her campaign to learn to meditate, including the weekend retreat, had been a stunt. She did it on Kathleen's advice. When I was in Colorado, the two had gone out for drinks. Seeing how disgruntled Vanessa was about my trip, Kathleen told her that if she didn't join my religion she would lose me.

"That's the stupidest advice I've ever heard."

"Maybe, but I was doing it for us."

"No, you were doing it for me, and you were lying."

"I was doing it for you *for us.* Don't you see?"

I didn't see, and after we hung up I didn't even know who she was. I was too creeped out to sleep that night. When we got on the phone the next night I broke up with her. I told her it didn't matter to me if she thought Buddhism was bullshit. It was the lying.

"That's all you're going to say?" I could tell she was furious—and it was nice, for a change, not to care about her anger.

"No," I said. "One other thing: we tried."

"Well then," she said, and hung up.

SHE CALLED THE next night asking if I would talk to the boys. Actually, she was pleading, and the boys were right there. She'd told them about our breakup while driving to a family dinner, and they freaked. They never made it to the restaurant. Instead, they turned around, came home, and called me. She apologized for springing this on me. I told her to put them on.

"Why do you hate us?" Austin said, choking on tears.

"Oh Austin, I don't hate you. I love you very much."

"Then why won't you visit us anymore?"

I tried to comfort him. Vanessa got back on the phone and sent the boys out of the room. She asked if we could remain friends. She said losing me as a friend would be ten times worse than our breakup. She wanted me to consider visiting her and the boys every now and then.

The boys would soon undergo their annual series of medical tests. The doctors were still trying to determine if they carried the disease that killed their father. It involved an exam at Children's National Hospital, followed by days of electrode monitoring. She said if I could be there when they went to the hospital, it would mean everything to the boys.

I agreed to come, and marked my calendar. She emailed me to confirm. I replied that I'd be there, like I said I would. She kept checking in to confirm, I kept telling her I'd be there, and confirming wasn't necessary. A few days before the appointment she sent three late-night text messages, all to confirm. I didn't reply to the texts, and instead emailed the next morning, told her I'd be there, and asked her to stop texting my phone. "Don't bother coming," she replied, and promised to mail me a check for the cost of the text messages.

THE NIGHT BEFORE the medical appointment, I knocked on a door 230 miles from my home. Nate answered, shouting, "Doug!"

"Doug's here!" said Austin. They were jumping up and down. Vanessa was sitting at the dining room table, still and watchful. I half expected her to tell me to leave.

"Bold move," she said, when we were alone in the kitchen.

"I'm sorry," I said. I didn't say anything else, and she didn't ask. I spent time with the boys, who had a lot they wanted to tell me. Nate was on the track team, running middle distance. "Those are the hardest races," I said. "Yeah," he replied. Austin asked how long I would stay, and tried to act nonchalant. We played some Nintendo together. I slept in the basement.

The next day, in the hospital waiting room, Vanessa pulled me aside to tell me that she would do all the talking, and that I was not to speak to the doctor or anyone else besides the boys. "You're here for them. Do you understand?" I nodded silently, eyes wide open. I was looking at a woman who'd lost her husband, and was frightened for her children, yet the only thing on her face was contempt for me. We went in, the boys took turns being examined, each of them high-fiving me when they hopped off the table. I left on a bus later that day.

The letter I put in the mail, wishing Vanessa well, wasn't hard to write. It was the other letter, the one I enclosed for the boys, that broke my heart.

> Sometimes people leave our lives, and we don't know
> why, but it doesn't mean they hate us. I love both of
> you, but I have to love you from a distance. It would
> mean a lot to me if you did the same.

They might have bonded with any man their mother chose, but they bonded with me. In between visits, they told their friends that I was big and strong enough to be in the NFL. That's love. When I last saw them they were seven and nine. Nate was nearly as tall as his mother. Austin was on track to grow even taller. By now, the doctors may have ruled out Brugada, for one or both of them, putting death far away, where it belongs.

EVEN BEFORE VANESSA revealed her lie, I knew the relationship needed to end. During my weeks in New York, I was crossdressing and going to the Cubbyhole, a lesbian bar on West Fourth Street. Just before Christmas I met a woman there named Salena. Much like the old cliché, we were strangers who locked eyes across a crowded room.

She was Indian American, a doctor doing an OB/GYN residency at a hospital uptown. She was my height, with long dark hair, a handsome face, and a clear intelligent voice. We didn't flirt; we didn't need to. We each seemed to possess a vast field of welcome for the other, something we discovered, moment by moment, as we spoke. We didn't have sex or get physical, but when I asked later why she had been so drawn to me, she shrugged and said, "Chick with a dick?" A person could be condemned for such a remark, but between us it was actually OK. "A lot of lesbians like penetration," she admitted. But she valued equally the "chick" part—*she saw me.*

We live in moments and nowhere else, though some moments may take a lifetime to understand. A woman points to the back of her neck and demands a kiss, then later promises never to pressure you for sex, and it may take years to know why you blurted out you loved her. Another woman sees you with so much aptitude it lights your way. Regardless of whether I'd ever meet Salena again, I knew—instantly—I couldn't be with Vanessa.

We had used each other. Vanessa wanted a replacement for her husband and a father for her children. I fell in love with a family, partly to heal my childhood. It was also, as it turned out, my last attempt at life as a man. I didn't know it at the time, but I was desperate to avoid transitioning, and the prospect of being alone for the rest of my life. I held out as long as I could.

A FAMILY IN DC

A woman is swatting a fly in her kitchen,
a Chinese woman, a widow with two small
half-Chinese boys who are sitting at the table,
watching their mother jump up (she's not so tall)
and swing murderously at something that lives
but seven days. I am the man in this picture—
or was, anyway—sitting with the boys at the table.
"You're rooting for the fly, aren't you?" she says,
glancing sidelong at me. The boys look at me too,
then back to her. They know I don't believe in
killing sentient beings. For all we know (and
I'd never say this aloud) the fly could be a visit
from their father, who collapsed just outside,
on the deck, two years earlier. But it's the boys

who interest me. They're deciding who to side with: the only parent they have left, or kooky, superfun Doug from New York City, who comes every other week and plays football with them, and builds shelves, and insists on a crazy prayer before meals, who their mother calls her "sexy man," making sure to get her long hair blown out on the day of his arrival. Or the fly—which is who I'd like them to side with, because I'll soon be gone.

In the Cabin of the Crazy One
2014

The San Luis Valley in south central Colorado is the size of the state of Connecticut and remarkably wide. It is flanked by the San Juan mountains to the west and the Sangre de Cristos to the east, and contains the headwaters of the Rio Grande. The valley is also amazingly flat. Looking west from the Baca Grande in the foothills of Kit Carson Mountain, everything seems laid out before you. It is as though an infinite vastness were knowable, though you cannot see most of the roads, or the herds of elk drifting across the valley floor. To the north, the Valley View Hot Springs ("clothing optional") hides in plain sight, as do the Great Sand Dunes—the tallest dunes in North America—to the south. Nor can you see the UFO Watchtower and Information Center, halfway to Alamosa on Route 17, even though its highway sign is a gigantic cutout of an alien with huge head and eyes, wearing coveralls and waving hi. The "tower" is merely a platform on a rooftop. You could view a UFO just as well from anywhere on the valley floor twelve feet below—but why take chances?

For decades, spiritual seekers have come to the Baca foothills outside the town of Crestone, which is home to various retreat centers, hermitages, and temples of Eastern and Western and New Age religions. Bejeweled shrines sit unprotected beside creek beds; massive stupas perch on outcroppings. Tibetans in particular are drawn here, having found the scenery powerfully reminiscent of the land from which they've been exiled since the late 1940s. Multicolored prayer flags, shredded by wind, festoon the Baca.

I have come here to do a twelve-day solo retreat in a cabin hidden among the pygmy pines. It is early February, and the cabin has a good woodstove. It has a bucket for a bathroom, a propane burner, two water coolers, and a faucet a quarter mile down the mountain. It is, in spiritual parlance, a very protected space, especially the upstairs loft, where I will practice ten hours a day before a window looking over the tops of the pinyons and junipers, and across the San Luis Valley.

I CAME TO the cabin to accomplish Guru Yoga, the fourth and final ngöndro practice Tibetan Buddhists must complete in order to receive the *abhisheka* blessing and progress to the high Tantric teachings and empowerments. To begin a session of Guru Yoga you need to briefly go through the three other ngöndros. This includes Vajrasattva mantra, a seated practice where you repeat a hundred-syllable Sanskrit chant while visualizing Vajrasattva (which means "indestructible being") in the form of an adolescent male seated cross-legged and floating above your head. As you say the mantra, Vajrasattva pours *amrita*, or nectar (literally "anti-death potion"), out the bottom of his body. The amrita enters you through the top of your head, flushes out your defilements, and washes down into the earth.

It's not an easy practice to get right, partly because there's never an experience of rightness. The goal is to be in a non-dual state, where there's no right or wrong, and no "you" to evaluate anything. Once it gets going, the visualization does what it wants. I've seen amrita come down as water, or vodka. At times it is sparkly, or silver like mercury. Once Vajrasattva poured a stream of live rats into me. It's a colorful religion.

But on day one of the retreat I felt completely stuck, even though I'd done the practice hundreds of times. I sat chanting the mantra, gazing inwardly upward at Vajrasattva, but he had nothing for me—no amrita, no vodka, no mercury, sewer rats, blood, pus, molasses, motor oil, nothing. Often you run into a wall several days in, after you've settled. That's when you find out what's really going on with you, at which point you might scream, or sing, or get violently ill, or lie curled up devastated for a few hours. But here was the wall, and my retreat had barely begun.

My mind went to Vajratopa, who is Vajrasattva's consort, and who often goes missing in the iconography. But she's there in the longer liturgical text, and in some of the illustrations, straddling Vajrasattva in *yab-yum*, or "primordial union"—literally fucking him, her haunches in his lap, her feet hooked at the ankles behind his waist. She is holding a knife in one hand and a skull cup in the other. I kept chanting, picturing them up there above my head. I hoped the nectar would pour from their union, enter my body and harmonize my masculine and feminine aspects, which seemed to be in a lifelong tug-of-war.

IN THE MONTHS before the retreat I'd been entertaining the possibility that I was "bi-gender." I watched YouTube testimonials of people who identified this way, examining their shifts between male and female presentation, wondering if a person could authentically be both. Watching female-to-male shifts brought on a grotesque fascination, while male-to-female videos filled me with euphoria, and envy.

In the fall of 2013, *Wabash Magazine* commissioned me to write a column for a series called "A Man's Life." My essay, "Rainbow Man," described a life of having been mistaken for gay. I mentioned the bullying I'd been subjected to in high school, and the theater teacher who'd groomed and molested me. Toward the end of the essay I pivoted to the subject of gender, and transsexuality. "In New York City," I wrote, "I know men less feminine than me who have undergone sex reassignment and live as women. And I know men less masculine than I am who don't get mistaken for being gay."

I'd been attending a "trans feminine spectrum" support group at the LGBT center. On the first Wednesday of each month, forty or so people crammed into a small room to commit this act of support. We tried arranging our chairs in a circle, but there were too many of us. The circle spread to the walls and then spiraled inward. We went around introducing ourselves and our pronouns, which varied from "she/her" to "he/him" to "either" to "I don't know" to "I don't care." (It would be another couple years before "they/them" would come on the scene.) There were trans women living full-time (*trans* had recently graduated from a prefix to a word), others presenting as men coming from work in suits and ties, and wayfaring souls reluctant to self-define. A tall fey person named Zingara, who wore a headscarf and hoop earrings, identified her gender as "just Zingara." A startlingly thin person, also in a headscarf, went by two initials, was a web coder, and practiced a spirituality that involved hula-hooping. I told them my name was Tina and that I identified as a crossdresser. I gave no pronouns, partly because everyone already referred to me as *she*; partly because I was old-school: if you have to ask the pronouns of someone in a dress named Tina, you deserve to be smacked with a handbag. A lot of the old guard, whose safety had depended on visual cues, found it crass to have to spell out pronouns. Val, the elder stateswoman of the group, said, "Pronoun: madam."

There were military vets, musicians, a junior high teacher, a pharmacist, a Metro North conductor, a bike messenger, an art school student. Many were unemployed, not all could afford the five-dollar requested donation. More than a few were addicts, or recovering addicts. Some showed up drunk or stoned, even though the rules forbade it. There were several new faces at every meeting, teenagers afraid (physically trembling) of being kicked out of their homes, millennials who'd recently migrated from a red state, or graduated college, seeking refuge in New York City.

The facilitators were two hyperfemme Latinas who called themselves "women of trans experience" and who liked to tell war stories about their days as street prostitutes. They seemed to think the solution to everyone's problems involved hormones, surgery, or a style makeover. There was a lot of passing privilege—people whose feminine looks gave them status, and the right to pontificate. The older participants dominated, and insisted on dispensing unsolicited advice (even though rule number 2 was "No giving advice"). Someone was worried about what starting on hormones would do to her sex life, and a jaded elder said, "Trust me, honey, you'll be dead below the waist." A newly transitioning person told us how everything went fine when she'd flown home to Louisiana for Thanksgiving, until her mother quietly suggested she not come back for Christmas. The facilitators tried to cheer her up, while others piled on with advice.

Val liked to lecture us " kids" about how lucky we had it. Toward the end of each session she'd regale us with a story about the old days, such as when she was thrown into "the paddy wagon" and charged with criminal impersonation. Her great sadness was the disappearance of the TV bars. "There's no place for us to go anymore," she lamented—not realizing those bars were gone because we could now go everywhere. (Though I admit, I shared some of her nostalgia for those enclaves.)

The discussions were free-for-alls. There were so many people, so little time. The important thing for me was the space itself, which was brimming with energy, and the sense of change. It was 2013. Trans fashion models were beginning to come out. Laura Jane Grace was fronting the punk band Against Me!, Laverne Cox would soon appear on the cover of *Time*. Amanda Simpson, a trans woman, was working in the Commerce Department for the Obama Administration. Ordinary trans people—quietly, one by one—were beginning to come out at their jobs and at colleges.

Yet the people in that room, including the facilitators, were in bad shape. There was a lot of PTSD, depression, addiction, eating disorders, suicidality. Many had far more pressing issues than gender. Then again, having your gender identity in a constant state of upheaval magnifies *every* issue. "How come we only meet once a month?" was a question repeated monthly. The unqualified facilitators, which was all the LGBT center would provide, never answered. When people who wished to remain anonymous objected to a sign-in sheet, an administrator came in and scolded us. The institutional transphobia was appalling: L, G, and B didn't give a fuck about T.

The most solid and helpful person in that group might have been Amanda, a smart, feminine trans woman who'd been living full-time for twenty years and had at one point run the group. She was tall and thin with dark hair and seemed quite at ease. She spoke freely, almost loosely, about having been an addict, and having had too much plastic surgery. I ran into her once in a thrift shop. I said hello and explained who I was. (I was in "guy mode," so she wasn't going to recognize me.) She was unfazed, and we exchanged numbers. A month later her phone call woke me at 3:00 a.m. Her speech was slurred and garbled. I heard other voices talking and shouting. It sounded like she was on the street. "Amanda?" I said. "Oh sorry wrong number," she blurted, and hung up.

I never saw her again. I asked about her each month at the meeting. Someone said they heard she was in the hospital, but didn't know which one. Amanda was the first of many I would see drop out of circulation, as if they'd fallen off a shelf. One moment a trans woman is before you, solid, alive, laughing, then you hear she was spotted sleeping in Port Authority, or you get a call from a psych ward, or worse.

I WASN'T DOING so well myself. After breaking up with Vanessa I'd plunged into a profound and puzzling depression. Puzzling because, getting into bed each night, I felt relieved to be alone. But when I woke up in the morning and put away my Murphy bed, I moved to the floor and lay staring at the ceiling, unable to face the day. Simple tasks, such as mailing a letter, felt impossible.

I hadn't worked a regular job since I'd returned from Oklahoma, and my unemployment insurance had run out. I'd received an MFA from Vermont College in 2012, and I was applying for faculty positions at universities. The applications were time-consuming, and often the colleges wound up hiring from within. I did some freelance editing, taught workshops in my living room and at conferences, published poems in good journals for little money. Being underemployed in New York is scary. *This is how people go homeless,* I told myself. I was spending savings on rent. I didn't eat out or go to movies.

I felt simultaneously panicked and indifferent about my economic survival. I'd look around at people working ordinary jobs—waiters, teachers, construction workers—as though they were performing superhuman feats. How did they get those jobs? What was it like to go to work each day? I couldn't fathom this, even though I'd worked since my teenage years, when I knew not to rely on my parents.

I would later learn the terrifying word "decompensation," which sounded like a financial term until I looked it up: "a breakdown in an individual's coping mechanisms resulting in progressive loss of functioning." Would my systems collapse like the towers on 9/11, each floor snapping like a twig from the weight of the floors above? Was six years of intense Buddhist practice, which encouraged me to renounce all hope and striving, making me decompensate? Each day, when I contemplated the Four Reminders—meant to turn the mind to meditation practice—the one about my "precious human birth" set me on edge, while the death reminder didn't faze me a bit.

Salena and I kept in touch after the night we locked eyes in the lesbian bar, though we didn't meet often. She was preparing for her medical boards, in addition to working a hospital residency. She was also the mother of a seven-year-old boy. They lived in an apartment near Carnegie Hall, along with her son's gay father and his husband. When we did get together it was just for a drink, once for a movie. I always showed up as Tina, since we both preferred that version of me. There was great warmth and mystery to our connection, but we hadn't a clue what to do about it. Salena had only partnered with women, and she'd just begun seeing someone in Sunset Park, which took up what little free time she had.

I had a brief relationship with a young woman named Liz, who managed a Starbucks in Philadelphia. Liz wanted to be a poet, and had talent, but was too depressed to do anything about it. We'd met at a writing conference held at a big hotel. She was tracking me, staring at me from the backs of rooms. She was tall, pretty, and lost. She was bisexual, and liked that I crossdressed. I liked her humor and directness. "I was going to give you a call last night," she once explained, "but then I didn't." We tried being boyfriend and girlfriend, but I sensed, after a disastrous road trip, it wasn't going to work. There was a huge age gap, and you could say our depressions didn't get along.

Still, we were very fond of each other, and remained friends. We liked to dress up and go out together, both in Philly and New York. The first time we did this we shared an unusual moment. After finishing my makeup I stepped into a skirt.

"What just happened?" she said, looking over at me.

"What?"

"You changed."

"Yeah, I put on a skirt."

"No." She narrowed her eyes and peered at me. "You

changed." There was a dumbfounded smirk on her face. "You're like . . . female."

"I would come out," I said to her later, "but I don't know what I'd come out *as.*"

"Who cares," she said, "as long as you come out to yourself."

THERE ARE MYRIAD ways in which trans people come out to themselves. Cracking your egg, it's called, or just cracking. First you're an egg, an unhatched, proto–trans person. You don't quite realize you're in a shell, or you may have a vague sense of a shell—of "shellness"—but you don't quite know what it is. Others may see your shell more than you do, though they can't see who, or what, is inside. Not until you crack.

I've known trans people who were cracked by something they saw in a book or magazine, a movie or TV show. Others are cracked by meeting someone trans, or the experience of performing in drag. Sometimes it's a sexual experience. Sometimes it's a near-death encounter, or the death of someone you're close to, making you stop and say, *What the hell am I waiting for?* Social media and the internet, with sites like Reddit and YouTube, may have hatched more of us than everything else combined.

When I think of trans people from past generations, I never cease to marvel at them. With so much danger, and so few things in their world to crack their egg, how had these Houdinis come out? I, on the other hand, was a reverse Houdini. I'd kept a woman's wardrobe my entire adult life, fed myself trans-related media, attended a trans support group (hello), and somehow still managed not to crack. In the end,

I needed fifty years of sadness, a remote cabin, and an outrageous religion to do it.

I didn't even do it. Vajratopa did.

SITTING IN THE loft of the cabin, chanting the hundred-syllable mantra, I was hoping Vajrasattva and Vajratopa could bring my masculine and feminine energies into balance. Instead, Vajratopa took over, pouring her skull cup of feminine nectar into the top of my head and down my spine. I felt myself shift into a female form—I don't know how else to say it—and energy coursed through me like never before.

A little later, Guru Yoga finished the job. In Guru Yoga practice, it is a teacher (guru) who sits above your head as you chant the simple mantra, *Hear my call*. You're calling the guru from afar. You say it a million times—*hear my call, hear my call*—like some lost child on a mountain. A black-and-white photograph of the guru, my teacher's teacher, sat on the shrine. I'd never seen this picture of him. He was dressed in a military uniform. His face was in three-quarter profile, looking to the side—though, as often happens in photos, he seemed to look everywhere. But I couldn't get him to look at me. Then I called to him as a woman, and our eyes met. *It's no problem*, his eyes said, *to be a woman*. I collapsed weeping. *You should be a woman*, he said.

I CLOSED MY morning practice and came downstairs for lunch, engaging in the ordinary activities of cooking, eating, washing, and one other thing: freaking out over what the hell went on in that loft. A key meditation instruction is "look again."

Don't come to conclusions, just come back and look again. That's what I did later that afternoon, again that evening, and the next morning. Each time I went upstairs and reentered practice, I was female. Each time I came downstairs to check on the fire or do chores or urinate, I was in shock.

At night, unable to sleep, I pictured living as a woman. I saw myself at a social gathering in a lush garden, standing near a tree in a print dress, holding court, smiling ear to ear as people came up to introduce themselves. A question arose from within: *You mean I actually get to be me?* The words were euphoric, and terrifying.

AS THE RETREAT stretched out, the womanly sense of myself I had in the loft, and at night in bed, began to extend into the rest of the space. After lunch I'd go for walks on the roads of the Baca, a circuit that took me across Spanish Creek, then down the long slope toward the valley floor. I wondered what it was to walk as a woman, or if I was in fact already a woman walking. Did people in the car approaching from far behind see a woman or a man walking the shoulder ahead in a knit cap, down jacket, and green trousers? I turned on Camino del Rey, and climbed back up the mountain. Another left brought me past the retreat center. If I texted Kathy Grant, the caretaker, I could schedule a shower. She'd unlock the side door and arrange to not cross paths with me, preserving my solitude. The first time I showered, I shaved my legs with great solemnity, relieved to know I'd never wear such body hair again.

Toward the end of the retreat I grew nervous and sleepless. Was I really going to do this? *Could I?* I feared the responses of others, the raised eyebrows of women who'd known me for years, men scratching their heads, former students typing question marks to one another. I wasn't so worried about the reaction of my family, whom I felt little connection to, but I dreaded the disapproval of Stephen Dunn, my poetry mentor, whom I admired immensely. Stephen was a very masculine person, who'd played NCAA basketball and loved to flirt with women. We enjoyed competing at Ping-Pong, and driving to casinos to play poker while discussing literature and sports and women. How would I ever tell Stephen? These fears soon gave way to deeper concerns: *What will I look like? How will I make a living? Will hormones make me impotent? Will they kill my creativity? Who will ever love me?*

But each morning upstairs, when I opened the day with *bodhicitta* practice, my heart broke open, and it was a woman's heart. As the sun rose over the mountains behind me, pulling in the shadows and flooding the valley with light, I was overwhelmed with compassion for the world's suffering. I wept for all the people I hadn't helped because I'd been so stuck in my own problems all my life.

On a final evening walk I looked up at the mountain, determined to state out loud: "I want to be a woman." My heart was in my throat, I could barely speak above a whisper. "I want to be a woman," I finally said, and the mountain said, "Fine by me." A tree said, "OK." "Like I care?" a chipmunk weighed in.

What visions do you trust? When you're alone in a cabin for twelve days and something shows up in your stillest moment, is it real, or is it in need of a reality check? Is reality, as the guru suggested, a fantastic rumor? Isn't depression, my most constant companion all these years, the result of being out of sync with reality? Could decades of thinking of myself as male be a grand illusion? Who would believe that? Did *I* believe it?

A last vision came to me while packing up to leave: a small girl, very thin, with bright, deep-set eyes, her orbital bones beginning to show. She was being held hostage. I only glimpsed her through a crack in a padlocked shack. She handed me a note on a scrap of paper. The note said, "Don't forget me." She was unsure I'd come back for her, yet I was her only hope, and she had no choice but to trust me. But did I trust *her?* Nothing in my life had worked out, and now here was this girl I'd never seen, pleading. Do I let go of everything, and base my life on her?

AFTER A RETREAT there is reentry, a return to the world of daily life. Reentries are precarious and seldom uneventful. I think of the Apollo 11 astronauts returning to earth, and how, if the angle of reentry was slightly off, the command module would skip like a stone off the atmosphere, or else burn up like a meteor. I had a lot of time—most of the retreat—to contemplate returning to my life, but no matter how hard I tried, I couldn't imagine it.

Just down the mountain was a friend. Liz had arrived in Crestone for a five-day program at the retreat center. She'd begun meditating months before, when she joined me for a half-day of group practice in New York. (I'd told her she was welcome to come, though it might be a cult. "How do you expect me to resist that invitation?" she said.)

In the residence hall, after we hugged, Liz stepped back and said, "What's going on?" I don't know what she saw. All I'd seen in the mirror—the first mirror I'd seen in a while—was a thousand-yard stare and someone who needed a shave.

"I want to show you something," I said.

I walked her up the mountain to the Cabin of the Crazy

One. We went up to the shrine room, now cleared and swept bare. The sun had just set, but there was still plenty of light in the valley. We stood at the window gazing out for a while. Then we sat on the floor facing each other with our legs outstretched.

"This is where it happened," I said.

"What happened?"

"I'm going to live as a woman."

"OK," she said. Then she narrowed her eyes, and tilted her head to the side.

"What?"

"You're not a Tina."

"No, I'm not."

She thought for a moment, cocked her head the other way, and held up a finger. "You're more of a Diana."

IT SHOULD BE mentioned that the Vajrayana Buddhist protocols I've described are considered restricted. Vajrayana itself is known as the "ear-whispered" lineage, and students are instructed to keep its methods and revelations secret. We even recite protector chants daily to remind us that wrathful beings stand ready to seize and devour "those who profess the tantras to all." It would seem, then, that I have sinned by divulging the details of my practice, so if I get struck by lightning—or abducted by a UFO—between now and the time you read this, you'll know why.

Personally I'm not worried, due to another Vajrayana teaching, which tells us that the highest spiritual truths are "self-secret." Even if such things were made explicit, it would still be impossible for someone of "degraded awareness" to see them. I ought to know: nothing could have been more self-secret than my own gender. Over the years, much of what I've detailed in this book was told to several therapists, none of whom so much as suggested I might be trans. But even if they had, it wouldn't have made a difference. There is simply no knowing a thing if it is self-secret, perhaps because that thing refuses to know *itself* in your presence. It is like a valley, spread out before you, hiding in plain sight.

The Thousand Gateless Gates
2015

I am sitting with five trans women in a circular booth at the Good Stuff Diner on Fourteenth Street. Together we are the Good Stuff Girls. We all met in the monthly support group at the LGBT center, which refuses, despite our pleas, to hold weekly meetings. So we come here each Wednesday night instead.

At the table with me are: Sandy, a married graphic artist; Marion, a computer systems analyst, also married; Jamie, a junior high school teacher; Christa, a rock guitarist and translator of Buddhist texts; and Kevin, a college student living with her parents in New Jersey, who has yet to choose a female name. Others join us from time to time, but we are the charter members of the Good Stuff Girls. We range in age considerably, though our trans ages are remarkably close, having begun hormone replacement therapy within months of one another. We compare notes on doctors, procedures, dosages, insurance. When one of us hires an attorney to help with her name change, all of us benefit from the advice. We talk about relationships, sex, travel, clothing. We make each other laugh, and we make each other safer.

The diner is overpriced, and the food isn't great, but the waiters know us, and will add on a table when more of us show up. This week Sandy and I arrived first, and the two of us had an interesting debate. Sandy had seen another trans woman on the subway, and wondered if she should have said hello. I knew the problem: on the one hand, you want to offer solidarity; on the other hand, it risks drawing attention to her, possibly outing her. Trans women become less passable, and potentially less safe, in pairs.

"What if," Sandy said, "you simply pointed to your wristwatch?"

"You mean like: *I clocked you*?"

"Yeah. But no one else will know."

"But you're still clocking her," said Marion, who had just joined us. "You're telling her she's not passable."

"Good point," said Sandy.

"But what trans girl passes with other trans girls?"

"Cosima," they said in unison. Cosima, a filmmaker in her early thirties, had joined us for the first time the month before. When she arrived she texted Sandy to say she was up front by the bar. A couple of us went looking for her, but couldn't spot anyone trans. Finally a gorgeous, soft-spoken Asian woman in a knit dress, with a mane of dark wavy hair, came back to our table. Even after fifteen minutes, I thought she might have the wrong table.

This week someone else is here for the first time, a man named Matthew. He is young, educated, well-dressed, with a neatly groomed beard reminiscent of George Michael. He quickly charms the Good Stuff Girls, a couple of whom have an instant crush on him.

Matthew is here to do research. A few weeks ago he woke from a long midday nap feeling like he was under a spell. He stumbled over to his computer, googled "Am I transgender?," and clicked on the first link. The screen went blank—except for the word "YES" plastered dead center. Since then,

Matthew has been speaking to every trans woman he can find, asking how we knew we were trans.

We go around telling our origin stories. Maybe the closest thing to Matthew's situation is Sandy, who hadn't longed to be female as a child (which is almost unheard of among trans women). Though her history of genderqueer role-play and sexual experimentation now make a lot of sense to her.

Matthew tells us it's only been a few years since the ordeal of coming out as gay. "I finally like my life," he says.

"So why put yourself through this?" Marion says.

"I just need to know."

"And what if you find out you're trans?"

"I'll do it, I'll transition."

I've never heard of anything like it: a person with no history of gender dysphoria, stepping toward a fire the rest of us spent our lives running from. *It was just a nap!* I want to tell him.

THE YEAR BEFORE, as I was starting to live part-time as a woman, I was given a coupon for a free tarot card reading with Flawless Sabrina. I was never drawn to fortune-tellers, though I wasn't about to turn this down. Flawless Sabrina, a.k.a. Mother Flawless, a.k.a. Jack Doroshow (she went by any pronoun), was a piece of living history. She'd been an impresario of drag beauty pageants in the 1960s, and the subject of the groundbreaking documentary *The Queen*. Her apartment near Central Park on the Upper East Side, where she'd been living since 1967, was a time capsule of Hollywood and drag memorabilia.

Flawless Sabrina was in her seventies, completely bald,

and wore no makeup. She laid out the tarot cards on a leather-top desk and instructed me to take a picture of them with my phone. She held forth for a while, offering generalities and suggestions about identity and life's journey, gesturing loosely with long arms. I saw someone accustomed to having her pronouncements heeded. She'd been a "mother" to a long line of drag queens and young queer femmes who'd crash-landed in New York City, starving for guidance and alternative family. I respected her, though her realm of glam and tarot cast no spell over me. I was neither coming from nor going toward a drag life. I was a different kind of artist, with no interest in "performing" gender. I thanked her, and tipped her, then went for a walk in Central Park—and *that* cast a spell.

It was a clear spring day, and the sun might as well have been starlight on another planet, for I had never walked in Central Park as a woman. I was wearing a wrap dress and strappy sandals, which I removed to stroll barefoot on the grass—another sublime first: walking on grass as a woman. It wasn't like trespassing; that feeling belonged to the past. It was more like being born as a fifty-year-old woman with no past.

There's a Russell Edson poem where a woman gives birth to a fully grown dentist. That's absurd of course, but to be a newly hatched trans person is no less absurd. You stumble gracelessly out of your shell, pieces of which stick to you like shrapnel, and there's no telling how the world will treat you, or who will be your friend. But what a world you see!

I put my sandals back on and walked over to the Ramble. I found a bench in the shade along a narrow path and called my friend, the poet Angelo Verga, who'd left a voicemail. Not yet having come out to Angelo, I talked on the phone in my male voice. I spoke as quietly as I could, fearing some passerby would notice the incongruence of the sound of me to the sight of me. Suddenly the space had collapsed and I was hiding on all sides, just moments after feeling euphoric.

I CALLED THIS my time of zigzagging, when radical shifts in my sense of belonging could turn a park bench into a prison. I first experienced this in the retreat cabin, when I leaned. While eating lunch, I spotted something moving out the corner of the window—a rabbit? the foot of an elk?—and I leaned to get a better look. Shifting my upper body from one shoulder to the other, I felt suddenly, irrevocably male. I scolded myself: *What did I think I was doing? I can't even* lean *like a woman.*

I zigzagged the first time I tried to pet a dog as a woman. Stooping down to greet a sweet-faced boxer, I suddenly felt like a fraud. I was sure the dog knew this, that the owner was about to say, "Please don't pet my dog." It was as though I'd collapsed out of my gender, but I didn't revert back to being a "he." Instead I dropped down to an "it," something unnatural, far lower than the dog. I was especially sensitive to laughter. If I heard someone laughing in my vicinity, I tensed up, certain they were laughing at me. There were, of course, plenty of things to laugh at besides me—I just couldn't think of any.

Maybe the scariest zigzag happened while watching the movie *American Hustle*. The movie concerns the FBI Abscam sting, though like nearly all Hollywood blockbusters, it offers sexy alluring women to gaze at—through the eyes of men who get to feast on their bodies. By reflex I started identifying with the men in the film. By the end of *American Hustle* I was totally estranged from myself, and freaking out about my transition.

Pop culture, I was realizing, roused powerful desires,

while giving you nowhere to be if you're trans. It was like riding in a sightseeing tram, thrilled at the view, then suddenly realizing you're not *in* the tram, but rather clinging to the outside in terror. A mere half hour of network TV could leave me feeling internally stranded. The commercials alone serve up enough chiseled men and radiant women to populate a Midwestern town—a town where there is no such thing as trans people.

So I stayed away from mass media, and sometimes I didn't even think about gender. I managed to spend most of a day forgetting I was in transition.

"That's good," my therapist said. (I was now seeing a therapist who specialized in gender.)

"It is?"

"Yes."

"Why is it good?"

"Everyone needs a break. Otherwise this gets too intense."

"But it made me wonder if gender was even an issue. For a moment transitioning seemed like a crazy dream."

"Do you think you're crazy?"

"No. But have you ever counseled someone who decided to stop and detransition?"

"I have."

"What happened?"

"There are only two reasons I've ever heard people give for desisting: not getting work and not getting touched."

FOR A TIME, my weeks were split into "Diana" days and "Doug" days. I dressed as a woman for psychotherapy on Tuesdays, and speech therapy and the Good Stuff Girls on Wednesdays. I was always Diana for doctor's appointments, and blood tests to check hormone levels. I could have done any of these things in guy mode, but the appointments provided structure in the beginning. I had a standing electrolysis appointment in Chelsea on Sundays, and needed to grow out my beard for a couple of days beforehand—these were Doug days. The transition seemed to have a pace that needed to be respected, lest I be overwhelmed. There couldn't be too many Diana days in a row—not yet—nor could I be Doug for too long. I was like two divers sharing one oxygen mask.

After therapy appointments I often shopped in thrift stores, indulging in the privilege of shopping for women's clothes as a woman. My crossdressing closet, geared toward going out at night, had lacked the everyday staples of a woman's wardrobe: scarves, belts, jeans, jackets, cardigans, camisoles, flats, boots, yoga clothing. Even if I had the income to shop retail, I'd still have preferred thrift stores for the wild variety, and the hidden gems. Other women had lived in these clothes, worn them to work, to PTA conferences, on dates, packed them into suitcases. I thought of writing an ode to the women of New York City, thanking them for my wardrobe. The poem would open on a crosstown bus, where a woman who's been looking over at me finally approaches and says, "You're wearing my sweater."

Every part of the city contained landmarks from my past—schools where I'd taught, dance studios I'd trained in, the building where I'd been a doorman, a restaurant where I'd eaten with my grandfather. I'd find myself passing by one of these places, thinking of the people I'd known there in another life. If they were still there, I could walk inside and meet them as a woman. On a trip to Brooklyn I took a detour down my old block to behold the rooming house where I'd once waited on the stoop for a car service, wearing a gold lamé skirt, about to combust with fear and excitement. I climbed the steps and gazed out from that stoop, rapt in wonder, grief, and gratitude.

Just walking the blocks of my current neighborhood as a woman, shopping in the supermarket, seeing the familiar cashiers, the manager who'd worked there for years, even the jerk behind the deli counter, could feel mystical. It was like I'd seen them in Oz, and was now seeing them in Kansas—or vice versa. I welcomed the simplest of errands—mailing a package, dropping off shoes to be repaired. I liked to go for frozen yogurt in Chelsea, then cross Eighth Avenue to a coffee shop, where I'd sit and write into the evening. Nothing important needed to happen on Diana days. Days that would have felt hollow and pointless in a previous life, now felt charmed and formative, like childhood.

SHE DEVOURED SOMETHING puffy, fast as a frog inhaling a fly.

"What just happened?" I said.

"It's going to take an hour on the elliptical to work off that cupcake."

"Is that what I have to start doing, now that I'm joining your team?"

"Why," she said, "would you ever want to join this team?"

The woman across the café table from me was tall and stunning. I would soon learn that she was in fact a fashion model. She was also a Ph.D. candidate in anthropology at Princeton, having previously graduated from Stanford. We had the same first name—though being from Romania, she pronounced it differently.

"Hey Diana," she texted a few days later. "I've got a few dresses which might fit you. Want to come over and see?" I happened to be at the Good Stuff Diner, hanging with my trans girlfriends. "I've been waiting for a text like this all my life," I told Marion, showing her my phone. When I got to Diana's apartment she confessed that she was bribing me. She did have dresses for me (and a couple of them fit), but what she really wanted was feedback on the first few pages of her Ph.D. thesis about an indigenous tribe in Brazil, which I gladly took a look at.

Diana was one person on the outside, and someone very different on the inside. On the outside, it would be hard to imagine a woman more set up for success and happiness in this culture. She was worldly, bright, spoke several languages, and had a modeling portfolio showing her on runways, yachts, and beaches in the Greek islands. Yet she didn't particularly enjoy being female. She was resentful, perhaps even jealous of men. She'd gotten a breast augmentation, only because she was attracted to younger men, and "that's what they like." No wonder she was puzzled that I would want to be on her team.

I didn't tell her this, but maybe the best thing about being on the team was knowing women like Diana in all of their reality. She might have shared such things about herself with a man, though I doubt it. Even if she did, it wouldn't have been while opening her closet, and pulling out dresses for me to try on.

EVERY THURSDAY I removed my nail polish, threw on trousers and a sweatshirt, and took the subway to the Upper East Side to give a poetry lesson to William Zinsser. Two years before, when progressive glaucoma had forced him to retire from writing prose, he called to ask if I thought I could teach him to write poetry. "Yes," I said in a heartbeat. If the author of *On Writing Well* couldn't be taught to write poetry, nobody could.

Bill was the reason I started publishing prose. We'd met at Stuyvesant, when my student teacher, the writer Carley Moore, invited him to visit our freshman comp class. He showed up the next week—free of charge—in a blazer, fedora, and sneakers. I invited him back to speak to the student newspaper editors about journalistic ethics. Then he invited me to lunch, which turned into a lunch date once a month for fifteen years. We'd meet in his office on East Fifty-Fifth Street, a room he rented from a midsize advertising firm. While the admen and -women buzzed about their business outside a door he kept open, Bill spent each day constructing some of the most elegant paragraphs in American nonfiction.

At lunch, Bill was interested in hearing about me. He was fascinated by how I put myself in places—jails, Oklahoma, solo retreats on mountains—he would never want to set foot in. "Now that's something I've never heard before," he'd sometimes say. "You should write about that." He'd follow up with a phone call the next day, mentioning again the thing he'd never before heard, reiterating that I should write about it.

"Have you started on that article yet?" he'd ask the next time we met.

"There *is* no article," I'd say, laughing. "I'm just a poet, Bill."

"Nonsense," he'd say.

He sent a letter through the U.S. mail (he had no email) sketching out the arc of a piece—"Here's how it could go . . ." Eventually I wrote it, for him, and mailed it to his office. It came back with a few edits in black fountain pen, and the word "good" next to a descriptive paragraph toward the end. His note on the title page: "Send this out."

"Have you sent it out yet?" he asked, next time at lunch.

Then came another phone call. "Get a pen," he said, and dictated a cover letter to the editor-in-chief of *The American Scholar.* "Now send out the fucking article!" he said. When it was accepted, he said, "We'll make a prose writer out of you yet."

Now it was my turn to make a poet out of Bill. His biggest obstacle to writing poetry was his belief that he possessed no interior life. He'd declared this to me years before, reclining on the beach below his summer home in Black Point, Connecticut. "How is that possible?" I asked. He pointed across the water, where the north fork of Long Island crouched low on the horizon. "If I were an introspective person," he said, "I'd be wondering about what's over there. But I'm not interested in what's over there." He said he didn't philosophize or ruminate, or write novels. But Bill's blindness would plunge him deep inside himself, whether he liked it or not.

THE FIRST POEM he wrote (he spoke while I typed, and we revised together) was inspired by a moment involving his young assistant, Audra. While cleaning out his files, she'd found some strangely textured paper and wanted to know what it was. Here's how that poem ended:

> As she left she thanked me profusely
> for letting her have the onion skin,
> as if I'd given her chocolate or diamonds.
> "I showed it to my boyfriend," she told me later,
> "We hung it from the ceiling."

"What do you think this poem is about?" I asked.
"Onion skin," he said.

"What do you think this poem is really about?"

"What's it about?" he asked.

"A love triangle."

"Beg pardon?"

On another visit his wife, Caroline, pulled me aside when I arrived, to tell me that they'd switched one of Bill's medications and he'd become disoriented. "He keeps asking for the time," she said, "and doesn't know where he is." She was tense and scared, near tears. She doubted that we would be able to write that day, but thought it would still be good if I visited. "He keeps asking for you," she said.

I greeted Bill at the dining-room table. He grabbed my hand as he always did, then reached for my shoulder, saying, "I am so glad you're here." As we ate the chicken sandwiches I'd brought, I could see he was not himself. But I took out my laptop and typed the following, which he delivered verbatim, holding up his sandwich like Yorick's skull:

> This piece of bread that I'm holding
> could be in Denver. It's nowhere.
>
> Up to a few weeks ago I could
> scroll back. If someone asked,
>
> "What's Burma like?" I could see it.
> How does it happen?

When I returned the next week his dosage had been worked out and he was back to his lucid self. I was excited to read him his poem from the week before. He couldn't for the life of him understand why I would praise it.

"What makes it good?" he wanted to know.

"It has space, Bill. It's not explaining or apologizing for itself."

"What's it about?" he asked.

"I think it's about surrendering to something."

Bill sat with that for a while, then said, "What if I don't like the poem?"

"That's OK," I said.

Soon after, he wrote a poem called "Beyond Directory Assistance," about his attempt to locate an old college friend, Arthur Morgan, by reaching out to Herb Hobler, the "class scribe":

> Neither man had turned up in class obituaries . . .
> where were they? I could only guess
> that they had moved to some penultimate
> port of call, some "Retirement Village"
> or "Assisted Living Facility" in some
> nameless town in nameless America,
> "to be near the children."

"We have to revise 'Beyond Directory Assistance,'" he said the following week. He'd managed to locate his two old Princeton friends, making the poem "untrue."

"Of course it's true," I said.

"How is it true?"

"The emotion is true. What if we just changed their names?"

"How about a footnote?" he asked.

"You're gonna have a footnote in a poem?"

We went back and forth like this for most of an hour, until

he said, "I think it's quite complete now as a poem—as long as you don't get three readers who say, 'I just saw them last week. They're alive and playing squash.'"

Bill was allowing me to pull him into poetry, a land he was entering with confusion and wonder, as his sight grew dimmer. Early in our work, he could still make out shapes and colors, and he had a lot of light sensitivity. He wore a baseball cap and kept the bill low, and yet he always took the chair opposite the long wall of windows facing north onto a Hitchcock-like cityscape of other apartments. But by the time I began hormone replacement therapy, his sight was completely gone. I could have come to him as a woman and he wouldn't have known. But he *would* have known, because the people around him—his doorman, his wife, his personal assistant, and later, his nurses—would surely have told him. Every Thursday Bill squeezed my hand and said, "I am so glad you're here," to a person named Douglas Goetsch who was fading out of existence.

I REALIZED THAT my previous resistance to getting a regular job may have been more about the worker than the work—because as a woman I would gladly do many jobs. *But who would hire me?* I knew a couple of local bartenders, and asked them if they thought their bosses would hire a trans woman with bartending experience. They weren't sure. By coincidence, I struck up conversations with two legal secretaries in the same week. Each was certain, given my typing speed and the fact that I'd been an English teacher, their firms would hire me. They said that all the lawyers cared about was productivity.

This led me to fantasize about transitioning as a legal secretary. Each day I'd put on the required corporate outfit—skirts and heels, nylons, earrings, makeup—and learn by osmosis to talk and act like a woman. I'd commiserate with the other legal secretaries about the hardships of our lot (whatever those were) in the ladies' room, or out for drinks together. Newer secretaries, hired after me, would not be sure if I was trans or not, and when they asked the others, they would have forgotten.

The fantasy of being "trained" as a woman, in a quintessentially feminine job, reminded me of the forced feminization tales in the magazines I used to read. The one constant in those stories (aside from the kink and soft porn) was the presence of women. Women "forced" the feminization, though on a deeper level they were permission givers. I also now realized those weren't crossdressing fantasies; they were, rather, transition fantasies, composed by people for whom transitioning wasn't an option. And here I was doing the same thing: sexualizing hardship to make life palatable.

My lifelong fixation on clothes also involved forced feminization. In my childhood mythology, feminine clothes *kept* girls female, turned tomboys *into* girls, and could turn *me* into a girl. Girls' clothes were sacred, the sole mechanism afforded me by this world for becoming who I was. At the same time, their clothes were lethal, also due to the world I was in. I knew, as a matter of safety, to associate femininity with danger and shame. It wasn't until I began transitioning that my shame around femininity started to unwind. Women's clothes were now my clothes. They lost a great deal of their erotic charge, and instead became a source of joy and well-being. (Not that it wasn't still fun to dress sexy.)

I was discovering things about gender identity that I'd never read in any book. It dawned on me, for example, that gender may be the only category of human experience where what you long to be is what you are. I'd always admired the clarity of the Bashō haiku—

The oak tree
doesn't seem to care
about flowers

Deep inside I had that same clarity—not caring about being a boy—though on the outside it brought me shame. I remember being with my mother in a department store in Huntington, Long Island, gazing up at mannequins cut off at the waist and mounted upside down above the hosiery aisles, their stockinged legs kicking up at the ceiling. I felt excitement staring at these legs, but also shame, and I looked away, fearing my mother would notice. Though I kept stealing glances, wishing I could trade places with those mannequins, even though they were inanimate objects. I would have preferred to be dead and buried in female clothes, rather than alive and male.

Another flash of insight came when I crossed a street and stepped up to a curb the way a woman steps up to a curb. I can't speak generally for how women vs. men step up to curbs, just that the feeling in my haunches was startlingly feminine, and different from any other instance in my life in which I'd performed that action. The moment was unforgettable, as was the curb (Greenwich Avenue and Thirteenth Street). I came to regard these moments as the inner transition, and there were innumerable gradations to it. You're walking down a street, something inside releases, and you're no longer performing femininity, or unperforming masculinity.

A similar thing was happening with my voice. I could not

pass vocally as a woman (few trans women can), but every now and then I said a word or phrase that sounded so womanly it startled me. At the NYU Speech Clinic I trained weekly in pitch, prosody, resonance, and articulation. But something else was needed—a release of fear and tension—in order to progress. "That sounded like shit," I said, after a vocal exercise. Darlene Monda, the clinic supervisor, rushed over and said, "Diana, could you try cursing more femininely?" So I tried, and that sounded like shit too. Then I went next door to Starbucks and ordered a "half decaf please," and the "please" was to die for.

The outer transition is well-marked—name change, hair, wardrobe, medical steps, coming out, etc. But the inner transition, the thousand gateless gates, and the somatic permission that blesses you from within, is something I'd never heard about.

I RECEIVED A call from Bill's wife, Caroline, asking me not to come to the apartment, but instead to go to Lenox Hill Hospital. Bill had suffered a mysterious fracture of his thighbone, but still wanted to see me. He was later moved to a long-term recovery facility. The building was gloomy; at times it was bedlam—anguished cries of patients echoing down halls. When I visited him there, Bill was in his room, alone and scared. He squeezed my hand and drew me close. He asked what time it was. He was worried the nurses would forget to give him his anxiety medication before they left for the night.

I went out to the nurse's station, introduced myself, and, throwing all egalitarian values to the wind, informed them that they had a celebrity patient on their hands. "That man," I said, pointing to Bill's room, "is a famous author and teacher.

Many people love him, and we need you to take good care of him."

Bill asked me to stay until he fell asleep. We talked, in quiet waves of conversation, as the sun went down. He told me how hard this part of the day had always been for him, even as a child. He told me about other fears, and chronic anxieties. It would have felt like a confession if he hadn't been speaking so plainly and without shame. In allowing me to comfort him, I think he saw not only that our friendship needed to shift, but that it could. He often joked self-effacingly about being a WASP, and subject to the formal stiffness of that privileged class. He'd even written a humorous article on the subject. But that evening I saw his utter grace: this man of towering faculties, opening his palms.

ON A THURSDAY after he'd returned home, Bill told me about a disturbing exchange he'd had with his assistant. Audra planned to move out of New York, and had posted an ad on Craigslist seeking her replacement. He asked her to read aloud through the stack of applications. When she came to someone who self-identified as transgender, he said, "What's that?" After she explained, he instructed her to move that application to the bottom of the pile. "Mr. Zinsser!" Audra scolded, shocked that he would do that.

"That girl," Bill said to me, "has no idea what I've written about Black people and civil rights." But he and Caroline, who had joined us at the table for lunch, wanted to know what *I* thought.

I won't ever be coming out to you, is what I thought. Here, in his search for a new assistant, was a trans person who had no chance at a job, because Bill didn't want someone like them—someone like me—anywhere near him.

I wasn't surprised by what he'd said to Audra. Claiming solidarity with Black people may seem like a bizarre cover for transphobia, though I'd seen it before: older Americans who feel their support for civil rights in the 1960s inoculated them from all other forms of prejudice. I knew that if I came out to Bill there was a good chance we would lose each other. I was being forced to make such judgment calls all the time—my survival depended on it.

Yet in some ways he understood me better than anyone. I keep going back to a day when he asked if I'd written anything new. I told him no, just a letter to a university looking for a poet.

"Let's hear it," he said.

After I read it, he thought for a moment.

"You haven't sent that off, have you?"

I had.

"It's not you."

"But they asked for my teaching philosophy."

"Why are you mentioning these other people?" (My letter made reference to some poets who had taught me.)

"Because I use some of their ideas when I teach. They're not mine."

"Who cares! I'm sure those ideas once weren't theirs either."

His criticism was even stronger the next morning, when he called on the phone to deliver a sermon (I wasn't allowed to speak) on the subject of not allowing others to define me. "I've been sitting here trying to figure out why you are holding yourself back," he said. "It's like you can't throw the switch." He ordered me to write another letter, one that would tell employers about the person he knew me to be. "You have taught people in some of the most godforsaken places," he said. "They need to know who you are. Throw the switch. Write it in the third person if you have to, and spare us your teaching philosophy. You're a poet, not a supplicant."

Before hanging up he said, "Do it for me."

What Bill said about holding myself back feels true, not just for me, but for every trans person I know. Until we are out, our lives are completely defined by others. We are afraid to ask for things, such as a job, or more appropriate clothing or pronouns—or a college recommendation. We are afraid to take up space. Bill had no clue about trans experience, but he sensed something missing in an otherwise accomplished person.

I rewrote the letter as he instructed. I wrote it for him, knowing I wouldn't have done it for myself. I think he knew that too. I read it back to him the next week. "Now *that's* a letter," he said.

I DIDN'T KNOW if I'd ever again "throw the switch" on love, nor did I think it was mine to throw. The fear of never being touched, which my therapist mentioned, was well-founded.

I'd go to the Cubbyhole, one of only a few women's bars in New York City, on "Margarita Night" (a.k.a. Tuesday) to have a drink, and observe how joyful the women were to be together. I was happy for them, but I also felt demoralized—how could I ever hope to be seen as female? Even as I felt more embodied, and made some friends there, I was physically irrelevant in that space. Occasionally an exceedingly drunk woman bodied up to me, then peeled away when she realized I was trans. Sometimes a butch woman felt license to drape an arm around my neck, which I didn't appreciate. "You're better-looking than most of my friends, *and they're women*," one of them blurted. "And you're almost good enough looking to be trans," I replied. I was intentionally misgendered fairly regularly, which sucked—though there will always be haters. My fear was that there would never be lovers.

Yet the Cubbyhole was where I met Salena. It was also where I met Jill, a pixie blue-eyed woman who walked in on a Friday night wearing a skirt suit, took one look at me, and said, "I love you." She was an attorney from Atlanta, here on business. This bar, she said, was her favorite place on earth. We hung out until closing, talking like old friends. She told me about a relationship she'd had with someone who'd begun to transition. I assumed the person was female to male, though Jill didn't indicate the direction, just that they had pulled away from her, which made her deeply sad. She texted me later that weekend, apologizing for being too tied up to meet again, and soon flew back to Atlanta. Months later, when I came out to myself in the retreat cabin, it was Jill I most wanted to tell.

I saw her again when I traveled through Atlanta around Christmas of 2014. She had a new girlfriend, and the two were planning to marry. They invited me out to a bar in a gay-friendly neighborhood, where they were meeting friends. Jill had been out her whole life, and this was her community. They welcomed me, and we had a great time, but I was quietly envious of their privilege. These gay women were schoolteachers, therapists, lawyers, researchers at the CDC. They owned houses, they were marrying and having families, they were part of the fabric of their city—while I didn't feel qualified to pet a dog.

The following summer I fell in love with a woman at a Buddhist program I was staffing in Colorado. We'd known each other a few years, but over the course of several late-night conversations, she revealed a depth and beauty I hadn't before seen. I couldn't stop thinking about her. Staff members weren't allowed to get romantically involved with participants until a program was over. After we'd each arrived back home, it was she who confessed to falling in love with me. In a lengthy email, she told me she felt a deep connection, and that she'd had erotic dreams of me. But the physical aspect of the dreams, the idea of sex with me, weirded her out, and she awoke feeling confused and shaken. Later in the same email, she told me about a man she'd met at another retreat a few years before. Both of them were in marriages at that time, but now they weren't, and she was moving to the West Coast to be with him. She said there was so much "yes" for him in her body. It was quite a letter. I have no doubt she considered herself bravely honest, as she told of her trans panic, and the man who rescued her.

When I look back on my relationships with women, none of which lasted longer than a year and a half, it's easy to see them as doomed. *How could it have worked*, I've thought, *if I couldn't be my true self?* Then again, these women had their issues too. They were beautiful, imperfect people, every bit as tangled as I was. Maybe the biggest difference between us was that their issues were culturally sanctioned, compared to matters of gender. I keep thinking back to Shauna, the struggling actress who, after I told her I was a crossdresser, cynically asked if I had any more "bombshells." I'd soon learn that she was a sex addict, that her previous boyfriend was an alcoholic, and that she was $100,000 in debt to her ex-father-in-law. Yet my deal was the "bombshell."

∙ ∙ ∙

IN JULY 2015, I endured eleven consecutive "Doug" days while teaching at the Iowa Summer Writing Festival. I was addressed as "Mr." and "sir," which actually felt weird. I wore a jean jacket in stifling heat to hide my budding breasts. I returned to New York and began living full-time as a woman. I didn't even realize I was doing it—I just noticed, midway through August, that my days were now all Diana days. So I bagged up my male clothes and hauled them, quietly and triumphantly, to thrift store donation counters.

I came out publicly in late September via the internet (as one does nowadays): a letter posted to Facebook, and a new web page with some pictures. In the weeks leading up to that, I came out in a series of emails to fellow writers, former students, and others. I sequenced the letters concentrically, beginning with those closest to me, then sending to wider circles. That way, the more people I informed, the less was at stake for me.

I notified my family last. I did this out of basic decency, so they'd hear it from me and not through online gossip. I reported my transition in the past tense, leaving no room for input, and I didn't ask them for anything. I had to get my father's email from one of my aunts. It was an address that combined his and his wife's name. My letter to my father brought a brief reply ("We are rooting for you") from my stepmother.

I told my brother over the phone. His initial reaction: "Don't tell me you're pulling a Bruce Jenner!" He tried to pull himself together, but he couldn't refrain from interrogating my decision. ("Wrong question," I kept having to say.) The next day I sent him a brief email, offering to stay in conversation, by phone or Skype, if it would help him understand and assimilate the news. I asked that he not send any long letters. Carl was a corporate CFO who subjected his employees, his children, and his estranged wife to endless screeds, which were insulting to their recipients. "No long letters," I pleaded.

That was on a Friday. Carl spent the weekend investigating me. He googled everything I'd written that he could find—"a treasure trove of my brother's life" he called it—and on Monday he sent me an email rendering his analysis of me in one insulting paragraph after another. He wouldn't use my name, referring to me throughout as "my brother." He reminded me that I was "a ladies' man," and reminisced about our "good times together," completely skipping over the pain and trouble I'd been in. He'd found my "Rainbow Man" essay, where I revealed that I was molested by my high school teacher, and bullied by my peers. He said he read "Rainbow Man" three times, and complimented me on the "amazing" writing, yet he made no mention of, nor expressed any compassion for, the suffering chronicled in that essay. He did find cause to mention—jokingly—my digestive issues as an infant, my smelly diapers filled with green shit.

Months before, I made the mistake of asking him if he still considered LGBT people sinners. "Well, yeah," he said. "But everybody sins. Just the other day I drove over the speed limit." I considered never coming out to him. Let him hear about my transition from my nephews.

"That seems like it would be an insult," my therapist said. She encouraged me to give him a chance.

I asked her how long it typically takes families to accept a trans member.

"Generally a year. Two if the family is religious."

"He doesn't get two years to treat me like shit."

"How long does he get?"

Carl and I had maintained contact as adults, speaking on the phone every few months, getting together once or twice a year. Our visits centered on sports and games (we played golf, and went to casinos). In a way this was fitting, since we hadn't played much together as children. But underneath, our childhood dynamic hadn't changed. He habitually called me "Uncle Doug"—even when his sons weren't present—defining me in terms of himself. He talked nonstop about his life, seldom asking about mine. Each of our phone calls began with a long monologue from him ("You gotta hear this," he'd insist), when all I wanted was a conversation. Year after year, he neglected to ask what I was doing for the holidays, many of which "Uncle Doug" spent alone. And he never once asked why I wasn't in contact with our mother.

I fault myself for never having addressed his bullying or his narcissism. I told myself I was waiting for him to change. In reality, I knew that if I confronted him he'd cut me off—and he was all I had left of family. His interminable email, which I'd urged him not to send, wasn't just transphobic; it was another chapter in a history of bullying and erasure, an attempt to come over the top (as they say in poker) and dominate the narrative.

I waited a week, then sent a brief reply, telling him to take as much time as he needed to process the news, but to stop vomiting that process on me. In the meantime, since he liked investigating, I recommended he google "how to respect a trans person"—"And if you don't want to learn that (and please be honest with yourself) we don't have to know each other." We haven't spoken since.

IF I EVER came out to Bill I would have waited, as long as it took, for him to understand. But I knew it would never come to that, for the time I was spending with him, the visits and the poetry lessons—and later, guided meditations, when he asked for help relaxing—was also hospice care.

Unable to adjust to being blind, he was in a state of increasing panic, and riddled with tension—most obvious in his hands, which were continuously trembling and clenching. He used them to feel his way along the walls, occasionally lunging for a doorjamb or light switch. Soon he required someone to lead him around his apartment, not arm in arm, but from in front, walking backward and holding both his hands, the way you'd support a beginning skater. You had to actively pull and lift him, because he leaned back, as though he were about to step into a chasm. Finally, for no medical reason, he surrendered to a wheelchair, and needed a twenty-four-hour nurse capable of lifting him.

Then the fractures came. After mysteriously breaking his femur, there were compression fractures in his thoracic spine, which curled his back. Bill, who took the stairs and went to the gym well into his eighties, had been unusually healthy. But the ordeal of blindness was crushing, day by day, the most optimistic person I've ever met. His systems were shutting down.

More and more he was prone to delusional states, which set Caroline on edge. But his waking reveries weren't fear-based, and I regarded them as a natural letting go. Sometimes he lay on the daybed in his study talking, in and out of coherence, about the past, or the arts, or the King James Bible. He gave a disquisition on the chord progression of Jerome Kern's "Ol' Man River"—complete with singing—that I wish I had on tape.

He still wrote poems with me on days when he could, and he wrote beautifully toward the end, with capacities he'd never before shown. His final poem, "The Psalm Writers," is a

wild and gorgeous ode to his favorite book of the Bible. It begins with a writer looking for a suitable rock to "scratch out" a
psalm, pivots stupendously to Tin Pan Alley and the scratch
sheets of Johnny Mercer's "Blues in the Night," then returns
to the biblical poet at the end:

> The work is done. He can go lie under the Eucalyptus tree
> and feel good about it. He has left something.
> Without that tree, he's a lot of places.
> He's without the interior impulse that caused him to pick
> out that jagged piece of granite in the middle of the Judean
> > Desert,
> to say, "Hey, may your life be as durable
> as that piece of granite over there."

Bill died on a Tuesday in May, five days after our last visit.
I got the call from his son, John, and attended his funeral the
next week at St. Bart's Church on Park Avenue. It was the last
time I've ever worn a man's suit and tie. Bill had joined that
church several years before, and cultivated a friendship with
the minister. He told me he wanted the person who would
preach his eulogy to have known him. Bill also arranged the
music for his memorial: Christian hymns, along with all four
verses of "America the Beautiful."

One of the things the great teachers do is prepare you for
their death. Not literally, not like training the minister. But
they give you confidence, they give you your life. Bill was my
mentor, my surrogate father, my student, but finally he was
my friend. I miss him still.

· · ·

IN OCTOBER 2015, I gave my first poetry reading after coming out. The artist Chris Eastland invited me to read in his painting studio, as part of an "open studios" event in the Gowanus section of Brooklyn. I wore a jean skirt, an orange tee with funky black print, black tights, and a colorful knotted scarf. Chris sat me in an antique high-backed chair and I felt like a queen.

I read from a new book of poems, *Nameless Boy,* the last volume I would publish under what is now my dead name. I didn't make a big deal about the fact that I was trans, nor did the poems in the book involve this aspect of me. At least that's what I thought—until the audience asked for an encore, and I read a poem about a man who has always thought himself capable of a back flip, but has never attempted one. Here's how it begins:

BACK FLIP

I bet I could do a back flip right now.
I've got a feeling they're not as hard
as we think. They're just dangerous.
I'm thinking of going for it right here
in my living room with no witness
except for the dog, who enjoys watching
me practice Tai Chi, as my wife walks
through snickering, "What're you going
to do, inner peace 'em to death?"

I'd written the poem six years earlier while in Oklahoma. I made up the part about the wife and the dog. But I also made up the man: it never once dawned on me that it was a poem about being in the closet. Here's how it ends:

. . . I see it as no harder than the leap
your average television detective makes
from one rooftop to another—which only
seems like a big deal because it's high up,
plus they're wearing suits and ties, the pursuit
of criminals being a formal occasion.
Anyhow I think I could cover that
no problemo—not only me but you too,
and that's my point: *a lot* of us could
do a back flip. We just *don't know it!*
We have *no idea* what we are capable of
and this is how the world keeps us in check—
everyone except for the stunt men,
and the ones who run off and join the circus,
or tear up their passports and go native,
or change their sex and become lounge singers,
or stand their ground in front of a tank.

If I do this back flip there's no telling
what I'll do next. Or maybe I'll keep it
a secret, and remain an ordinary civilian,
humble and quiet as I've been,
though with the knowledge
of what I'm capable of
buzzing inside me.

After the reading I signed some books, crossing out *Doug-las*, writing in *Diana*, and wishing people luck with their own back flips.

Epilogue: Mother's Day
2019

I often think about a fifty-five-year-old African American military vet who wore one of her wife's dresses to a support meeting I attended in 2014. She was crying because she waited too long to transition. No, she was bawling, doubled over, heaving and sobbing for a long time. I was fifty, and I wanted to say something positive about transitioning late. I'm glad I didn't. Her abject grief, for decades of a life not lived in her gender, consecrated that space. The tide of that grief wouldn't roll over me for a few more years. I don't know if it will ever recede.

The experiences of late and early transitioners are like night and day. Early transitioners were unable to conceal, from themselves or others, the fact that they were trans. Late transitioners were unable to unearth it. Trans women's history has centered on early transitioners, which makes sense: they were the ones who were out, struggling to survive in the face of violence, poverty, AIDS; they were the ones marching, and forming alternative families and communities. Meanwhile, late transitioners struggled to live as men, often (though not always) engaging in crossdressing. Many of the crossdressers I knew in the 1980s and '90s were trans and didn't know it. But I have yet to meet a trans person of any age who isn't filled with regret for not transitioning sooner.

How can you spend your life face-to-face with an essential

fact about yourself and still not see it? That's what people in general want to know about us. Some are curious and open-minded enough to stay for the answer. These are your friends. Others pose the question while frowning. They see trans people as, at best, confused, at worst dissembling, dangerous, and subhuman. That's actually a big part of the answer to the question: if you saw that you were trans, you'd be powerfully compelled to transition, and if you did that you would be in danger from those who regard you as subhuman.

In my case, three big things stood in the way of knowing myself: culture, family, and love. There have always been trans people, but the culture I grew up in did not include or show them to me, and so I felt like the only one in the world configured as I was, despite the fact that there are millions of us. There were kids like me in every town, each of us certain we were alone.

But even if a culture doesn't reflect you, a loving family still might see you, or at least provide a space for you to tell them who you are. Had I been in a family that was less frozen, had there been love in the house and people I could confide in, I might have been confirmed (or at least felt safe enough to try on those Mary Jane shoes in my cousin's closet). Even a family you resist can define you. If the people in your house have violated, bullied, and neglected you, it will be hard to identify as trans, because you will be busy identifying as worthless.

Something else: the psychological marks of child abuse and incest, and of closeted trans people, can appear identical: toxic shame, withdrawal, dissociation, depression, loss of identity, sexual confusion, inability to trust, or bond with others, or stand up for oneself. The two are like twins, and like twins they are two different things, which can easily pass for one another. Had I been able to separate my abuse issues from my gender identity I might have transitioned twenty years earlier. Then again, to have sorted any of this out feels like a miracle.

As for the third obstacle, what could possibly compete with the yearning to live in your gender? Answer: for me, the love of a woman. I had no intrinsic desire to be male, but I had a body that many women desire. In the culture in which I grew up, these two goals—to live in my gender, and female companionship—were incompatible. If any of my relationships had worked out, I might never have come out to myself. When they didn't work out, I felt something way beyond the usual breakup devastation. I felt existentially doomed.

WHEN I FINALLY decided to transition, I sensed a need for a vow. In Buddhism, when you take a vow you surrender everything. You become a refugee and receive a new name. There's no bargaining, no preconditions. I asked myself, *Am I willing to surrender everything, in exchange for living as a woman?* I was sure to lose friends. I would never have children. I might never have a partner, or a job. I could lose all sexual function. That's what I said yes to in the cabin. If some of those things—things most people live for—came back to me, it would be gravy. I am fairly certain the converse is true for anyone reading this: if you were offered everything you wanted, in exchange for being unable to live in your gender, you wouldn't take that deal, which is the deal forced on every trans person at birth.

But when I came out as trans, there was, built into it,

a second coming out that I had not anticipated. A few days after leaving the cabin I listened to Tami Simon give refuge vows to a group of new practitioners at the retreat center. Tami, an out lesbian, made sure to mention that our lineage of enlightened beings included many queer people, and for the first time I realized *that word included me*. I'd been labeled queer all my life, and all my life people were mistaken. Now they weren't. Gender identity and sexual orientation are said to be two different things—and they are. One concerns the gender of who you love, the other is the gender you are. Yet the two are deeply intertwined: a person's sexual orientation is defined by the gender identity of who they love.

"So you're a lesbian?" said Kathy. Kathy Collins was my high school writing teacher, with whom I'd never lost touch. She was also a lesbian. "I prefer the word 'queer,'" I said. The point was that I wasn't straight, even though for decades I had identified as straight. How do I go about *this* transition? Would I like queer sex? How is it done? How is it found? Would I have a queer community, and would it be different from my trans community?

A couple years ago an extensive survey asked, "Would you date a trans person?" and the results, especially with regard to trans women, were devastating. Dating sites such as OK-Cupid that had long ago banned the question, "Would you date a Black person?" now freely ask, "Would you date a trans person?"—thereby enabling cisgender people to publicly deem us unworthy of being in partnership. I already knew, from my experiences at the Cubbyhole, that lesbians did not include someone like me in their plans. Bisexuals and pansexuals, on the other hand, were more flexible. So were trans people—and I of course tossed out all plans when I made my vow to give up everything. And I *did* give up everything, so why did I care so much about this? I cared because, having survived my transition, I wanted a full life.

I COULD NEVER quite figure out what to do on Mother's Day, but in 2019 I wanted to connect with my grandmother, who grew up in Bensonhurst. (Bens*onhoist*, as my grandfather said—as in, "When Grandma and I kept company, I'd take the Coney Island line to Bensonhoist.") I too took the Coney Island line—now known as the D train—to a solid beige zone on the New York City subway map I'd stared at for years. I didn't have an address, but I walked some of the streets— perhaps unknowingly passing her house. I planned to stay awhile in the neighborhood, find a coffee shop to write in.

Instead of writing, I looked again at an email from a journalist in California named Leslie, my grandmother's niece. Leslie had found me through her cousin Eric, my grandmother's nephew, a retired professor living in Paris. "Dear Diana," she wrote, "I've been wanting to introduce myself to you for a long time, and now Eric has written saying you want the Bensonhurst address where they grew up." But all she had was a photo of a white three-story clapboard house, which she attached. The number 22 was visible above the door when I zoomed in, but nobody knew the street. I typed "22" plus my grandmother's maiden name into Google—a total shot in the dark—and whaddaya know: the first link took me to a page listing her address. I opened a new window, typed the address into Google Maps and there it was: the house, still white, on a block in Bath Beach, the small neighborhood abutting Bensonhurst to the south (though perhaps it was all Bensonhoist in my grandfather's day).

I looked again at the web page that had given me the

address, and saw my mother's name. (I hadn't noticed it at first because she'd remarried and changed her name.) Google had linked me to a page my mother had created on a family ancestry site, a community of do-it-yourself genealogists obsessed with their roots. The page for my grandmother linked to other pages my mother maintained. She'd been spending years digging into hospital records, death certificates, census bureau records, immigration records, records in Eastern Europe, sleuthing out changes of address, changes of name and employment. She'd written brief, factual accounts of ancestors she hadn't known, and longer, opinionated narratives about people she did know.

Then I read *her* biography, a series of aggrieved, self-aggrandizing paragraphs written by her in the third person. The text wrapped around several photos. Looking at her made me cringe. My mother's narrative featured what she wanted to feature, and left out what she wanted to leave out—I suppose we all do that. Among the things she left out: me.

Under the category "Descendants," alongside my brother's name, which appeared in full, was "private son (1960s-unknown)." Maybe the bylaws of online genealogy require consent in order to name a person, but what struck me was the "son" part. There was no way she did not know about my transition. My brother surely would have told her, or one of my three adult nephews, or cousin Eric in Paris, or the hours she spent ransacking the internet. I'd been out for five years, living and writing as a woman.

Happy Mother's Day, I told myself.

THE BLOCK WAS claustrophobic, narrow houses on small lots, parked cars flanking both sides of the street. A coupe and a minivan were wedged between the curb and front door of number 22, more vehicles in the driveway running beside the house, which extended back farther than I expected. No telling how many people lived there, or how many times the place had been sold and repossessed in the ninety years since my grandmother lived there.

It was crowded *then*. Grandma had five siblings (one was a half-sibling) in addition to her parents, an aunt, and a boarder who lived with them. She was the third oldest. Her lungs were unhealthy. I knew a few other facts, but not many. Mostly I pictured the spirit of my grandmother—a spirit I knew intimately—as a young person navigating what had to be an extraordinarily complicated household. I wondered what alliances and hazards, what generosities and secrets had shaped her into a taciturn, steadfast young woman. Her own life was so silent and invisible, as were the lives of so many women then. After high school she worked as a secretary and stenographer. She was late to marry, had one child, and when her daughter became pregnant a second time she anticipated me with excitement. She loved me before I was even born. She thought I'd be a girl. She was right.

I stood across the street under a tree, gazing at the modest facade of her childhood house, silently thanking her for getting through whatever she got through, feeling overwhelmed with gratitude for a woman whose life, by some miracle, intersected with mine just enough to nourish me forever. She died in a hospital bed in Florida minutes after I arrived from New York. She squeezed my hand with a grip that astounded me, then turned her head to the window and closed her eyes.

• • •

SOON AFTER COMING out, I received a call from a writer named Carolyn Hays. We'd once been colleagues at a writing conference and exchanged books. After congratulating me, she informed me that the youngest of her four children is a trans girl. We had a long talk on the state of trans rights and health care. (No one is more savvy about such things than the parents of trans kids.) Over time, I got to know Carolyn's remarkable family, particularly that daughter, Addy, who came out to her parents as soon as she could speak.

A few years ago I stopped by their house while driving home from a poetry conference. Addy, who was eleven at the time, knew I'd be coming, and she prepared a rather extensive dance presentation to her favorite K-pop music, complete with costume changes. She couldn't have been more girly, or more free. She knew I was trans, and I sensed that mattered to her, but we didn't discuss it. She wasn't particularly talkative, though she was alert and quite witty, like her mother.

Perhaps some of that alertness came from living in stealth. Addy has never come out at school. Few people outside of her family know she is trans, which means the whole family is in stealth. Coming out is up to her, of course, and it has only occurred to me recently that she may not even identify as trans, never having experienced a *transit*—Addy has only ever known herself to be a girl.

Even before telling her parents, she was sending signals, trying to get them to see she was a girl "on the inside and the outside." Sometimes Carolyn wonders what it was like for her as an infant. We now know about the biological impact of a mother's gaze. What is the effect on a child, she wonders, of being misgendered in your mother's gaze? I don't know the answer, but as far as I'm concerned, just asking the question puts Carolyn in the hall of fame of mothering.

She recently showed me a manuscript, a book-length "love letter" to her daughter, to be read when she is an adult. In the book, Addy comes across as a wisdom figure, and the rest of the family, her parents and three older siblings, are trying to catch up to who and where she is, while fiercely protecting her from outside threats (and there have been threats). Maybe the most remarkable passage in the book is this:

> I was only vaguely aware of the construction of your self through memory, at the time. But it's become important to me now that you don't have to create a hidden self—a library of outward facing stunt books like the ones in Jay Gatsby's library. I don't want you to lock away the girl inside of you. Because I believe that that girl would continue to grow up inside of you—a girl who becomes a woman. I imagine the trans person who transitions late in life being reunited with that self. They finally get to know the girl they were but never fully got to be. She exists, of course. She was there all along.
>
> I want that girl to exist from the inside out, without boundaries. I believe that this was what you meant when you said I'm a girl on the inside and the outside. You were refusing these demarcations. I want you to build a full rich library of your girlhood—not the story of someone you had to pretend to be, but your *true* self. I want your brain to hold onto those memories, to layer one on top of the next, to construct a story of you.

Nobody quite understands gender dysphoria, other than the fact that it makes trans lives extremely precarious. Some have called it "gender sadness." *Phor* is from the Greek, meaning to "carry" or "bear"; *dysphoros* being "hard to bear." I've likened it to falling out of your gender, which is like the ground suddenly dropping out, gutting you of all sense of your own humanity. I don't have a single trans friend who doesn't wonder, on a daily basis, if their life will be viable. I also don't know any trans adults blessed with a memory of a childhood in their gender—or for that matter, a mother with the aptitude of Carolyn.

Not long ago, she asked if I'd be Addy's trans godmother. I'm not sure either of us knows exactly what that will mean, and of course I said yes. Whenever I look at Addy, and she looks at me, I get the feeling we each can see the future.

Acknowledgments

This book could not have been completed without the support and vision of others. First among them are Laurie Shapiro, a friend and force of nature, and Colin Dickerman, who was the editor at Farrar, Straus and Giroux who acquired this book because—and only because—he believed in it.

My thanks to the editors Robert Wilson and Bruce Falconer at *The American Scholar*, where I wrote the "Life in Transition" blog from 2015 to 2016, and where parts of "The Fabric Factory" and "In the Cabin of the Crazy One" first appeared. And to Rachel Arons, deputy culture editor at *The New Yorker*, where sections of "The Thousand Gateless Gates" were first published (under the title "Teaching William Zinsser to Write Poetry").

My gratitude to Jenna Johnson at FSG, whose editing helped me develop and shape this memoir. To Eleanor Jackson, a valued agent, and an incredibly insightful reader, and to Mary Herzog, who supplied insight and agency of a different kind. To Lisa Bankoff, who helped steward this project in its early stages. For their advice and expertise I thank Don Wiese, Kate Garrick, Ellen Scordato, Marvin Artis, Kevin O'Connor, Brenda Copeland, Callie Garnett, David Faux, Frederick T. Courtright, Maureen Daniels, and David Groff—the kindest man in publishing.

A spectacularly generous grant from Julie Fowler afforded

me time and a cabin by a lake, where I wrote the hardest of these chapters. My thanks to her, and to Sister Maureen Mulcrone, who arranged a writer-in-residency with the Sisters of Mercy outside Detroit, where I received sanctuary to rival any von Trapp.

To friends and first draft readers along the way, for their time, company, and insight: Beth Rigazio, Alex Neustein, Erin Stuckey, Angela Patrinos, Oliver Klicker, Thea Cook, Tom Peele, Kathy Collins, Ryan Davenport, and John Loonam.

For help with the most vexing questions, I counted on Julianna Baggott and Inés Garland, whose phones were always charged. Thank you.

Finally, I pour one out for the millions of trans people who've come before, and lived through unfathomable hardships—some publicly, most unknown and closeted, warriors all.

Diana Goetsch is an American poet and essayist. Her poems have appeared widely, in *The New Yorker*, *Poetry*, *The Gettysburg Review*, *Ploughshares*, *The Best American Poetry*, and the Pushcart Prize anthology, and in the collections *Nameless Boy* and *In America*, among others. She also wrote the "Life in Transition" blog at *The American Scholar*. Her honors include fellowships from the National Endowment for the Arts, the New York Foundation for the Arts, and the New School, where she served as the Grace Paley Teaching Fellow. For twenty-one years Goetsch was a New York City public school teacher, at Stuyvesant High School and at Passages Academy in the Bronx, where she ran a creative writing program for incarcerated teens.